# Hot Springs and Hot Pools of the Northwest

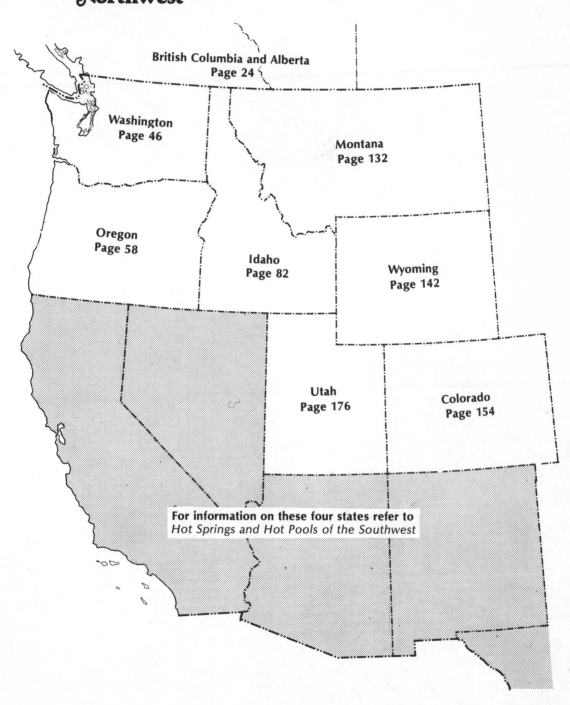

British Columbia and Alberta
Page 24

Washington
Page 46

Montana
Page 132

Oregon
Page 58

Idaho
Page 82

Wyoming
Page 142

Utah
Page 176

Colorado
Page 154

**For information on these four states refer to**
*Hot Springs and Hot Pools of the Southwest*

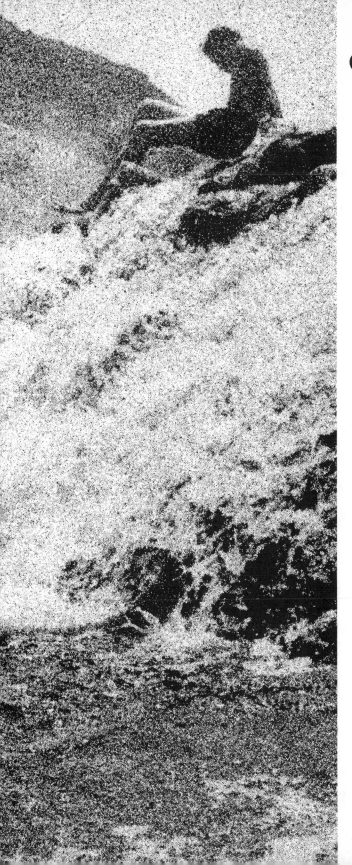

INCLUDING SOUTHWESTERN CANADA

# Hot Springs and Hot Pools
### of the Northwest

COLORADO • WYOMING
IDAHO • MONTANA
OREGON • UTAH
WASHINGTON

Jayson Loam and Marjorie Gersh

Wilderness Press
Berkeley

## Grateful acknowledgements to:

NOAA/Scientist Joy Ikelman for introducing me to 1:250,000 USGS overlays at the Boulder, Colorado, data center; D.H. Herchmer, Regional Recreation Officer of the British Columbia Ministry of Forests, for invaluable information on primitive Canadian hot springs; Merna Forster, Chief Park Interpreter at Jasper National Park, for meeting my deadline with photos of Miette Hot Springs; to the U.S. Department of Agriculture Forest Service—Northern Region—for their tips on keeping the "wild" in wilderness; to all National Forest, National Park and Bureau of Land Management personnel for their patient courtesy and generous cooperation; to the hot-spring soakers who agreed to be in the photographs; to the resort owners for their hospitality; and to Tom Winnett, my publisher, and to his staff, for supporting my experiments in distribution and promotion.

Copyright © 1980, 1986 by Jayson Loam and Marjorie Gersh
First Edition 1980
SECOND EDITION 1986
Cartography, design, layout and production by Jayson Loam
Library of Congress Card Catalog Number 85-41028
ISBN 0-89997-067-2
Manufactured in the United States of America
Published by Wilderness Press
                  2440 Bancroft Way
                  Berkeley, CA 94704
                  Write for free catalog

Library of Congress Cataloging-in-Publication Data

Loam, Jayson.
    Hot springs and hot pools of the Northwest.

    Includes index.
    1. Health resorts, watering-places, etc.--
Northwestern States--Directories.  2. Health resorts,
watering-places, etc.--Canada, Western--Directories.
3. Hot springs--Northwestern States--Guide-books.
4. Hot springs--Canada, Western--Guide-books.
I. Gersh, Marjorie, 1942-    .  II. Title.
RA807.N93L623  1986      613'.122'025795        85-41028
ISBN 0-89997-067-2 (pbk.)

**Dedication:**

**To the spirit that created All That Is, especially hot springs.**

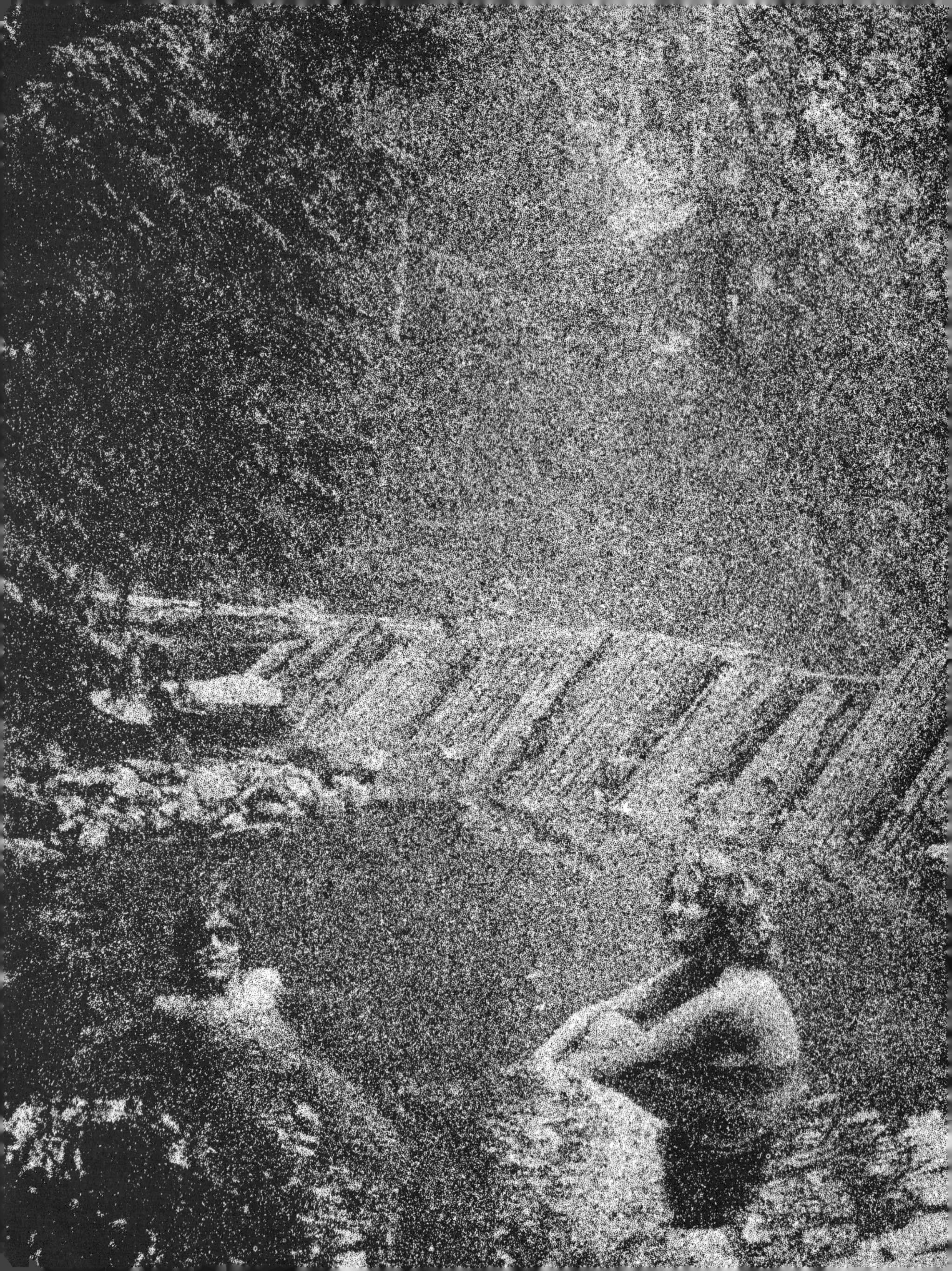

# Contents

# THE AUTHORS' PAGE

Long before the white man arrived to "discover" hot springs, the Indians believed that the Great Spirit resided in the center of the earth and that "Big Medicine" fountains were a special gift from their creator. When the red men retreated, or were pushed, away from their sacred "smoking waters," they took their traditional bathing rituals with them, leaving us spiritually poorer.

It is our hope that you will create your own personal ritual of appreciation as you soak in peace.

*Jayson Loam*

*Marjorie Gersh*

If you are not the owner of the copy you are reading, and would like to have a copy of your own, here are several suggestions:

1. Use the key maps in this book to look up the nearest hot-spring resort or rent-a-tub facility and write down the phone number. Call them and ask if they have a copy of this book in stock. If they do, reserve yourself a copy, and while you are at it, make a reservation to take a soak when you go to pick it up. If they don't have it in stock, ask them to order it for you directly from the publisher.

2. Phone your nearest book store, or hiking and camping store, and ask them if they have a copy in stock, or if they are willing to order it for you. Most of these retailers already carry the Wilderness Press line of books so they should be able to give you fast service.

3. If all else fails, send your prepaid order directly to the publisher. Make your check or money order payable to Wilderness Press. Prices including postage are:

**Southwest** (192 pages) $13.95

**Northwest** (192 pages) $13.95

Wilderness Press
2440 Bancroft Way
Berkeley, CA 94704

At least one of our readers is going to find a mistake in this book. If we knew where it was, we would fix it, but we need your help to find it and tell us about it. It is O.K. to write us a nasty letter giving us a bad time for being wrong, but don't forget to include the right information. We may squirm a little, but it is more important that we make a correction in the next revision.

As the months roll by, several readers are going to notice that the conditions at this location or that location have changed since this book was published. We don't really want a nasty letter about such a change, but we would appreciate your letting us know about it.

We don't expect very many new hot springs to start flowing, but some closed springs may reopen, and we're sure that more rent-a-tub establishments will be built. If you find out about any kind of a new place to put your body in hot water, please write to let us know about it. Thank you very large.

You don't even have to send us any information. It is O.K. to just write and say something nice, if that is how you feel.

Jayson & Marjorie
c/o Wilderness Press
2440 Bancroft Way
Berkeley, CA 94704

# PRIMITIVE HOT SPRINGS ● The Original Real Thing

If you are interested in geothermal springs, it is likely that you have a mental picture of your ideal primitive hot spring, and it is possible that your picture will contain some of the elements described below.

Crystal-clear water, of course, with the most beneficial combination of minerals, but with no slimy algae or rotten-egg smell. Water temperature that is "just right" when you step in, whatever that means for you. A picturesque, rock-rimmed pool, with a soft, sandy bottom, divided into a shallow section for lie-down soaks and a deeper section for sit-up-and-talk soaks. Gorgeous natural surroundings, with grass and trees, plus an inspiring view of snow-capped mountains. A location so remote that you have the place to yourself, and can skinny-dip if you choose, but not so remote that you get too tired from a long hike. Finally, if you like to camp out, a lovely campground, with rest rooms, conveniently nearby, or, if you prefer more service, a superior motel/restaurant just a short drive down the road.

There probably isn't a single actual spring that has all the elements in your ideal mental picture, but the search for a close approximation could be most enjoyable. This book is intended to help make your personal goethermal exploration effective and rewarding.

The "good book" for all hot-spring seekers is the *Thermal Springs List of the United States,* published by the National Oceanic and Atmospheric Administration. At first glance, it is thrilling to see nearly 800 locations in the seven northwest states, but a closer look shows that several hundred have temperatures below 90°, and therefore don't really qualify as "hot". Still, it is tempting to assume that all the remaining 500 are ideal primitive hot springs, just waiting to be enjoyed.

Unfortunately, the reality is somewhat different. After many months and thousands of miles of field research, we found that nearly 150 of the locations are on private property, not open to the public, and another 150 are in Yellowstone Park, where Park regulations forbid public use. Of the remaining 200, more than 100 are developed commercial hot-springs resorts or plunges, leaving less than 100 still in the primitive state. You can maximize your

▲
▼ Scalding water (above) must be mixed with creek water (below) before it can be enjoyed without injury. Both photos were taken at *Bonneville Hot Springs,* page 120, #573.

▲ Some volunteer groups who prefer clothing optional are able to work with the Forest Service. See *Terwilliger*, page 72, #428.

▲ It is possible for open-minded people to adopt a group policy of clothing optional without trauma. See *McCredie*, page 68, #423.

chances of finding your ideal primitive hot spring by heading for the state of Idaho, which has more of them than all the rest of the western states put together.

Do your preliminary exploration at home with the help of this book, then get out there and put your body in the water, again and again.

The first paragraph of each listing is intended to convey the general appearance, atmosphere and surroundings of the location, including the altitude, which can affect local weather conditions. The phrase "Open all year." does not imply that all roads and trails are kept open, regardless of snow falls or fire seasons. Rather, it means that there are no seasonally-closed gates or doors, as at some commercial resorts.

Soaking-pool descriptions start with the geothermal water temperature and include any applicable primitive temperature-control techniques. "Volunteer-built pool" usually implies some crude combination of at-hand material, such as rock and sand. River-edge and creek-edge pools are vulnerable to complete washouts during high runoff months, so some volunteers have to start over from scratch every year.

With regard to skinnydipping, you had best start from the hard fact that any private-property owner, county administration, park superintendent or forest supervisor has the authority to prohibit "public nudity" in a specific area or in a whole forest or park. Whenever a ranger station has to deal with repeated visitor complaints about nude bathers at a specific hot spring, it is likely that the area will be posted with NO NUDE BATHING signs, and you could get a citation without warning by ignoring them.

The absence of NO NUDE BATHING signs does not necessarily imply an official clothing-optional policy. Posted signs may have been torn down by aggressive skinnydippers, or a forest-wide ban on public nudity may have been signed but never posted. However, the absence of a posted sign at least will give you the opportunity to explain to an official that you had no intent to offend, and that you are quite willing to comply with the rule, now that you know it exists.

At any unposted hot spring it is unlikely that you will be hassled unless the ranger or sheriff is responding to a complaint. Therefore, your most important goal should be to make sure there is no complaint. If you are skinnydipping when other people arrive on the scene, don't wait for them to express their approval or disapproval; offer to work out a compromise which is mutually acceptable to all those present.

The description of each primitive hot spring includes a reference to the local bathing suit customs, insofar as they could be determined. Our purpose is to help both skinnydippers and suit-wearers to find like-minded friends. Our hope is that if both groups happen to occupy an unposted primitive hot spring, they will be willing to support personal freedom of choice and mutually consent to a policy of clothing-optional.

By their nature, primitive hot springs do not have customer services available at the site, except, in some cases, nearby areas where overnight parking is not prohibited. Therefore, the distances to such services are included in each description. See the following section on MAPS AND DIRECTIONS for the various methods of finding primitive hot springs.

# DEVELOPED GEOTHERMAL SITES ■ Fancier than the Real Thing

In nearly every state most of the hot-mineral-water locations usable by the public are on private property that has been "improved" by the construction of pools, buildings and fences. The variety of for-a-fee facilities and services at these sites covers such a wide range that it is impractical to employ any kind of conventional five-star rating system. Therefore, the intent of this book is to provide enough factual information for you to decide whether a specific location will meet your basic needs. Then you can make a direct request for current rates and any additional data required for you to make a fully informed decision.

Around the turn of the century, hot-spring-resort owners made a point of emphasizing the mineral analysis of their geothermal water. The closer the

analysis to that of Germany's Baden Baden Spa, the higher the quality of the water, and, by implication, the more diseases it could "cure". Modern medicine no longer gives credence to such cures, and most of today's customers are more concerned about *added* chemicals, such as chlorine, so mineral-analysis data are not included in this book.

For safety and sanitary reasons a "source" hot spring is usually covered over and the mineral water piped to the area chosen for commercial development. Some resorts use individual bathtubs or

 These sparkling new pools in Olympic National Park are a fine example of good commercial development. See *Sol Duc*, page 50, #331.

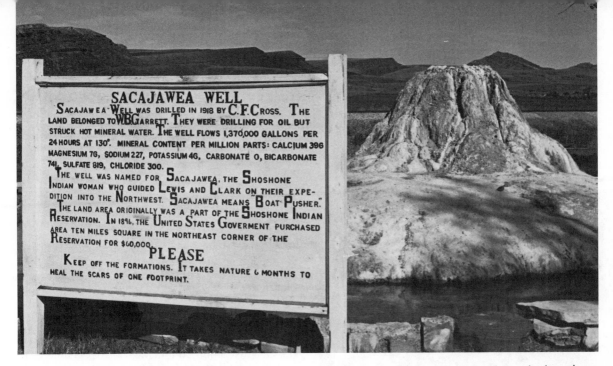

SACAJAWEA WELL

Sacajawea Well was drilled in 1918 by C.F.Cross. The land belonged to W.B.Garrett. They were drilling for oil but struck hot mineral water. The well flows 1,370,000 gallons per 24 hours at 130°. Mineral content per million parts: Calcium 396 Magnesium 76, Sodium 227, Potassium 46, Carbonate 0, Bicarbonate 741, Sulfate 819, Chloride 300.

The well was named for Sacajawea, the Shoshone Indian woman who guided Lewis and Clark on their expedition into the Northwest. Sacajawea means "Boat Pusher." The land area originally was a part of the Shoshone Indian Reservation. In 1896, the United States Goverment purchased area ten miles square in the northeast corner of the Reservation for $60,000.

PLEASE

Keep off the formations. It takes nature 6 months to heal the scars of one footprint.

▲ Hot wells are not included on lists of hot springs but they supply some fine mineral-water resorts. See *Fountain of Youth*, page 113, #706.

▼ Some of the mineral-water resorts have added health clubs, with hydrojet pools, at an extra charge. See *Glenwood Springs*, page 162, #824A.

private in-room hydropools, which are drained and cleaned after each customer, thereby eliminating the need for chemical water treatment. There are also a few locations that have enough rate-of-flow-through in some of their smaller soaking pools to meet local health-department standards without adding any chemicals. However, most pools, especially larger swimming pools, require at least some minimum treatment. Still, the chlorine levels are far less than those found in urban tap-water municipal pools. Each location listing includes a description of the kind and quantity of tub or pools or whatever is offered as a place to put your body. For example, if the only choice is an individual claw-footed bathtub in a separate men's or women's bathhouse, you will not be able to organize a co-ed social occasion. On the other hand, if all pools are communal co-ed, with bathing suits required, you will not be able to have a private soak in the nude. Nearly all the commercial resorts and plunges require that bathing suits be worn, and provide separate locker and shower rooms. However, there are a few developed geothermal sites that have a management policy of clothing-optional. Clearly, there is no such thing as a "typical" hot-spring resort.

Just as clearly, there is no such thing as a "typical" hot-spring resort customer. Upscale travelers take only a couple of suitcases and require hotel-type accommodations, with private bath, plus a restaurant/bar/disco on the premises. Budget travelers take a tent and cooking gear, requiring only a reasonably level low-cost space (with rest rooms) in which to set up camp. In between are owners of RV's, trailers, campers, vans and station wagons, who may like a few nights "camped out" in the woods, but who can afford indoor accommodations and restaurant meals whenever they choose. In order that you may make your choice, each listing provides a general idea of the services available on the premises, the credit cards accepted, if any, and the approximate distances to other services.

13

# TAP-WATER HOT TUBS □ Almost as Good as the Real Thing

According to one version of a popular myth, the very first personal hot tub was created by a group of Santa Barbara residents who loved a hot soak but were tired of making a long gravel-road trip over the mountains to Big Caliente Hot Spring. Initially, the whole unit consisted of a redwood water tank and a manually controlled gas water heater. By the time commercial versions started selling to Marin County residents in the 1960's each unit had a filter, pump, thermostat, hydrojets, built-in seat and thermal cover. Sales of contoured fiberglass and acrylic personal hot tubs have surpassed the sales of wood tubs as the combined total has now surged into the hundreds of thousands per year, nationwide.

In the 1970's many resort hotels and motels responded to customer demand by installing communal hydrojet hot pools for their registered guests. By the 1980's nearly all new hotel/motel construc-

▲ Very few rent-a-tub places have this degree of indoor/outdoor flexibility, especially nice in winter. See *Waterhole #1*, page 129, #589.

▼ Newer rent-a-tub construction has gone from wood tubs to colorful tile and rest areas. See *Just For The Health Of It*, page 80, #444C.

▲ The popularity of hot tubbing has inspired at least one community-owned plunge to add two hot pools. See *Emerald Pool*, page 70, #425B.

▼ Converted older motels, with bathrooms and resting space in each unit, make fine rent-a-tub sites. See *First Resort*, page 158, #813A.

## OUR RULES
- NO DRUGS OR ALCOHOL ON THE PREMISES.
- NO FOOD IN THE SPA ROOMS.
- NO GLASS CONTAINERS IN SPA ROOMS.
- NO SOAPS OR OILS IN SPAS.
- MINORS MUST BE ACCOMPANIED BY PARENTS OR LEGAL GUARDIAN.
- PLEASE HELP US MAINTAIN A QUIET & RELAXING ATMOSPHERE BY KEEPING VOICES LOW.

## THE WATER
- TEMPERATURE MAINTAINED AT 102°F.
- AUTOMATIC CHLORINATORS MAINTAIN FREE CHLORINE AT 2-3 PPM.
- PH MAINTAINED AT 7.2 - 7.6.
- FILTERS ARE DIATOMACEOUS EARTH WITH A 10 MINUTE SYSTEM TURN OVER RATE.
- GROUPS ARE SCHEDULED 15 MINUTES APART TO INSURE PROPER FILTRATION.

## BE CAREFUL
- THE SURFACE AROUND SPAS IS SLIP RESISTANT, BUT ENTER & EXIT SPAS WITH CAUTION.
- WE RECOMMEND A MOMENT'S PAUSE WHEN LEAVING SPA TO LET YOUR BODY ADJUST.
- WE ARE NOT RESPONSIBLE FOR LOST ITEMS LEFT ON THE PREMISES.
- WE WILL CHECK WITH YOU ON THE HALF HOUR TO INSURE EVERYTHING IS SATISFACTORY.

ONSEN *trusts your stay with us will be*

▲ This list is not typical for all rent-a-tub establishments, but all of them do have rules and cautions. See *Onsen*, page 70, #825A.

tion has included a hydropool, plus, in many cases, several de luxe suites, each with its own in-room hydropool.

During the same decades there has been a parallel proliferation of private-space rent-a-tub establishments to serve those city dwellers who want only a private one-hour soak at a reasonable price. Most of the metropolitan areas now have more rent-a-tub locations than there are hot-spring resorts within 100 miles. Just as in Santa Barbara, many years ago, avoiding a long drive is sufficient reason to soak in a tub of tap water, even though it is not the real thing.

Thanks to home hot tubs, hotel/motel hydropools and rent-a-tub establishments, there are now millions of people who have learned to enjoy a social soak without ever having visited a hot-spring resort or experienced a primitive natural hot spring. There are also thousands of hot-spring enthusiasts who, while traveling. would be willing to settle for a tap-water hot soak, if only they knew were to find one. This book is intended to serve all hot-soak buffs by

helping them to treat themselves to the best hot springs or hot pools available under their particular circumstances.

Information on rent-a-tub businesses includes the kind, quantity and location of tubs, chemical treatment of the water, miscellaneous services available on the premises and credit cards accepted. Additional information, rates, reservations and directions, if needed, should be obtained by telephone. Several nudist/naturist parks with hot pools have been included for the benefit of those skinny-dippers who are willing to arrange for a temporary guest pass onto property that is not open to the public on a drive-in basis. Hotel/motels with hydropools (communal and/or in-room) get a three-line listing for the convenience of travelers who are willing to become registered guests in order to have a hot soak.

It is easy to disparage all tap-water hot tubs because they are not the real thing, but to a tense, tired body, they are a lot better than nothing.

15

# PR + MH + CRV — On-Site Accommodations and Local Amenities

▲ This location is coded MH only because
the pool is not available by the hour
or the day. See *Burgdorf*, page 131, #592.

This quick-reference coding appears at the beginning of each commercial location listing:

PR = Tubs or pools for rent by hour, day or treatment.

MH = Rooms, cabins or dormitory space for rent
by day, week or month.

CRV = Camping or vehicle overnight parking
spaces, sometimes with hook-ups, for rent
by day, week, month or year.

Within each listing there is specific information
about the accommodations indicated by the gen-
eralized code.

The PR code obviously applies to rent-a-tub
establishments, and it is also used for those hot-
spring resorts that admit the public to their pools on a
day-rate basis. This code is not used on hotel/mo-
tel/resort locations where pool use is restricted to
registered guests.

The MH code covers every kind of overnight
sleeping accommodations, including tents and
rental trailers as well as rooms, cabins and dormi-
tories. When you phone for reservations, ask enough
questions so that you will know what to expect when
you arrive.

The CRV code is very general, indicating that there
is some kind of outdoor space in which some kind of
overnight stay is possible. Some locations permit
tents, many do not. Some have full hookups for RV's,
most do not. Read the listing description and then
ask plenty of questions when you phone for reservations. When CRV appears in a three-line listing, that
location (along with a description of the facilities)
can be found in most standard RV travel guides.

All commercial locations that offer some form of
meals, groceries, gasoline, etc. are identified, along
with a list of credit cards accepted. Approximate
distances are given for any services or amenities not
available on the premises, in order that you can plan
appropriate shopping along the way. When in doubt,
phone the commercial resort for current information and directions to whatever store, restaurant or
service station you might need. When you are out in
the wide open spaces, it is a good idea to ask the
knowledgeable local resort owner to help you find
your way.

▲ PR only applies to this location, which does not offer motel or RV units. See *Steamboat*, page 156, #803.

▼ RV accommodations as well as pool day use are available here, so the coding given is PR + CRV. See *Belmont*, page 177, #902.

▼ This location has it all so it carries the maximum coding, PR + MH + CRV. See *Doe Bay Resort*, page 57, #358.

# MAPS AND DIRECTIONS — Getting There Is Everything

The key map for each state (and Canada) shows the approximate locations of various kinds of hot springs and hot tubs. Each map carries the message, "This map is designed to be used with a standard highway map." because the key map is too small to provide all the mileage and other information you need to navigate efficiently. This is especially true in congested metropolitan areas which usually appear in large-scale inserts within standard highway maps. The circles and squares in the key map are identified by location numbers, and the listing information for those locations appears in numerical order on the pages following each key map.

Detailed maps and directions are not provided for rent-a-tub establishments or for hotel/motel three-line listings. The street address is usually self-explanatory, and if not, directions can be requested when you phone for reservations.

Directions are provided for hot-spring resorts in order for you to approximate where the location is relative to major towns and highways as shown on your standard highway map. A precautionary telephone call is recommended, even if you don't need room or space reservations, just to make sure that the place is still open and that the directions are still valid. Hot-spring resorts are usually somewhat off the beaten path, local highway routes may change, and the resort may change owners. Few experiences are more frustrating than making a long drive, expecting a delicious soak, only to find the place is closed and you have another long drive to somewhere else, without that soak.

Nearly all primitive hot springs are located in a national forest or a national park, and the name of the specific forest or park is shown under *Source Maps:* at the bottom of each such listing. Your first move is to obtain that map, because the directions given in the listing will probably refer to forest road numbers and other landmarks not shown on any other map. Even if a specific hot spring is not shown on the forest or park map, you will still need that map in order to follow the directions leading to the spring. Some listings will also have adjoining supplementary maps, designed to be used in conjunction with the basic forest or park map.

This book is not intended to be your sole source for hiking to remote and hazardous hot-spring locations, especially those in wilderness areas. Instead, you are provided with general information and then referred to the appropriate district ranger station for the required maps and authentic information on the degree of difficulty. There, you will also be supplied with current data on trail, weather and fire-season conditions, plus the correct procedure for trailhead check in and check out. A lot of the fun of reaching a fabulous primitive spring is lost if you don't live to come back and brag about it.

► The map reproduced on the facing page is a small section of the Forest Service map for the Fairfield Ranger District of the Sawtooth National Forest. Directions given in this book often use the Forest Service road numbers and refer to landmarks on these maps.

U.S. DEPARTMENT OF AGRICULTURE
FOREST SERVICE
JOHN R. MC GUIRE, CHIEF

# SAWTOOTH NATIONAL FOREST

## FAIRFIELD RANGER DISTRICT

▲
▼ Refer first to the Region B map on page 92, and find locations #537, #538 and #539, then find them on this map. *Lightfoot Hot Springs* also appears but it was omitted from the directory because it was a slimy ditch. *Preis, Worswick* and *Skillern Hot Springs* were included with photos when space permitted. The Forest Service map includes the trail to *Skillern Hot Springs*, which could not be adequately shown on the Region B map.

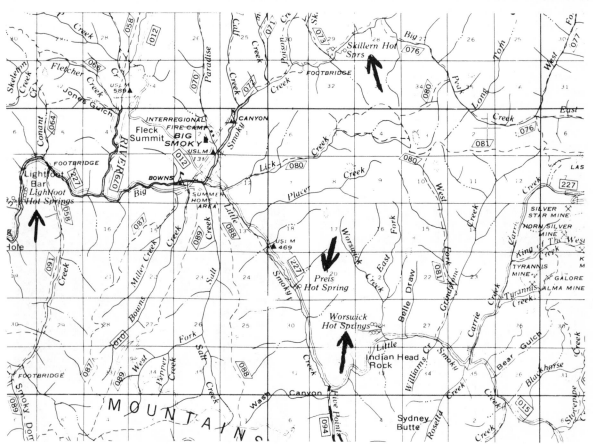

# NATIONAL FORESTS AND PARKS — Heroes in Smokey Hats

This is an enthusiastic testimonial and an invitation to join us in supporting the work of the U.S. Forest Service, the National Park Service and the Canadian National and Provincial park services.

During our last ten years of hot-spring chasing, we have been in dozens of Forest Service ranger stations, to buy maps and to ask questions. We have always received prompt, courteous service, even when an office was also busy handling the complex administration of the "Land Of Many Uses." Beyond that initial courtesy we also received the benefit of alert, informed interest in what we were trying to do, and the kind of help we needed. There was a willingness to phone another ranger station, if necessary, to put us in touch with the ranger or supervisor who could respond to our requests. This cheerful, efficient cooperation was evident at all Forest Service offices in the 11 western states.

Nearly all primitive hot springs are in national forests, and many commercial hot-spring resorts are on private land surrounded by national forest. If you are heading for either type of location, make your first stop a local ranger station, buy a forest map, and let them know what you would like to do in addition

to putting your body in hot water. They are good friends as well as public servants.

National park personnel also get high marks for courtesy, but in the seven northwest states only Olympic National Park permits the public to soak in hot-spring water. The official attitude at other parks is that geothermal water is "holy," to be seen but not touched, to be preserved but not used. Hopefully, they will eventually realize that the "natural state" of a hot spring is when it is providing healing warmth to a human body.

Parks Canada has built large and beautiful public facilities at Radium Hot Springs, at Banff, and at Miette. The Provincial Park Service of British Columbia was very responsive to our need to locate and identify those primitive springs that could be legally used by the public.

The following material is adapted from a brochure issued by the Forest Service—Northern Region, U.S. Department of Agriculture. Please do your part to take care of natural beauty while you visit, to show your appreciation for those who have taken care of it all year in order that you may have a place worth visiting.

▼ Trailhead bulletin boards and location markers are just a few visible signs of valuable Forest Service work.

# Keeping the 'Wild' in Wilderness

Each Forest visitor has a personal responsibility to help manage and preserve our natural environment. This is especially important in wilderness and other undeveloped areas.

These wilderness tips are designed to help you minimize your impact on areas you visit.

## Plan Ahead

- Learn as much as you can about the area you plan to visit.
- Become familiar with rules and regulations for the area.
- For current and specific information, contact the National Forest headquarters or Ranger District for the area you plan to visit.
- Select areas not heavily used.
- Consider practicing minimum-impact camping.
- Anticipate possible emergencies: be prepared.

## Equipment and Supplies

- Use dark or natural-colored tents and packs.
- To conserve firewood, use a portable stove for cooking.
- Leave radios at home.
- Bring a whistle, mirror, and a bright piece of cloth for emergencies.
- Carry food in plastic containers.
- Bring a trash bag for packing garbage out.
- Bring a lightweight digging tool (plastic trowel) for use in disposing of human waste and digging "no trace" fire holes.

Proper equipment and supplies can help make your wilderness visit rewarding and enjoyable. To reduce the weight of your pack, repack food in plastic containers. Many wilderness travelers desire an atmosphere of serenity. Bright colors and loud noise can infringe upon this value.

Most of us enjoy an open fire, but some wildlands are feeling the impact of too many campfires. Consider the option of using a portable stove.

# Travel - Hikers

- Prevent erosion: Do not cut across switchbacks.
- Do not hang signs or ribbons or otherwise mark trees to identify cross-country travel routes.
- Keep trails clean.
- Avoid spooking horses. Step off on the lower side of the trail to permit stock to pass.

Most trails get you from one place to another. Early in the spring and in higher elevations, trails can be wet and soft. Cutting across trail switchbacks can create erosion and soil loss. If you hike or ride cross country, select routes on hard ground. If your group must cross a tundra or meadow, spread out to avoid trampling a path through the vegetation.

Generally, horses have the right of way on trails. When approached by stock, step off on lower side of trail until stock passes. This alerts the stock to your presence, reducing the possibility of spooking the animals.

## Campsites

- Select campsites well away from lakes, streams, and trails.
- Protect live trees and brush from axe and knife.
- Don't build lean-to's, bough beds, or fire rings.
- Return your camp area to its natural condition.
- Select campsites with adequate drainage; avoid ditching around tent.
- Avoid locating campsites in areas that contain delicate plants.

Careful selection of your campsite helps preserve the wilderness atmosphere of solitude, even in popular areas. Choose your site thoughtfully; use it lightly. Leave the area clean and in its natural condition.

## Water

- Bring potable water from home.
- Boil or treat all open water used for drinking.

Increasing occurrences of back-country dysentery, caused by giardia, demonstrates the impact water pollution has in the wilds. Giardia is transmitted by water contaminated by animal or human waste. Consider most water found in the back country to be contaminated even though it appears clean and may be running rapidly. Don't take a chance. Contaminated water can give you dysentery and spoil your visit.

# Smoking

- Do not smoke while riding or hiking.
- Limit smoking to safe areas.
- Make sure your ashes are cool before they are discarded.
- Dispose of cigarette filters by burning or packing them out.

# Sanitation - Pollution

- Prevent water pollution: Do not wash yourself, utensils, or clothing in lakes or streams.
- Dispose of wash water in a hole dug well away from campsites, lakes, and streams.
- Pack out all unburnables: food waste, containers, cans, and aluminum foil.
- Dispose of human waste in a hole located well away from campsites, lakes, and streams. Cover with sod or topsoil.
- Dispose of fish entrails by burying.

Help protect the wilderness from pollution and degradation by practicing a no-trace ethic. Even biodegradable soap is a stress on the environment; do as much of your cleanup as possible with soapless, hot water.

If soap is used, wash yourself, dishes, and clothing from a basin. Dispose of the waste water in a hole located well away from lakes or streams. Cover the hole before you break camp.

Human waste and toilet paper, when disposed of properly, will be taken care of by nature in a short time. If you fish, dispose of entrails by burning completely, burying, or packing them out. Leave a clean camp. Pack out all unburnable material, including aluminum foil.

# Courtesy

- Maintain solitude: Keep noise to a minimum.
- Leave pets at home.
- Keep groups small.
- Leave a clean camp.
- Don't litter.
- If you pack it in, pack it out.
- Be courteous in sharing the trail with others.

Solitude is an important part of a wilderness visit. Minimize your impact on others. While many more are using the back country, there are still opportunities for a quality experience, provided we are all conscientious visitors.

## MAP AND DIRECTORY SYMBOLS

● Unimproved natural mineral water pool
■ Improved natural mineral water pool
□ Gas-heated tap or well water pool

——— Paved highway
– – – Unpaved road
········ Hiking route

PR = Tubs or pools for rent by hour, day or treatment
MH = Rooms, cabins or dormitory spaces for rent by day, week or month
CRV = Camping or vehicle parking spaces, some with hookups,
      for rent by day, week, month or year

# Canada

This map was designed to be used with a standard highway map

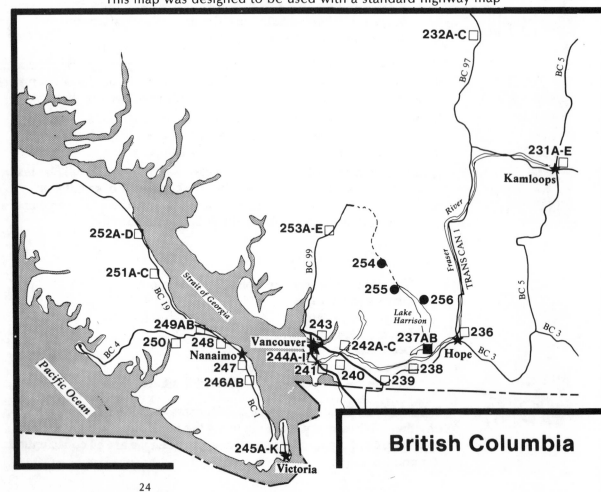

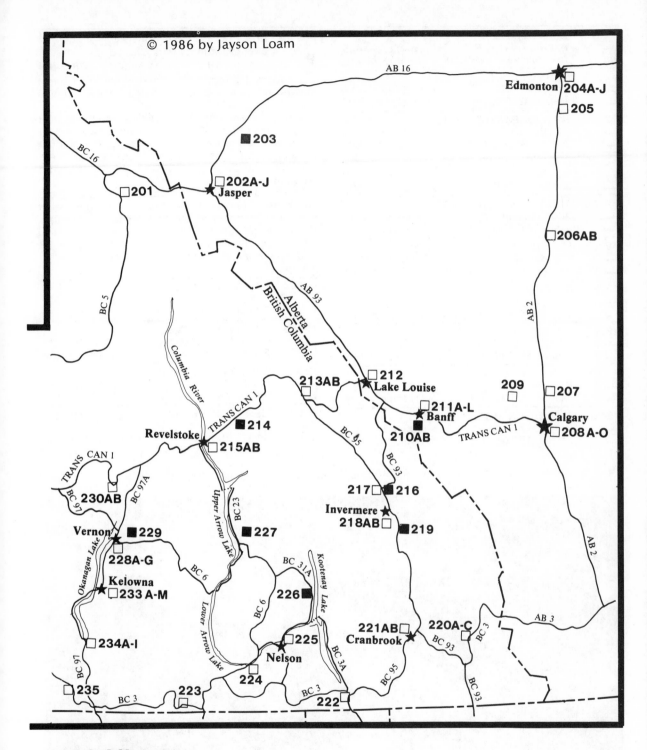

© 1986 by Jayson Loam

AB 16

Edmonton 204A-J

205

BC 16

203

206AB

202A-J
Jasper

201

BC 5

Alberta
British Columbia

AB 93

212
Lake Louise

213AB

209

207

Columbia River

TRANS CAN 1

214

211A-L
Banff

210AB

Calgary

208 A-O

Revelstoke

215AB

BC 95

BC 93

TRANS CAN 1

TRANS CAN 1

230AB

BC 97

BC 97A

Upper Arrow Lake

BC 23

217  216

Invermere
218AB

219

AB 2

Vernon

229

228A-G

BC 6

Okanagan Lake

Kelowna

233 A-M

BC 31A

Kootenay Lake

227

BC 6

226

221AB
Cranbrook

220A-C

BC 93

AB 3

234A-I

Lower Arrow Lake

225

Nelson

224

BC 3A

BC 95

BC 93

BC 97

235

BC 3

223

BC 3

222

**and Alberta**

25

| #201 | SARAK MOTEL | | |
| :-- | :-- | --: | --: |
| ☐ | Yellowhead Hwy 5 | (604) 566-4445 | |
| | Valemount, BC V0E 2Z0 | Hydropool MH | |

| #202A | MARMOT LODGE | | |
| :-- | :-- | --: | --: |
| ☐ | P.O. Box 687 | (403) 852-4471 | |
| | Jasper, AB T0E 1E0 | Hydropool MH | |

| #202B | SAWRIDGE HOTEL JASPER | | |
| :-- | :-- | --: | --: |
| ☐ | P.O. Box 2080 | (403) 852-5111 | |
| | Jasper, AB T0E 10E | Hydropool MH | |

| #202C | DIAMOND MOTEL | | |
| :-- | :-- | --: | --: |
| ☐ | P.O. Box 757 | (403) 852-4535 | |
| | Jasper, AB T0E 1E0 | Hydropool MH | |

| #202D | ANDREW MOTOR LODGE | | |
| :-- | :-- | --: | --: |
| ☐ | 200 Connaught Dr. | (403) 852-3394 | |
| | Jasper, AB T0E 1E0 | Hydropool MH | |

| #202E | MOUNT ROBSON MOTOR INN | | |
| :-- | :-- | --: | --: |
| ☐ | P.O. Box 88 | (403) 852-3327 | |
| | Jasper, AB T0E 1E0 | Hydropool MH | |

| #202F | CHATEAU JASPER | | |
| :-- | :-- | --: | --: |
| ☐ | P.O. Box 1418 | (403) 852-5644 | |
| | Jasper, AB T0E 1E0 | In-room hydropools MH | |

| #202G | JASPER PARK LODGE | | |
| :-- | :-- | --: | --: |
| ☐ | P.O. Box 40 | (403) 852-3301 | |
| | Jasper, AB T0E 1E0 | Hydropool MH | |

| #202H | LOBSTICK LODGE | | |
| :-- | :-- | --: | --: |
| ☐ | P.O. Box 1200 | (403) 852-4431 | |
| | Jasper, AB T0E 1E0 | Hydropool MH | |

| #202I | JASPER INN MOTOR LODGE | | |
| :-- | :-- | --: | --: |
| ☐ | P.O. Box 879 | (403) 852-4461 | |
| | Jasper, AB T0E 1E0 | Hydropool MH | |

# # 203   MIETTE HOT SPRINGS
### Jasper National Park Box 10
### Jasper, AB T0E 1E0 Canada          PR + MH

A modern clean and proper Parks Canada communal plunge, in a remote part of beautiful Jasper National Park. Elevation 4,500 ft. Open all year.

Natural mineral water flows out of several springs at temperatures up to 130° and is piped to two outdoor pools, where it is treated with chlorine. The outdoor swimming pool and outdoor soaking pool are maintained at approximately 102°. Bathing suits are required.

Locker rooms, cafe, rooms and cabins are available on the premises. It is 11 miles to a store, service station and overnight camping and 14 miles to RV hook-ups. No credit cards are accepted.

Directions: From the city of Jasper, drive 42 km (26 miles) north on AB 16, then follow signs southeast to the springs.

| #204A | EDMONTON INN | | |
| :-- | :-- | --: | --: |
| ☐ | 11830 Kingsway Ave. | (403) 454-9521 | |
| | Edmonton, AB T5G 0X5 | Hydropool MH | |

| #204B | CHATEAU LACOMBE | | |
| :-- | :-- | --: | --: |
| ☐ | 101st St. and Bellamy Hill | (403) 426-6611 | |
| | Edmonton, AB T5J 1N7 | Hydropool MH | |

| #204C | CAPILANO MOTOR INN | | |
| :-- | :-- | --: | --: |
| ☐ | 9125 50th St. | (403) 465-3355 | |
| | Edmonton, AB T6B 2H3 | Hydropool MH | |

| #204D | BEST WESTERN BEVERLY CREST MOTOR HOTEL | | |
| :-- | :-- | --: | --: |
| ☐ | 11310 109th St. | (403) 479-2042 | |
| | Edmonton, AB T5G 2T7 | Hydropool MH | |

▼ *Miette Hot Springs:* When construction is completed, this will be another Parks Canada jewel.

▲ When *Miette Hot Springs* reopens in 1986 these Rocky Mountain sheep will surrender this parking area to visitors seeking a soak.

| | | |
|---|---|---|
| **#204E** ☐ | ALBERTA PLACE APARTMENT HOTEL<br>10049 103rd St.<br>Edmonton, AB T5J 2W7 | (403) 423-1565<br>Hydropool  MH |
| **#204F** ☐ | SHERATON-CARAVAN HOTEL<br>10010 104th St.<br>Edmonton, AB T5J 0Z1 | (403) 423-2450<br>Hydropool  MH |
| **#204G** ☐ | SANDMAN INN<br>17635 Stony Plain Rd.<br>Edmonton, AB T5S IE3 | (403) 483-1385<br>Hydropool  MH |
| **#204H** ☐ | THE NISKU INN<br>P.O. Box 336<br>Edmonton, AB T0C 2G0 | (403) 995-7744<br>Hydropool  MH |
| **#204I** ☐ | THE MAYFIELD INN<br>16615 109th Ave.<br>Edmonton, AB T5P 4K8 | (403) 484-0821<br>Hydropool  MH |
| **#204J** ☐ | FOUR SEASONS HOTEL<br>10235 101st St.<br>Edmonton, AB T5J 3E9 | (403) 426-7111<br>Hydropool  MH |
| **#205** ☐ | LEDUC INN<br>5705 50th St. N.<br>Leduc, AB T9E 2Y8 | (403) 986-6550<br>Hydropool  MH |
| **#206A** ☐ | NORTH HILL INN<br>7150 50th Ave.<br>Red Deer, AB T4N 6A5 | (403) 343-8000<br>Hydropool  MH |
| **#206B** ☐ | GREAT WEST INN<br>6500 67th St.<br>Red Deer, AB T4P IA2 | (403) 342-6567<br>Hydropool  MH |
| **#207** ☐ | HORSEMAN MOTEL<br>521 3rd Ave. N.E.<br>Airdrie, AB T0M 0B0 | (403) 948-2233<br>Hydropool  MH |

| | | |
|---|---|---|
| **#208A** ☐ | PORT-O-CALL INN<br>1935 McKnight Blvd. N.E.<br>Calgary, AB T2E 6V4 | (403) 276-8411<br>In-room hydropools  MH |
| **#208B** ☐ | THE WESTIN HOTEL<br>4th Ave. at 3rd St.<br>Calgary, AB T2P 2S6 | (403) 266-1611<br>Hydropool  MH |
| **#208C** ☐ | SANDMAN INN<br>888 7th Ave. S.E.<br>Calgary, AB T2P 3V3 | (403) 237-8626<br>Hydropool  MH |
| **#208D** ☐ | FOUR SEASONS CALGARY<br>110 9th Ave. S.E.<br>Calgary, AB T2G 5A6 | (403) 266-7331<br>Hydropool  MH |
| **#208E** ☐ | GLENMORE INN<br>2720 Glenmore Trail S.E.<br>Calgary, AB T2C 2E6 | (403) 279-8611<br>Hydropool  MH |
| **#208F** ☐ | SHERATON CAVALIER<br>2620 32nd Ave. N.E.<br>Calgary, AB T1Y 6B8 | (403) 291-0107<br>Hydropool  MH |
| **#208G** ☐ | VILLAGE PARK INN<br>1804 Crowchild Trail N.W.<br>Calgary, AB T2M 3Y7 | (403) 289-0241<br>Hydropool  MH |
| **#208H** ☐ | MARLBOROUGH INN<br>1316 33rd St. N.E.<br>Calgary, AB T2A 6B6 | (403) 248-8888<br>Hydropool  MH |

*Sunny Chinooks Family Nudist Recreation Park:*
The members, and their tropical plants,
flourish in the warm temperatures and the
high humidity of this indoor hydrojet pool.

| #208I | HOSPITALITY INN | |
|---|---|---|
| | 135 Southland Dr. S.E. | (403) 278-5050 |
| | Calgary, AB T2J 5X5 | Hydropool MH |

| #208J | DELTA BOW VALLEY | |
|---|---|---|
| | 209 Fourth Ave. | (403) 266-1980 |
| | Calgary, AB T2G 0C6 | Hydropool MH |

| #208K | BEST WESTERN HOSPITALITY INN—SOUTH | |
|---|---|---|
| | 135 Southland Dr. S.E. | (403) 278-5050 |
| | Calgary, AB T2J 5X5 | Hydropool MH |

| #208L | BLACKFOOT INN | |
|---|---|---|
| | 5940 Blackfoot Trail | (403) 252-2253 |
| | Calgary, AB T2H 2B5 | Hydropool MH |

| #208M | CARRIAGE HOUSE MOTOR INN | |
|---|---|---|
| | 9030 MacLeod Trail S. | (403) 253-1101 |
| | Calgary, AB T2H 0M4 | Hydropool MH |

| #208N | CROSSROADS MOTOR HOTEL | |
|---|---|---|
| | 2120 16th Ave. N.E. | (403) 277-0161 |
| | Calgary, AB T2E 1L4 | Hydropool MH |

| #208O | CHATEAU AIRPORT | |
|---|---|---|
| | 2001 Airport Rd. | (403) 276-9881 |
| | Calgary, AB T2E 6Z8 | Hydropool MH |

## #209 SUNNY CHINOOKS FAMILY NUDIST RECREATIONAL PARK

☐ P.O. Box 486        (403) 932-6633
Cochrane, AB T0L 8W0    PR + MH + CRV

Rustic and secluded nudist park on 40 wooded acres, an hour's drive from Calgary. Elevation 4,500 ft. Open May through September.

Gas-heated well water is used in an indoor hydropool maintained at 102° to 104° and treated with bromine. Gas-heated well water is also used in an outdoor swimming pool maintained at 80° and treated with chlorine. Clothing is always prohibited in the pools, and, weather permitting, prohibited everywhere on the grounds.

A cafe, convenience store, cabins and trailer rentals, overnight camping and RV hook-ups are available on the premises. It is 17 miles to a service station. No credit cards are accepted.

Note: This is a membership organization not open to the public for drop-in visits, but prospective members may be issued a guest pass by prior arrangement. Telephone or write for information and directions.

## #210A UPPER HOT SPRING

■ **Banff National Park Box 900**
**Banff, AB T0L 0C0**        **PR**

A modern clean and proper Parks Canada communal plunge, surrounded by the beautiful scenery of Banff National Park. Elevation 4,200 ft. Open all year.

Natural mineral water flows out of a spring at temperatures ranging from 90° to 108°, depending on snow run-off conditions, and is piped to an outdoor swimming pool where it is treated with chlorine. Water temperature in the swimming pool is slightly lower than the current spring output temperature. Bathing suits are required.

Locker rooms are available on the premises. It is one mile to a cafe, store, service station and motel, and two miles to overnight camping and RV hook-ups. No credit cards are accepted.

Directions: From the south end of Banff Avenue, follow signs to the spring.

*Upper Hot Springs, Banff National Park:*
► Parks Canada has a knack of building lovely
hot-springs facilities in a way which makes
the most of the spectacular scenery.

## #210B CAVE AND BASIN HOT SPRING
**Banff National Park Box 900**
**Banff, AB T0L 0C0**                                    **PR**

■

A modern clean and proper Parks Canada communal plunge, with many technical and historical exhibits for visitors, surrounded by the beautiful mountain scenery of Banff National Park. Elevation 4,200 ft. Open all year.

Natural mineral water flows out of a cave at approximately 85°, into an outdoor natural rock basin and then into a large outdoor swimming pool, which maintains a temperature of approximately 80°. The public may enter and observe the cave pool through a short tunnel, and the basin pool may be seen from an observation deck, but bathing in either one is prohibited. The swimming pool, which is treated with chlorine, is available to the public. Bathing suits are required.

Locker rooms are available on the premises. It is one mile to a cafe, store, service station and motel rooms, and two miles to overnight camping and RV hook-ups. No credit cards are accepted.

Directions: From the south end of Banff Avenue, follow signs to the spring.

◄ *Cave & Basin Hot Spring, Banff National Park:* Natural stone arches protect bathers from the wind while preserving the breathtaking vistas.

▼ The entrance lobby at *Cave & Basin Hot Spring* has bilingual displays to educate visitors.

| #211A | TUNNEL MOUNTAIN CHALETS | |
|---|---|---|
| ☐ | P.O. Box 1137 | (403) 762-4515 |
| | Banff, AB T0L 0C0 In-room hydropools MH | |
| #211B | TRAVELLER'S INN | |
| ☐ | P.O. Box 1017 | (403) 762-4401 |
| | Banff, AB T0L 0C0 In-room hydropools MH | |
| #211C | BANFF PARK LODGE | |
| ☐ | P.O. Box 2200 | (403) 762-4433 |
| | Banff, AB T0L 0C0 In-room hydropools MH | |
| #211D | RED CARPET MOTOR INN | |
| ☐ | 425 Banff Ave. | (403) 762-4184 |
| | Banff, AB T0L 0C0 | Hydropool MH |
| #211E | ASPEN LODGE | |
| ☐ | 501 Banff Ave. | (403) 762-4418 |
| | Banff, AB T0L 0C0 | Hydropool MH |
| #211F | BANFFSHIRE INN | |
| ☐ | 537 Banff Ave. | (403) 762-2201 |
| | Banff, AB T0L 0C0 | Hydropool MH |
| #211G | BANFF SPRINGS HOTEL | |
| ☐ | P.O. Box 960 | (403) 762-2211 |
| | Banff, AB T0L 0C0 | Hydropool MH |
| #211H | BEST WESTERN SIDING 29 LODGE | |
| ☐ | P.O. Box 1387 | (403) 762-5575 |
| | Banff, AB T0L 0C0 | Hydropool MH |
| #211I | DOUGLAS FIR RESORT | |
| ☐ | P.O. Box 1228 | (403) 762-5591 |
| | Banff, AB T0L 0C0 | Hydropool MH |
| #211J | INNS OF BANFF PARK | |
| ☐ | P.O. Box 1077 | (403) 762-4581 |
| | Banff, AB T0L 0C0 | Hydropool MH |
| #211K | PTARMIGAN INN | |
| ☐ | P.O. Box 1840 | (403) 762-2207 |
| | Banff, AB T0L 0C0 | Hydropool MH |
| #211L | SUNSHINE VILLAGE RESORT | |
| ☐ | P.O. Box 1510 | (403) 762-3381 |
| | Banff, AB T0L 0L0 | Hydropool MH |
| #212 | LAKE LOUISE INN | |
| ☐ | P.O. Box 209 | (403) 522-3791 |
| | Lake Louise, AB T0L 1E0 | Hydropool MH |
| #213A | GOLDEN RIM MOTOR INN | |
| ☐ | P.O. Box 510 | (604) 344-2216 |
| | Golden, BC V0A 1H0 | Hydropool MH |
| #213B | RONDO MOTEL | |
| ☐ | 904 Park Dr. | (604) 344-5295 |
| | Golden, BC V0A 1H0 | Hydropool MH |

*Canyon Hot Springs:* Even the smaller private commercial hot springs in this area have the benefit of snow-capped mountains with trees.

### #214    CANYON HOT SPRINGS

P.O. Box 3030                    (604) 837-2526
Revelstoke, BC V0E 2S0        PR + CRV

Well-kept commercial plunge with creekside camping spaces, surrounded by the beautiful scenery below Glacier National Park. Elevation 2,000 ft. Open May 15 to September 15.

Natural mineral water flows out of a spring at 85° and is gas-heated as needed, as well as being treated with chlorine. The outdoor swimming pool is maintained at 80°, the outdoor soaking pool at 104°. Bathing suits are required.

Locker rooms, cafe, store and overnight camping are available on the premises. It is 12 miles to a service station and 21 miles to a motel and RV hook-ups. Visa and MasterCard are accepted.

Location: 21 miles east of Revelstoke on Canada 1.

---

#215A    SANDMAN INN
P.O. Box 2329                    (604) 837-5271
Revelstoke, BC V0E 2S0        Hydropool  MH

#215B    BEST WESTERN WAYSIDE INN
P.O. Box 59                      (604) 837-6161
Revelstoke, BC V0E 2S0        Hydropool  MH

### #216    RADIUM HOT SPRINGS

P.O. Box 220                    (604) 347-9622
Radium Hot Springs, BC V0A 1M0
                                PR + MH + CRV

A modern, clean and proper Parks Canada communal plunge, with adjoining commercial services, surrounded by the beautiful mountain scenery of Kootenay National Park. Elevation 2,800 ft. Open all year.

Natural mineral water flows out of five springs at a combined temperature of 117°, and is piped to two outdoor pools, where it is treated with chlorine. The swimming pool is maintained at a temperature of 82° to 83° and the soaking pool is maintained at a temperature of 98° to 103°. Bathing suits are required.

Locker rooms and a cafe are available on the premises, with rooms, overnight camping and RV hook-ups available nearby. It is two miles to store and service station. No credit cards are accepted.

Directions: Follow signs one mile east from the West Gate of Kootenay National Park.

---

#217    THE CHALET
Hwys 93 and 95                   (604) 347-9305
Radium Hot Springs, BC V0A 1M0
                                Hydropool  MH

*Radium Hot Springs:* This sparkling plunge building is operated by Parks Canada staff but a change to private operation is likely.

The modern lodge installation above *Radium Hot Springs* is a private franchise operation.

The Canadian bilingual tradition appears on all *Radium Hot Springs* signs and literature.

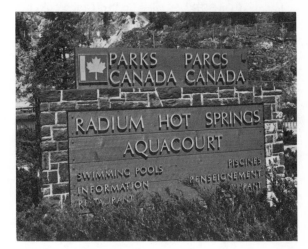

| #218A | INVERMERE INN | |
|---|---|---|
| ☐ | P.O. Box 2340 | (604) 342-9246 |
| | Invermere, BC V0A 1K0 | Hydropool MH |

| #218B | PANORAMA RESORT | |
|---|---|---|
| ☐ | on Toby Creek Rd. | (604) 342-6941 |
| | Invermere, BC V0A 1K0 | Hydropool MH |

### #219 FAIRMONT HOT SPRINGS RESORT
■ P.O. Box 10      (604) 345-6311
**Fairmont Hot Springs, BC V0B 1L0**
**PR + MH + CRV**

Famous large destination resort and communal plunge, beautifully landscaped and surrounded by the forested mountains of the Invermere Valley. Elevation 2,100 ft. Open all year.

Natural mineral water flows out of three springs at temperatures of 108°, 112° and 116°, and is piped to the resort pools, where it is treated with chlorine and cooled with creek water as needed. The outdoor public plunge area includes a swimming pool maintained at a temperature of 89°, a diving tank maintained at a 87° and a soaking pool maintained at a temperature of 102° to 104°. The lodge area, available only to registered guests, includes an outdoor soaking pool maintained at 102° to 104°, an indoor soaking pool maintained at 108° to 112°, and a cold water plunge maintained at 60°. The lodge also has two co-ed saunas. Bathing suits are required.

Locker rooms, massage, cafe, store, service station, hotel rooms, overnight camping (no tents), RV hook-ups, saddle horses, tennis, golf and skiing are available on the premises. Visa, MasterCard and American Express are accepted.

Location: On BC 93, 64 miles north of Cranbrook and 100 miles south of Banff.

| #220A | THREE SISTERS MOTEL | |
|---|---|---|
| ☐ | P.O. Box 280 | (604) 423-4438 |
| | Fernie, BC V0B 1M0 | Hydropool MH |

| #220B | ANCO MOTEL | |
|---|---|---|
| ☐ | P.O. Box 1230 | (604) 423-4492 |
| | Fernie, BC V0B 1M0 | Hydropool MH |

| #220C | CEDAR LODGE MOTEL | |
|---|---|---|
| ☐ | P.O. Box 1477 | (6O4) 423-4438 |
| | Fernie, BC V0B 1M0 | Hydropool MH |

| #221A | TOWN & COUNTRY MOTOR INN | |
|---|---|---|
| ☐ | 600 Cranbrook St. | (604) 426-6683 |
| | Cranbrook, BC V1C 3R7 | Hydropool MH |

| #221B | BEST WESTERN COACH HOUSE MOTOR INN | |
|---|---|---|
| ☐ | 1417 Cranbrook St. N. | (604) 426-7236 |
| | Cranbrook, BC V1C 3S7 | Hydropool MH |

▲ *Fairmont Hot Springs Resort:* This privately owned hot-spring facility has a cleanliness policy equal to that of the Parks Canada pools.

▲ This sign on the *Fairmont Hot Springs Resort* pool area fence is a reminder that the English tradition of proper dress is strong in Canada.

These *Fairmont Hot Springs* pools are for daily public use. A major forest fire is the source of the smoke obscuring the nearby mountains.

The covered walkway provides easy winter access for *Fairmont Hot Springs* lodge guests, for whom this tiled pool is reserved.

# CAVES

Recommended
maximum
time in caves
10 to 15 minutes

Children
must be
accompanied
by an adult
all times

▲ *Ainsworth Hot Springs:* Those who like higher temperatures and 100% humidity need only walk a few yards back into these geothermal caves.

◄ The *Ainsworth* cold pool has its own waterfall.

▼ These free-form *Ainsworth* pools overlook the lake and provide a wide range of temperatures.

| #222 | SUNSET MOTEL | |
| --- | --- | --- |
| ☐ | P.O. Box 2186 | (604) 428-2229 |
| | Creston, BC V0B 1G0 | Indoor hydropools MH |

| #223 | WESTERN TRAVELLER | |
| --- | --- | --- |
| ☐ | 1591 Central Ave. | (604) 442-5566 |
| | Grand Forks, BC V0H 1H0 | Hydropool MH |

| #224 | FIRESIDE MOTOR INN | |
| --- | --- | --- |
| ☐ | 1810 8th Ave. | (604) 365-2126 |
| | Castlegar, BC V1N 2Y2 | Hydropool MH |

| #225 | WILLOW BAY MOTEL | |
| --- | --- | --- |
| ☐ | on Hwy 3A | (604) 825-9421 |
| | Nelson, BC V1L 5P4 | Hydropool MH |

## #226 AINSWORTH HOT SPRINGS

■ P.O. Box 1268     (604) 229-4248
**Ainsworth Hot Springs BC V0G 1A0**

**PR + MH**

Modern, well-equipped multi-pool plunge, including historic walk-in geothermal caves, overlooking beautiful Kootenay Lake. Elevation 1,900 ft. Open all year.

Natural mineral water flows out of five springs at temperatures ranging from 110° to 117°. All pools are treated with chlorine. The outdoor swimming pool and connected hydrojet pool are maintained at 85° to 95°. The water in the caves ranges from 106° to 110° and is circulated to the connected outdoor soaking pool, where it ranges from 104° to 106°. There is a ledge in the cave which may be used as a steambath. There is also an outdoor cold pool containing creek water ranging from 40° to 60°. Bathing suits are required.

Locker rooms and sleeping rooms are available on the premises. It is one block to a cafe and store, three miles to overnight camping and nine miles to a service station. No credit cards are accepted.

Location: On BC 31A, 12 miles south of Kaslo.

## #227 NAKUSP HOT SPRINGS

■ P.O. Box 280
     Radio Tel. N688499 Nakusp JS
**Nakusp, BC V0G 1R0**     **PR + MH + CRV**

Modern, clean, city-owned plunge, with creek-side camping spaces, surrounded by beautiful mountain scenery. Elevation 2,200 ft. Open all year.

Natural mineral water flows out of springs at 135°, and is piped to two outdoor pools, where it is treated with chlorine. The swimming pool is maintained at 100°, the soaking pool at 110°. Bathing suits are required.

Locker rooms, cabins and overnight camping are available on the premises. It is eight miles to a cafe, store, service station and RV hook-ups. Visa cards are accepted.

Directions: From a junction on BC 23 one mile north of Nakusp, follow signs eight miles east to the plunge.

▲ *Nakusp Hot Springs:* The campground and cabins rented to tourists help support this fine pool for day use by the town residents.

▼ The *Nakusp Hot Springs* pools are for social soaking; there is no deep end for diving.

▲ *Cedar Springs:* This facility combines some of the best features of urban rent-a-tub places with the attraction of natural mineral water.

▼ The architecture at *Cedar Springs* is that of a resort, not that of a medical cure center.

| #228A | VERNON LODGE HOTEL |  |
|---|---|---|
| ☐ | 3914 32nd St. | (604) 545-3385 |
|  | Vernon, BC V1T 5P1 | Hydropool  MH |

| #228B | BEST WESTERN VILLAGER MOTOR INN |  |
|---|---|---|
| ☐ | 5121 26th St. | (604) 549-2224 |
|  | Vernon, BC V1T 8G4 | Hydropool  MH |

| #228C | MIDWAY MOTEL |  |
|---|---|---|
| ☐ | 4006 32nd St. | (604) 549-1241 |
|  | Vernon, BC V1T 5P1 | Hydropool  MH |

| #228D | HILLSIDE PLAZA INN |  |
|---|---|---|
| ☐ | 4100 32nd St. | (604) 549-1211 |
|  | Vernon. BC V1T 5P1 | Hydropool  MH |

| #228E | SCHELL MOTEL |  |
|---|---|---|
| ☐ | 2810 35th St. | (604) 545-1351 |
|  | Vernon. BC V1T 6B5 | Hydropool  MH |

| #228F | TIKI VILLAGE MOTOR INN |  |
|---|---|---|
| ☐ | 2408 34th St. | (604) 545-2268 |
|  | Vernon, BC V1T 5W8 | Hydropool  MH |

| #228G | WESTGATE MOTOR INN |  |
|---|---|---|
| ☐ | 4204 32nd St. | (604) 542-0314 |
|  | Vernon, BC V1T 5P4 | Hydropool  MH |

### #229  CEDAR SPRINGS

■ RR 3                              (604) 542-5477
Vernon, BC V1T 6L6            PR + CRV

Recreation-oriented plunge with large wood decks, cedar pools and a private tub, on a tree-covered hillside near a ski area. Elevation 4,000 ft. Open all year.

Natural mineral water flows out of a spring at 50°, is heated with propane as needed and is treated with chlorine. The outdoor swimming pool is maintained at 75° in the summer and 80° to 95° in the winter. The large cedar outdoor hydrojet pool is maintained at 103° and the outdoor soaking pool is maintained at 108°. The indoor private-space cedar pool is maintained at 102°. Bathing suits are required except in the private space.

Locker room, juice bar and Tillicum mineral water by the glass, bottle or case are available on the premises. Overnight camping, RV hook-ups, cross-country skiing and ice-skating are available near-by.

It is six miles to a cafe, store, service-station and motel. Visa cards are accepted.

Directions: From 27th Street (BC 97) in Vernon go north on 48th Avenue (Silver Star Road) five miles to Tillicum Valley Road. Turn right and follow signs one mile to plunge.

▲ This indoor tub at *Cedar Springs* is especially popular with wintertime ski-slope visitors, who must reserve it many weeks in advance.

**#230A**  SALMON ARM MOTOR HOTEL
☐  P.O. Box 909                    (604) 832-2129
   Salmon Arm, BC V0E 2T0          Hydropool  MH

**#230B**  BEST WESTERN VILLAGE WEST MOTOR INN
☐  P.O. Box 3308                   (604) 832-9793
   Salmon Arm, BC V0E 2T0          Hydropool  MH

**#231A**  DOME MOTOR INN
☐  555 W. Columbia St.             (604) 374-0358
   Kamloops, BC V2Z 1K7            Hydropool  MH

**#231B**  KAMLOOPS TRAVELODGE
☐  430 Columbia St.                (604) 372-8202
   Kamloops, BC V2C 2T5            Hydropool  MH

**#231C**  THE PLACE INN
☐  1875 Hwy 5S                     (604) 374-5911
   Kamloops, BC V2C 1W8            Hydropool  MH

**#231D**  PANORAMA INN
☐  610 W. Columbia St.             (604) 374-1515
   Kamloops, BC V2C 1L1            Hydropool  MH

**#231E**  LAC LE JEUNE RESORT
☐  P O. Box 3215                   (604) 372-2722
   Kamloops, BC V2C 6B8            Hydropool  MH

**#232A**  RED COACH FLAG INN
☐  170 N. Cariboo Hwy              (604) 395-2266
   100 Mile House, BC V0K 2E0      Hydropool MH

**#232B**  108 HILLS HEALTH AND GUEST RANCH
☐  Box C-26, 108 Ranch            (604) 791-5225
   100 Mile House, BC V0K 2E0      Hydropool MH

**#232C**  108 MOTORLODGE
☐  RR 1, 108 Ranch                 (604) 791-5211
   100 Mile House, BC V0K 2E0      Hydropool MH

**#233A**  SIESTA MOTEL
☐  3152 Lakeshore Rd.              (604) 763-5013
   Kelowna, BC V1Y 1W4             Hydropool  MH

**#233B**  SANDMAN INN
☐  2130 Harvey Ave.                (604) 860-6409
   Kelowna, BC V1Y 6G8             Hydropool  MH

**#233C**  BEST WESTERN COUNTY INN
☐  2402 Hwy 97 N.                  (604) 860-1212
   Kelowna, BC V1X 4J1             Hydropool  MH

**#233D**  BIG WHITE MOTOR LODGE
☐  1891 Parkinson Way              (604) 860-3982
   Kelowna, BC V1Y 7V6             Hydropool  MH

**#233E**  CASA LOMA RESORT
☐  2777 Casa Loma Rd.              (604) 769-4630
   Kelowna, BC V1Z 1T7             Hydropool  MH

**#233F**  DILWORTH MOTOR LODGE
☐  1755 Dilworth Dr.               (604) 762-9666
   Kelowna, BC V1Y 7V3             Hydropool  MH

**#233G**  KELOWNA MOTOR INN
☐  1070 Harvey Ave.                (604) 762-2533
   Kelowna, BC V1Y 3H1             Hydropool  MH

**#233H**  LODGE MOTOR INN
☐  2170 Harvey Ave.                (604) 860-9711
   Kelowna, BC V1Y 6G8             Hydropool  MH

**#233I**  PANDOSY INN
☐  3327 Lakeshore Rd.              (604) 762-5858
   Kelowna, BC V1Y 1W5             Hydropool  MH

**#233J**  STETSON VILLAGE MOTEL
☐  1455 Harvey Ave.                (604) 762-6000
   N. Kelowna, BC V1Y 6E9          Hydropool  MH

**#233K**  LAKE OKANAGAN RESORT
☐  P.O. Box 1321 Sta. A            (604) 764-3511
   Kelowna, BC V1Y 7V8             Hydropool  MH

**#233L**  KELOWNA TRAVELODGE
☐  1780 Glenmore St.               (604) 762-3221
   Kelowna, BC V1Y 3H2             Hydropool  MH

**#233M**  CAPRI HOTEL
☐  1171 Harvey Ave.                (604) 860-6060
   Kelowna, BC V1Y 6E8             Hydropool  MH

**#234B**  GOLDEN SANDS MOTEL
☐  1028 Lakeshore Dr.              (604) 492-4210
   Penticton, BC V2A 1C1           Hydropool  MH

**#234C**  THE DELTA LAKESIDE
☐  21 Lakeshore Dr. W.             (604) 493-8221
   Penticton, BC V2A 7M5           Hydropool  MH

**#234D**  BOWMONT MOTEL
☐  80 Riverside Dr.                (604) 492-0112
   Penticton, BC V2A 5Y3           Hydropool  MH

**#234E**  BEL-AIR FLAG INN
☐  2670 Skaha Lake Rd.             (604) 492-6111
   Penticton, BC V2A 6G1           Hydropool  MH

▲ *The Harrison Hotel:* This full-service resort hotel provides a buffet lunch and bar service at this swimming pool in the central patio.

► Convivial sing-alongs make the rafters ring in this hot-pool building, adjoining the main pool, on the grounds of the *Harrison Hotel.*

| #234F | SANDMAN INN | | |
|---|---|---|---|
| ☐ | 939 Burnaby Ave. | (604) 493-7151 | |
| | Penticton, BC V2A 1G7 | Hydropool | MH |
| #234G | PENTICTON TRAVELODGE | | |
| ☐ | 950 Westminster Ave. | (604) 492-0225 | |
| | Penticton, BC V2A 1L2 | Hydropool | MH |
| #234H | PENTICTON INN | | |
| ☐ | 333 Martin St. | (604) 493-0333 | |
| | Penticton, BC V2A 5K7 | Hydropool | MH |
| #234I | BEST WESTERN TELSTAR MOTOR INN | | |
| ☐ | 3180 Skaha Lake Rd. | (604) 493-0311 | |
| | Penticton, BC V2A 6G4 | Hydropool | MH |
| #235 | CATHEDRAL LAKES RESORT | | |
| ☐ | RR 1 | (604) 499-5848 | |
| | Cawston, BC V0X 1C0 | Hydropool | MH |
| #236 | RED ROOF INN | | |
| ☐ | P.O. Box 795 | (604) 869-5311 | |
| | Hope, BC V0X 1L0 | Hydropool | MH |

## #237A THE HARRISON HOTEL

**■**

**(604) 521-8888**
**Harrison Hot Springs, BC V0M 1K0**
**PR + MH**

Attractive, large destination resort located on the south shore of beautiful Lake Harrison. This well-managed facility offers an unusually wide range of recreation activities. Elevation 47 ft. Open all year.

Natural mineral water flows out of a spring at 140° and is piped to cooling tanks before being treated with chlorine. The Olympic-size outdoor swimming pool is maintained at 82°, the indoor swimming pool at 94° and the indoor soaking pool at 104°. The men's and women's sections of the health pavilion each contain a Roman bath in which the temperature is controllable. Massage services and Roman baths are available to the public, but all other facilities are reserved for registered guests only. Bathing suits are required in all public areas.

A restaurant, bungalows, rooms, children's programs, tennis, golf, pickle ball, curling (winter), boat cruises and boat rental are available on the premises. It is three blocks to a store, service station, overnight camping and RV hook-ups. Visa, MasterCard, American Express, Carte Blanche, Enroute and Diners Club are accepted.

Location: 65 miles east of Vancouver at the south end of Harrison Lake. Phone for rates, reservations and directions.

*Harrison Hot Springs Public Pool:* The same spring which supplies the hotel, two blocks away, also supplies this well-kept plunge.

## #237B HARRISON HOT SPRINGS PUBLIC POOL

**■**

**c/o Harrison Hotel**
**Harrison Hot Springs, BC V0M 1K0     PR**

Large, modern, indoor communal plunge, owned and operated by the hotel, available to the public. Elevation 47 ft. Open all year.

Natural mineral water is drawn from the same spring that supplies the hotel. It is treated with chlorine, and maintained at 100° in the swimming pool. Bathing suits are required.

Locker rooms are available on the premises. All other services are within three blocks. Visa and MasterCard are accepted.

Location: On the main intersection at the beach in Harrison Hot Springs.

*Sunny Trails Club:* From the deck of their cabin these residents have a view of the pool area and hot tub in the adjoining building.

| #238 ☐ | SPORTSMAN FLAG INN |  |
|---|---|---|
| | 48000 Yale Road. E. | (604) 792-2020 |
| | Chilliwack, BC V2P 6H4 | Hydropool MH |

| #239 ☐ | BEST WESTERN BAKERVIEW MOTOR INN |  |
|---|---|---|
| | 34567 Delair Rd. | (604) 859-1341 |
| | Abbotsford, BC V2S 1H4 | Hydropool MH |

| #240 ☐ | SUNNY TRAILS CLUB |  |
|---|---|---|
| | Box 1 9900 162A St. | (604) 581-1353 |
| | Surrey, BC V3R 4B6 | PR + CRV |

An ideal northwest nudist park with 30 secluded wooded acres of trees and grass, a small running stream, and many residents, conveniently located within an hour of downtown Vancouver. Elevation 700 ft. Open all year.

Gas-heated tap water is used in an enclosed fiberglass hydropool which is maintained at 104°, and in an outdoor swimming pool which is maintained at 80°. Both pools are treated with chlorine. Bathing suits are prohibited in the pools. There is no requirement of full nudity regardless of weather conditions, but posted signs state that individual dress is expected to conform to that of the majority at any given time.

Facilities include a wood-fired sauna, cafe, overnight camping and RV hook-ups. It is three miles to a store and service station and 5 miles to a motel. No credit cards are accepted.

Note: This is a membership organization not open to the public for drop-in visits, but prospective members may be issued a guest pass by prior arrangement. Telephone or write for information and directions.

| #241 ☐ | TSAWWASSEN INN |  |
|---|---|---|
| | 1741 56th St. | (604) 943-8221 |
| | Delta, BC V4L 2B2 | In-room hydropools MH |

| #242A ☐ | SQUIRE FLAG INN |  |
|---|---|---|
| | 631 Lougheed Hwy | (604) 931-4433 |
| | Coquitlam, BC V3K 3S5 | Hydropool MH |

| #242B ☐ | COQUITLAM TRAVELODGE |  |
|---|---|---|
| | 725 Brunette Ave. | (604) 525-7777 |
| | Coquitlam, BC V3K 1C3 | Hydropool MH |

| #242C ☐ | BEST WESTERN COQUITLAM MOTOR INN |  |
|---|---|---|
| | 319 North Road | (604) 931-9011 |
| | Coquitlam, BC V3K 3V8 | Hydropool MH |

| #243 ☐ | INTERNATIONAL PLAZA HOTEL |  |
|---|---|---|
| | 1999 Capilano Rd. | (604) 984-0611 |
| | N. Vancouver, BC V7P 3E9 | Hydropool MH |

| #244A ☐ | GRANADA MOTOR INN |  |
|---|---|---|
| | 9020 Bridgeport Rd. | (604) 270-6030 |
| | Richmond, BC V6X 1S1 | Hydropool MH |

| #244B ☐ | AIRPORT INN RESORT—A DELTA HOTEL |  |
|---|---|---|
| | 10251 St. Edward's Dr. | (604) 278-9811 |
| | Richmond, BC V6X 2M9 | Hydropool MH |

| #244C ☐ | RICHMOND INN |  |
|---|---|---|
| | 7551 Westminster Hwy | (604) 273-7878 |
| | Richmond, BC V6X IA3 | Hydropool MH |

| #244D ☐ | LAKE CITY MOTOR INN |  |
|---|---|---|
| | 5415 Lougheed Hwy | (604) 294-4751 |
| | Burnaby, BC V5B 2Z7 | Hydropool MH |

| #244E ☐ | SANDMAN INN—GEORGIA STREET |  |
|---|---|---|
| | 180 W. Georgia St. | (604) 681-2211 |
| | Vancouver, BC V6B 4P4 | Hydropool MH |

| #244F ☐ | SHERATON LANDMARK HOTEL |  |
|---|---|---|
| | 1400 Robson St. | (604) 687-0511 |
| | Vancouver, BC V6B 1B9 | Hydropool MH |

| #244G ☐ | FOUR SEASONS VANCOUVER |  |
|---|---|---|
| | 791 W. Georgia | (604) 689-9333 |
| | Vancouver, BC V6C 2T4 | Hydropool MH |

| #244H ☐ | WESTIN BAYSHORE |  |
|---|---|---|
| | 1601 W. Georgia | (604) 682-3377 |
| | Vancouver, BC V6G 2V4 | Hydropool MH |

| #244I ☐ | BEST WESTERN MOTOR INN |  |
|---|---|---|
| | 3075 Kingsway | (604) 430-3441 |
| | Vancouver, BC V5R 5J8 | Hydropool MH |

| | | |
|---|---|---|
| **#244J** ☐ | INTERNATIONAL PLAZA HOTEL<br>1999 Marine Drive<br>Vancouver, BC V7P 3E9 | (604) 984-0611<br>Hydropool MH |
| **#244K** ☐ | ABERCORN INN<br>9260 Bridgeport Rd.<br>Vancouver, BC V6X 1S1 | (604) 270-7576<br>Hydropool MH |
| **#244L** ☐ | JOHNNY CANUCK MOTOR INN<br>3475 E. Hastings St.<br>Vancouver, BC V5K 2A5 | (604) 294-4751<br>Hydropool MH |
| **#245A** ☐ | VICTORIA REGENT HOTEL<br>1234 Wharf St.<br>Victoria, BC V8W 3H9 | (604) 386-2211<br>In-room hydropools MH |
| **#245B** ☐ | CANTERBURY FLAG INN<br>310 Gorge Rd. E.<br>Victoria, BC V8T 2W2 | (604) 382-2151<br>Hydropool MH |
| **#245C** ☐ | COLONY MOTOR INN<br>2852 Douglas St.<br>Victoria, BC V8T 4M5 | (604) 385-2441<br>Hydropool MH |
| **#245D** ☐ | HARBOUR TOWERS HOTEL<br>345 Quebec St.<br>Victoria, BC V8V 1W4 | (604) 385-2405<br>Hydropool MH |
| **#245E** ☐ | HUNTINGDON MANOR INN<br>330 Quebec St.<br>Victoria, BC V8V 1W3 | (604) 381-3456<br>Hydropool MH |
| **#245F** ☐ | LAUREL POINT INN<br>680 Montreal St.<br>Victoria, BC V8V 1Z8 | (604) 386-8721<br>Hydropool MH |
| **#245G** ☐ | OXFORD CASTLE INN<br>133 Gorge St.<br>Victoria, BC V9A 1L1 | (604) 388-6431<br>Hydropool MH |
| **#245H** ☐ | RED LION MOTOR INN—WESTWATER'S<br>3366 Douglas St.<br>Victoria, BC V8Z 3L3 | (604) 385-3366<br>Hydropool MH |
| **#245I** ☐ | ROYAL SCOT MOTOR INN<br>425 Quebec St.<br>Victoria, BC V8V 1W7 | (604) 388-5463<br>Hydropool MH |
| **#245J** ☐ | SPORTSMAN MOTOR INN<br>1850 Douglas St.<br>Victoria, BC V8T 4K6 | (604) 388-4471<br>Hydropool MH |
| **#245K** ☐ | DUTCHMAN INN MOTEL<br>2828 Rock Bay Ave.<br>Victoria, BC V8T 4S1 | (604) 386-7557<br>Hydropool MH |
| **#246A** ☐ | YELLOW POINT LODGE<br>RR 3<br>Ladysmith, BC V0R 2E0 | (604) 245-7422<br>Hydropool MH |
| **#246B** ☐ | INN OF THE SEA RESORT<br>3600 Yellow Point Rd.<br>Ladysmith, BC V0R 2E0 | (604) 245-2211<br>Hydropool MH |
| **#247** ☐ | BEST WESTERN HARBOURVIEW<br>MOTOR INN<br>809 Island Hwy. S. RR 1<br>Nanaimo, BC V9R 5K1 | (604) 754-5252<br>Hydropool MH |
| **#248** ☐ | SCHOONER COVE RESORT AND MARINA<br>RR 2, Box 12<br>Nanoose Bay, BC V0R 2R0 | (604) 468-7691<br>Hydropool MH |
| **#249A** ☐ | QUALICUM COLLEGE INN<br>427 College Rd.<br>Qualicum Beach, BC V0R 2T0 | (604) 752-9262<br>Hydropool MH |
| **#249B** ☐ | OLD DUTCH INN (BY THE SEA)<br>2690 Island Hwy<br>Qualicum Beach, BC V0R 2T0 | (604) 752-6974<br>Hydropool MH |
| **#250** ☐ | RODEWAY INN<br>4277 Stamp Ave.<br>Port Alberni, BC V9Y 7X8 | (604) 724-3344<br>Hydropool MH |
| **#251A** ☐ | WASHINGTON INN<br>1001 Ryan Rd.<br>Courtenay, BC V9N 3R6 | (604) 338-5441<br>Hydropool MH |
| **#251B** ☐ | THE WESTERLY HOTEL<br>1590 Cliffe Ave.<br>Courtenay, BC V9N 2L1 | (604) 338-7741<br>Hydropool MH |
| **#251C** ☐ | BEST WESTERN THE POINTE-<br>WATERFRONT RESORT<br>4330 Island Hwy.<br>Courtenay, BC V9N 5M8 | (604) 338-5456<br>Hydropool MH |
| **#252A** ☐ | AUSTRIAN CHALET VILLAGE MOTEL<br>462 S. Island Hwy<br>Campbell River, BC V9W 1A5 | (604) 923-4231<br>Hydropool MH |
| **#252B** ☐ | BENNETT'S POINT RESORT<br>RR 1<br>Campbell River, BC V9W 2E7 | (604) 923-4281<br>Hydropool MH |
| **#252C** ☐ | CAMPBELL RIVER LODGE<br>1760 Island Hwy<br>Campbell River, BC V9W 2E7 | (604) 287-7446<br>Hydropool MH |
| **#252D** ☐ | ANCHOR INN<br>261 Island Hwy<br>Campbell River, BC V9W 2B3 | (604) 286-1131<br>Hydropool MH |
| **#253A** ☐ | CARLETON LODGE<br>P.O. Box 519<br>Whistler, BC V0N 1B0 | (604) 932-4183<br>Hydropool MH |
| **#253B** ☐ | DELTA MOUNTAIN INN<br>4050 Whistler Way<br>Whistler, BC V0N 1B0 | (604) 932-1982<br>Hydropool MH |
| **#253C** ☐ | WHISTLER CREEK LODGE<br>2021 Karen Crescent<br>Whistler, BC V0N 1B0 | (604) 932-4111<br>Hydropool MH |
| **#253D** ☐ | BLACKCOMB LODGE<br>4220 Gateway Dr.<br>Whistler, BC V0N 1B0 | (604) 669-4155<br>Hydropool MH |
| **#253E** ☐ | WHISTLER VILLAGE INN<br>P.O. Box 190<br>Whistler, BC V0N 1B0 | (604) 932-4004<br>Hydropool MH |

# THE PAMPERED AND THE PRIMITIVE

Most hot spring visitors patronize those convenient and comfortable establishments that offer tiled pools, hot showers, a restaurant and a souvenir shop, with nearby overnight accommodations. However, a hardy minority make a point of seeking out those remote and primitive hot springs that are inconvenient and often inaccessible.

Many of them are on or near logging roads, which means that quite often public access is prohibited from 6 a.m. to 6 p.m. during logging season, and that the road could be closed by slides, washouts, snow, high fire danger, and actual forest fires. In other words, access to primitive hot springs is a sometimes thing. Therefore, the best first step toward reaching any specific hot spring is to contact the Provincial Ministry of Forests District Office for the area and inquire about current conditions. Then, if access is possible, you can obtain an area map and first-hand directions at a Forest Service office.

(NOTE: Office hours are 8:30–4:30, Monday–Friday only)

- Please help keep the sites clean and preserve the natural beauty of the areas.
- Do not cut live trees for firewood nor live boughs for bedding.
- Light campfires only in designated areas and never leave a campfire unattended.
- Pack out all garbage and litter if barrels are not provided.

FUTURE NOTE: There are a few primitive hot springs that could not be included because of special restrictions—which might be lifted at any time. When you inquire at a District Office about any of the following locations, also ask for information on additional locations available to the public.

---

## #254 SKOOKUMCHUCK HOT SPRINGS (LILLOOET) (St. Agnes Well)

**non-commercial**
**South of the town of Pemberton, B.C.**

Two large fiberglass soaking tubs in a small clearing near a logging road along the Lillooet River. Elevation 100 ft. Open all year; however, the road is not plowed in winter.

Natural mineral water flows out of a spring at 129°. Volunteers have mounted the two halves of a fiberglass storage tank near the spring, using long pieces of PVC pipe to bring a gravity flow of hot mineral water. Other pieces of PVC pipe are used to bring a gravity flow from a cold-water spring. Water temperature within each tub is controlled by mixing the hot and cold water. One of the tubs is in the open, the other is under a crude A-frame shelter. In the absence of posted rules, the use of bathing suits is determined by the consent of those present.

There are no services available, but there are numerous nearby self-maintained camping areas along the logging road and at the site itself.

► *Skookumchuck Hot Springs (Lillooet):* Pool temperature is controlled by moving the pipe.

Directions: From the town of Mt. Currie, go approximately 34 miles south on the logging road along the Lillooet River. At BC Hydro tower #682 turn right onto a camping-area access road and go ¼ mile to spring. Caution: this dirt road may require a 4-wheel-drive vehicle when wet.

The hot springs are located on private property and use is permissable without the consent of the property owner. Please respect the hot springs and adjacent property. Pack out all garbage.

◄ *Clear Creek Hot Springs:* Technically the bath tub makes this an "improved" site, but the conditions are still clearly primitive.

## #256 CLEAR CREEK HOTSPRINGS
Along the Northeast side of Harrison Lake, B.C.     **non-commercial**

Two small wooden tubs and two old porcelain bathtubs are located near a log cabin along Clear Creek, approximately 35 miles up the east side of Harrison Lake from Harrison Hot Springs and 6 miles east of the lake up Clear Creek. Elevation approximately 2,200 ft. Hot springs open all year: however, road passable only in summer and only to 4x4's. A spring percolates from the ground at 95° and volunteers have constructed two wooden tubs connected to the springs with long lengths of PVC pipe. There are two conventional bathtubs which can also be used for soaking.

There are few amenities available in the area other than the log cabin and an outhouse nearby. The springs are located on an active mineral claim which was initially prospected by a woman who built the cabin and an Olympic-sized swimming pool about 15 years ago. The pool is largely filled with algae and silt and not used by bathers any longer.

Directions: From the town of Harrison Hot Springs head up the east side of Harrison Lake for about 33 miles to the logging camp at Big Silver Creek. Stay on the main logging road for another 5 miles and look for a narrow road going off to the right. This is the old mining road up Clear Creek, and it is extremely rough in places. It is drivable with a narrow 4x4 for most of the 6 miles to the hot springs and cabin, which are located on the right side of the creek. It will take 2–3 hours to drive from Harrison Hot Springs to the Clear Creek Road, and considerably longer if you walk up the road. There are no posted rules or restrictions for use of the site, but anything packed in should be packed out, including garbage.

## #255 SLOQUET CREEK HOTSPRINGS
Near the North end of Harrison Lake, B.C.     **non-commercial**

Several springs seep from the rocks above Sloquet Creek and flow along the ground before dropping over a short waterfall and forming a small pool which is too hot for bathing. Several other springs percolate from the ground, and volunteers have constructed small natural-rock pools for bathing along the creek. The hot springs are located about 62 miles south of Mt. Currie, near the Lillooet River and just NW of Harrison Lake, elevation approximately 1000 ft. Water temperature varies between 135° and 155°.

Few services are available in the area, though there is a logging camp at Port Douglas, at the head of Harrison Lake. Walk-in camping is possible near the springs.

Directions: From the town of Mt. Currie, go about 57 miles south on the logging road along the Lillooet River to a bridge that crosses the river to the west side. Turn left, cross Fire Creek, and go south 2 miles to a second creek, where you go right. Follow this creek (Sloquet) for about 3.4 miles on an old logging road that takes you to a bridge across North Sloquet Creek. The bridge is washed out and you must cross the creek on foot on a large log. Follow the logging road until you reach an obvious clearing, which can be used for camping. There is a trail leading downhill from the clearing to the creek and the hot springs. It will take 2–3 hours to drive from Mt. Currie and an additional 45 minutes to walk the remainder of the logging road to the hot springs. There are no posted rules or regulations for use of the site, but anything packed in should be packed out, including garbage.

# Washington

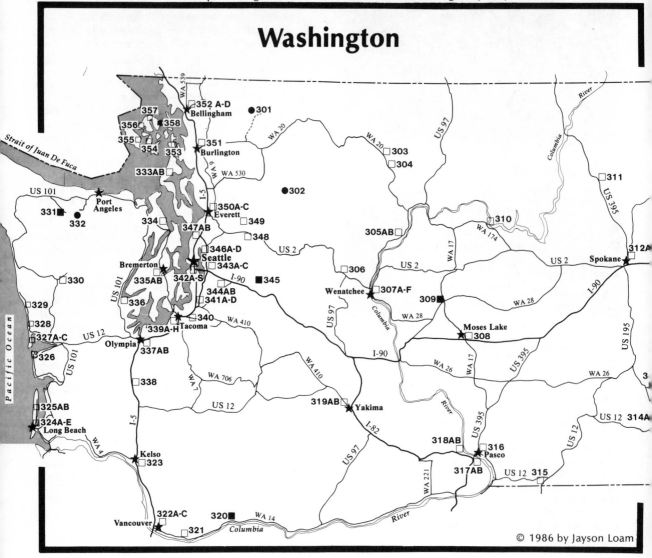

© 1986 by Jayson Loam

## MAP AND DIRECTORY SYMBOLS

● Unimproved natural mineral water pool

■ Improved natural mineral water pool

□ Gas-heated tap or well water pool

――――― Paved highway

– – – – – Unpaved road

·····∿····· Hiking route

PR = Tubs or pools for rent by hour, day or treatment

MH = Rooms, cabins or dormitory spaces for rent by day, week or month

CRV = Camping or vehicle parking spaces, some with hookups,
for rent by day, week, month or year

## #301   BAKER HOT SPRINGS
**North of the town of Concrete**
**non-commercial**

Charming, primitive spring located at the end of an easy 600-yard path through the lush green timber of Mt. Baker National Forest. Elevation 2,000 ft. Open all year.

Natural mineral water bubbles up into the bottom of a large, round, volunteer-built soaking pool at 109°. Water temperature in this sandy-bottomed pool is controlled by admitting or diverting the water from a small, adjacent cold stream. The apparent local custom is clothing optional. Conscientious visitors have kept the area litter free. Please help to maintain this standard.

There are no facilities on the premises and no overnight camping is permitted. However, there is a Forest Service campground within three miles. All other services are located 20 miles away, in Concrete.

Directions: From WA 20, five miles east of Hamilton, turn north on Grand Creek Road toward Baker Lake. Just beyond Park Creek Campground, near the head of the lake, go left on FS 1144 and after 3.2 miles watch for an unusually large parking area on both sides of the gravel road. (If you reach a U turn to the left, with a branch road going off to the right, you have gone too far.) An unmarked trail to the hot springs starts with wood steps visible at the north end of the parking area. Follow the easy trail west to the spring.

Source map: *Mt. Baker—Snoqualmie National Forest* (hot spring not shown).

 *Baker Hot Springs:* This lovely pool is a primitive hot spring at its best. However, be sure to bring along your insect repellent.

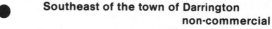

## #302   KENNEDY HOT SPRING
**Southeast of the town of Darrington**
**non-commercial**

A popular scenic hot spring, five miles in on a trail that connects with the Pacific Crest Trail one mile farther on. Located in a rugged canyon of the White Chuck River in the Glacier Peak Wilderness. Elevation 3,300 ft. Open all year.

Natural mineral water flows out of a spring at 96° directly into a 4′ by 5′ cedar-plank soaking pool. Even though this spring is a five-mile hike from the nearest road, there is no assurance of quiet privacy during the busy summer months, especially on weekends. There are no posted clothing requirements, which leaves it up to the mutual consent of those present.

There are no facilities on the premises. It is 15 miles to a Forest Service Campground and 30 miles to all other services.

Directions: From the town of Darrington, take FS 20 southeast approximately eight miles to the intersection with FS 23. Drive to the end of FS 23, which is the trailhead for Trail 643 up White Chuck Canyon. Consult with the Ranger Station in Darrington regarding weather and trail conditions before starting this trip.

Source map: *Mt. Baker—Snoqualmie National Forest.*

| #303 | SUN MOUNTAIN LODGE |
|---|---|
| ☐ | P.O. Box 1000     (509) 996-2211 |
| | Winthrop, WA 98862     Hydropool MH |

| #304 | IDLE-A-WHILE MOTEL |
|---|---|
| ☐ | P.O. Box 575     (509) 997-3222 |
| | Twisp, WA 98856     Hydropool MH |

| #305A | CAMPBELL'S LODGE & COTTAGES |
|---|---|
| ☐ | P.O. Box 278     (509) 682-2561 |
| | Chelan, WA 98816     Hydropool MH |

| #305B | DARNELL'S RESORT MOTEL |
|---|---|
| ☐ | P.O. Box 506     (509) 682-2015 |
| | Chelan, WA 98816     Hydropool MH |

| #306 | ENZIAN MOTOR INN |
|---|---|
| ☐ | 590 Hwy 2     (509) 548-7612 |
| | Leavenworth, WA 98826     Hydropool MH |

| #307A | AVENUE MOTEL |
|---|---|
| ☐ | 720 N. Wenatchee Ave.     (509) 663-7161 |
| | Wenatchee, WA 98801     Hydropool MH |

| #307B | FOUR SEASONS INN |
|---|---|
| ☐ | 11 W. Grant Rd.     (509) 884-6611 |
| | Wenatchee, WA 98801     Hydropool MH |

| #307C | HOLIDAY LODGE |
|---|---|
| ☐ | 610 N. Wenatchee Ave.     (509) 663-8167 |
| | Wenatchee, WA 98801     Hydropool MH |

| #307D | THE UPTOWNER MOTEL |
|---|---|
| ☐ | 101 N. Mission     (509) 663-8516 |
| | Wenatchee, WA 98801     Hydropool MH |

| #307E | CHIEFTAIN MOTEL |
|---|---|
| ☐ | 1005 N. Wenatchee     (509) 663-8141 |
| | Wenatchee, WA 98801     Hydropool MH |

| #307F | BEST WESTERN RIVERS INN |
|---|---|
| ☐ | 580 Valley Mall Parkway     (509) 884-1474 |
| | East Wenatchee, WA 98801     Hydropool MH |

| #308 | MOSES LAKE TRAVELODGE |
|---|---|
| ☐ | 316 S. Pioneer Way     (509) 765-8631 |
| | Moses Lake, WA 98837     Hydropool MH |

WE DON'T SWIM IN YOUR TOILET SO PLEASE DON'T PITTLE IN OUR POOL!

## #309    NOTARAS LODGE
■    **242 Main St. E.**     **(509) 246-0462**
       **Soap Lake, WA 98851**     **PR + MH**

Large, new, western-style log-construction motel with in-room jet tubs and a public bathhouse. Open all year.

Natural mineral water is obtained from the city water system through an extra pipe which supplies Soap Lake water at temperatures up to 95°. Three of the motel units are equipped with in-room jet tubs built for two. All rooms have an extra spigot over the bathtub to supply the hot mineral water whenever desired. There is also a bathhouse building containing a sauna and three private-space, old-fashioned single bathtubs, plus a fresh-water hydrojet pool maintained at 95° to 100°. The bathhouse facilities are available to the public.

Massage and motel rooms are available on the premises. All other services are within five blocks. Visa and MasterCard are accepted.

Location: On WA 17 in the town of Soap Lake.

| #310 | COULEE HOUSE MOTEL |
|---|---|
| ☐ | Roosevelt and Birch Sts.     (509) 633-1101 |
| | Coulee Dam, WA 99116     Hydropool MH |

| #311 | NORDIG MOTEL |
|---|---|
| ☐ | 101 W. Grant St.     (509) 935-6704 |
| | Chewelah, WA 99109     Hydropool MH |

| #312A | RAMADA INN |
|---|---|
| ☐ | P.O. Box 19228     (509) 838-5211 |
| | Spokane, WA 99219 |
| | In-room hydropools MH |

| #312B | CAVANAUGH'S INN AT THE PARK |
|---|---|
| ☐ | W. 303 N. River Dr.     (509) 326-8000 |
| | Spokane, WA 99201     Hydropool MH |

| #312C | CAVANAUGH'S RIVER INN |
|---|---|
| ☐ | 700 Division St.     (509) 326-5577 |
| | Spokane, WA 99202     Hydropool MH |

| #312D | QUALITY INN VALLEY |
|---|---|
| ☐ | N. 905 Sullivan Rd.     (509) 924-3838 |
| | Spokane, WA 99214     Hydropool MH |

| #312E | BEST WESTERN TRADE WINDS MOTEL |
|---|---|
| ☐ | 907 W. 3rd Ave.     (509 838-2091 |
| | Spokane, WA 99204     Hydropool MH |

| #312F | BEST WESTERN TRADE WINDS NORTH |
|---|---|
| ☐ | 3033 N. Division     (509) 326-5500 |
| | Spokane, WA 99207     Hydropool MH |

| #312G | LINCOLN CENTER MOTOR INN |
|---|---|
| ☐ | 827 W. First Ave.     (509) 456-8040 |
| | Spokane, WA 99204     Hydropool MH |

| #312H | QUALITY INN NORTH |
|---|---|
| ☐ | 7111 N. Division     (509) 467-3838 |
| | Spokane, WA 99208     Hydropool MH |

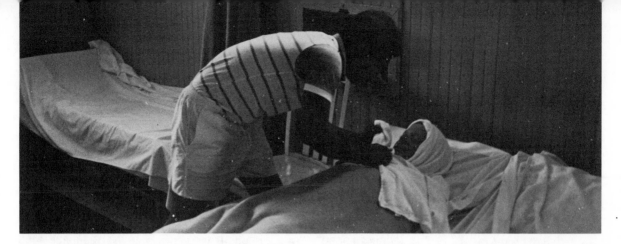

**#312I QUALITY INN SPOKANE HOUSE**
P.O. Box 91 (509) 838-1471
Spokane, WA 99210 Hydropool MH

**#312J TRAILER INNS**
on 4th Ave. (509) 535-1811
Spokane, WA 99202 Hydropool CRV

**#313 QUALITY INN—PARADISE CREEK**
S.E. 1050 Johnson Ave. (509) 332-0500
Pullman, WA 99163 In-room hydropools MH

**#314A PUB AND TUB**
821 6th St. (509) 758-2500
Clarkston, WA 99403 PR

Combination tavern and rent-a-tub facility in downtown Clarkston. Open all year.

Private-space pools using chlorine-treated tap water are for rent to the public by the hour. There are four enclosed outdoor tubs in which the temperature is maintained at 98° to 102°. No credit cards are accepted.

Phone for rates, reservations and directions.

**#314B BEST WESTERN RIVERTREE INN**
1257 Bridge St. (509) 758-9551
Clarkston, WA 99403 Hydropool MH

**#315 COUNTRY ESTATES MOBILE PARK**
on Larch Rd. (509) 529-5442
College Place, WA 99324 Hydropool CRV

**#316 APPLE INN**
1800 W. Lewis St. (509) 547-0791
Pasco, WA 99301 Hydropool MH

**#317A CLOVER ISLAND INN**
435 Clover Island (509) 586-0541
Kennewick, WA 99336 Hydropool MH

**#317B CAVANAUGH'S MOTOR INN**
1101 N. Columbia Center Blvd.
(509) 783-0611
Kennewick, WA 99336 Hydropool MH

**#318A HOLIDAY INN**
1515 George Washington Way
(509) 946-4121
Richland, WA 99352 Hydropool MH

*Carson Hot Mineral Springs Resort:* A bathhouse patron receives the traditional sweat wrap from an attendant after each soak.

**#318B DESERT GOLD MOTEL & TRAILER PARK**
on US 12 (509) 627-1000
Richland, WA 99352 Hydropool CRV

**#319A COLONIAL MOTOR INN**
1405 N. First St.
(509) 453-8981
Yakima, WA 98901 Hydropool MH

**#319B TRAILER INNS**
on N. First St.
(509) 452-9561
Yakima, WA 98901 Hydropool CRV

**#320 CARSON HOT MINERAL SPRINGS RESORT**
P.O. Box 370 (509)427-8292
Carson, WA 98610 PR + MH + CRV

Picturesque, historic resort which prides itself on having used "the same bath methods for over 100 years." Elevation 300 ft. Open all year.

Natural mineral water flows out of a spring at 126° and is piped to men's and women's bathhouses. There are eight claw-footed enamel tubs in the men's bathhouse, and six in the women's. Temperature is controllable in each tub, which is drained and filled after each use, requiring no chemical treatment. An attendant, who is with you at all times, applies a sweat wrap after the soak. Bathing suits are *not* required in the bathhouses, which are available to the public as well as to registered guests.

Television, radio, newspapers and telephones are not available on the premises. Massage, restaurant, hotel rooms, cabins, overnight camping and RV hook-ups are available. A store and service station are within two miles. Hiking and fishing are nearby. Visa and MasterCard are accepted.

Directions: From the intersection of WA 14 and Bridge of the Gods go east on WA 14 and watch for signs. Phone for rates, reservations and further directions, if necessary.

| #321 ☐ | BRASS LAMP MOTOR INN<br>544 6th St.<br>Washougal, WA 98671 | (206) 835-8591<br>Hydropool MH |
|---|---|---|
| #322A ☐ | SHILO INN—HAZEL DELL<br>13206 Hwy 99<br>Vancouver, WA 98665 | (206) 573-0511<br>Hydropool MH |
| #322B ☐ | SHILO INN—DOWNTOWN<br>401 E. 13th St.<br>Vancouver, WA 88601 | (206) 696-0411<br>Hydropool MH |
| #322C ☐ | MARK 205 MOTOR INN<br>221 N.E. Chkalov Dr.<br>Vancouver, WA 98664 | (206) 256-7044<br>Hydropool MH |
| #323 ☐ | BEST WESTERN ALADDIN MOTOR INN<br>310 Long Ave.<br>Kelso, WA 98626 | (206) 425-9660<br>Hydropool MH |
| #324A ☐ | CHAUTAUQUA LODGE<br>205 W. 14th St. N.<br>Long Beach, WA 98631 | (206) 642-4401<br>Hydropool MH |
| #324B ☐ | OCEAN LODGE<br>P.O. Box 337<br>Long Beach, WA 98631 | (206) 642-2777<br>Hydropool MH |
| #324C ☐ | OUR PLACE AT THE BEACH<br>1309 Ocean Blvd.<br>Long Beach, WA 98631 | (206) 642-3134<br>Hydropool MH |
| #324D ☐ | THE BREAKERS<br>P.O. Box 428<br>Long Beach, WA 98631 | (206) 642-2727<br>Hydropool MH |
| #324E ☐ | SURFSIDE INN<br>31512 J Place<br>Long Beach, WA 98631 | (206) 665-521l<br>Hydropool MH |
| #325A ☐ | THE PARK MOTEL<br>P.O. Box 339<br>Ocean Park, WA 98640 | (206) 665-4585<br>Hydropool MH |
| #325B ☐ | OCEAN PARK TOURIST CAMP<br>on 259th Place<br>Ocean Park, WA 98640 | (206) 665-4585<br>Hydropool CRV |
| #326 ☐ | CANTERBURY WESTPORT MOTEL<br>P.O. Box 349<br>Westport, WA 98595 | (206) 268-9101<br>Hydropool MH |

| #327A ☐ | THE SANDS RESORT<br>Ocean Shore Blvd.<br>Ocean Shores, WA 98569 | (206) 289-2444<br>Hydropool MH |
|---|---|---|
| #327B ☐ | DISCOVERY INN<br>P.O. Box 2<br>Ocean Shores, WA 98569 | (206) 289-3371<br>Hydropool MH |
| #327C ☐ | THE CANTERBURY INN<br>P.O. Box 310<br>Ocean Shores, WA 98569 | (206) 289-3317<br>Hydropool MH |
| #328 ☐ | BEACHWOOD RESORT<br>P.O. Box 116<br>Copalis Beach, WA 98535 | (206) 289-2177<br>Hydropool MH |
| #329 ☐ | OCEAN CREST RESORT<br>on SR 109<br>Moclips, WA 98562 | (206) 276-4465<br>Hydropool MH |
| #330 ☐ | LAKE QUINALT<br>P.O. Box 7<br>Quinault, WA 98575 | (206) 288-2571<br>Hydropool MH |

## #331 ■ SOL DUC HOT SPRINGS RESORT
**P.O. Box 2169**      **(206) 327-3583**
**Port Angeles, WA 98362**      **PR + MH**

Extensively modernized historic resort surrounded by the evergreen forest of Olympic National Park. Elevation 1,600 ft. Open early May to the end of September. (All year operation will be possible when planned highway improvements are completed. Phone for status of construction.)

Natural mineral water flows out of a spring at 128° and is piped to a heat exchanger, where it heats the shower water and the chlorine-treated creek water in the swimming pool. The cooled mineral water is then piped to three large outdoor soaking pools, which are maintained at 101° to 105° on a flow-through basis, requiring no chemical treatment of the water. These pools are equipped with access ramps for the convenience of handicapped persons. There are also four indoor private-space fiberglass hydrojet pools supplied with mineral water maintained at 101° on a flow-through basis. All pools are available to the public as well as to registered guests. Bathing suits are required except in private spaces.

Locker rooms, cafe, store and cabins are available on the premises. It is ¼ mile to a National Park campground, 15 miles to a service station and 30 miles to RV hook-ups. MasterCard and Visa are accepted.

Directions: From US 101, two miles west of Fairholm, take Soleduc River Road 11 miles south to resort.

Source map: NPS *Olympic National Park.*

*Sol Duc Hot Springs Resort:* These lovely tiled pools were designed for family fun; as well as for soaking and swimming.

*Sol Duc* even has four private-space hot tubs in a building near the pools, thereby bringing the modern comfort of rent-a-tub stores to a hot spring in the mountains.

Wise visitors to *Olympic Hot Springs* check water temperatures before plunging in. This pool, on a summer day, is nearly 110°.

*Olympic Hot Springs:* The largest of the several pools is this last vestige of an old, long-since-abandoned commercial resort.

# Hot Springs

Indians, pioneers and 1920s travellers bathed in these pools. According to legend, both the Olympic and Sol Duc Hot Springs (in Soleduck Valley) are the result of hot tears shed by two creatures who fought a frustrating battle neither could win. The tears at Olympic Hot Springs range from lukewarm to 188°F.

Sol Duc and Olympic Hot Springs are chemically similar. Ordinary surface water seeps down until it reaches the earth's hotter interior. Then, through cracks in the rock, steam and heated water rise to form the springs.

The National Park Service will maintain modern bathing facilities at Sol Duc and keep these Olympic Hot Springs in a natural state. Enjoy them, but help us preserve these "legendary tears." Please do not litter, or use plastic liners, or alter the pools in any way.

Chemistry of Olympic Hot Springs

| Chemical | Parts per million |
|----------|-------------------|
| Chlorine | 0.4 to 0.7 |
| Sodium | 39 to 79 |
| Potassium | 0.7 to 1.5 |
| Silica | 30 to 120 |

The waters are an alkaline pH 9.5.

Legendary Lightning Fish

52

## #332   OLYMPIC HOT SPRINGS   (see map)
### South of Port Angeles   non-commerical

Several user-friendly primitive springs surrounded by lush rain forest at the end of an easy two-mile hike in Olympic National Park. Elevation 1,600 ft. Open all year.

Natural mineral water flows out of several springs at temperatures ranging from 100° to 112°. Volunteers have built a series of rock-and-sand soaking pools which permits the water to cool down to comfortable soaking temperatures. Official notices prohibiting nudity are posted often and promptly torn down, resulting in considerable uncertainty. Rangers have been observed issuing a citation after someone complained or after bathers didn't heed orders to dress. However, rangers have not made special trips to the area for the purpose of harassment.

Conscientious visitors have kept the area litter-free. Please do your part to maintain this standard.

There are no services on the premises, but there is a walk-in campground within 200 yards. It is eight miles to a cafe, store and service station, seven miles to a campground, and 20 miles to a motel and RV hook-ups.

Directions: From the city of Port Angeles, go ten miles west on US 101, turn south and follow signs to Elwha Valley. Continue south on paved road as it winds up Boulder Creek canyon to where the road is closed due to slide damage. Park and walk the remaining two miles on the damaged paved road to the old end-of-road parking area. At the west end of that parking area is an unmarked, unmaintained path which crosses Boulder Creek and then leads into the hot-spring area. Most, but not all, paths indicate the presence of a nearby spring.

Source map: NPS *Olympic National Park.* (hot springs not shown)

▲ This *Olympic Hot Springs* pool is on a cliff just above the tumbling waterfalls of Boulder Creek, which is fed all year by melting snow.

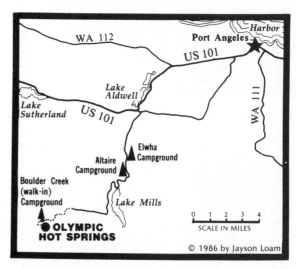

© 1986 by Jayson Loam

| #333A | COACHMAN INN | |
|---|---|---|
| ☐ | 5563 Hwy 20 | (206) 675-0727 |
| | Oak Harbor, WA 98277 | Hydropool  MH |
| #333B | THE AULD HOLLAND INN | |
| ☐ | on WA 20 | (206) 675-2288 |
| | Oak Harbor, WA 98277 | Hydropool  MH |
| #334 | THE RESORT AT PORT LUDLOW | |
| ☐ | 781 Walker Way | (206) 437-2222 |
| | Port Ludlow, WA 98365 | Hydropool  MH |

#335A SPA WORLD
☐ 2130 6th St.         (206) 373-8727
Bremerton, WA 98312       PR

Newer rent-a-tub establishment, built and operated by a hot tub dealer, on a main street in western Bremerton. Open all year.

Private space pools, using bromine-treated tap water, are for rent to the public by the hour. There are seven fiberglass hydrojet pools in private rooms, with the water maintained at 102° to 104°. There is also a communal sauna. Bathing suits are required in the sauna but not in private rooms. Visa and MasterCard are accepted.

Phone for rates, reservations and directions.

#335B BAYVIEW INN
☐ 5640 Kitsap Way       (206) 373-7349
Bremerton, WA 98312   Hydropool MH

#336 ALDERBROOK INN
☐ on WA 106         (206) 898-2200
Union, WA 98592     Hydropool MH

#337A VANCE TYEE MOTOR INN
☐ 500 Tyee Dr.        (206) 352-0511
Olympia, WA 98502    Hydropool MH

#337B OLYMPIA'S WESTWATER INN
☐ 2300 Evergreen Park Dr.  (206) 943-4000
Olympia, WA 98502    Hydropool MH

#338 ECONO LODGE
☐ 702 Harrison Ave.    (206) 736-2875
Centralia, WA 98531
                In-room hydropools MH

#339A ROYAL COACHMAN MOTOR INN
☐ 5805 Pacific Hwy E.   (206) 922-2500
Tacoma, WA 98424  In-room hydropools MH

#339B BEST WESTERN EXECUTIVE INN
☐ 5700 Pacific Hwy E.   (206) 922-0080
Tacoma, WA 98424    Hydropool MH

#339C APPLE INN
☐ 1811 S. 76th St.     (206) 473-7100
Tacoma, WA 98408    Hydropool MH

#339D BEST WESTERN TACOMA INN
☐ 8716 S. Hosmer St.   (206) 535-2880
Tacoma, WA 98444    Hydropool MH

#339F TACOMA DOME HOTEL
☐ 2611 East E St.      (206) 572-7272
Tacoma, WA 98421    Hydropool MH

#339G SHERATON-TACOMA HOTEL
☐ S. 13th St. & Broadway Plaza (206) 572-3200
Tacoma, WA 98402    Hydropool MH

#339H KINGS MOTOR INN
☐ 5115 Pacific Hwy E.   (206) 922-3636
Tacoma, WA 98454    Hydropool MH

#340 NORTHWEST MOTOR INN
☐ 1409 S. Meridian     (206) 842-2600
Puyallup, WA 98271   Hydropool MH

#341A GRAND CENTRAL SAUNA & HOT
☐ TUB CO.
32510 Pacific Highway South
                (206) 952-6154
Federal Way, WA 98003      PR

One of a chain of urban locations, established by Grand Central, a pioneer in the private rent-a-tub business. Open all year.

Private-space hot pools using chlorine-treated tap water are for rent to the public by the hour. 19 indoor tubs are maintained at temperatures from 102° to 104°. Each unit contains a sauna. No credit cards are accepted.

Phone for rates, reservations and directions.

#341B AUBURN MOTEL
☐ 1202 Auburn Way S.   (206) 833-7470
Auburn, WA 98002    Hydropool MH

#341C BEST WESTERN PONY SOLDIER INN
☐ 1521 D St. N.E.      (206) 939-5950
Auburn, WA 98002    Hydropool MH

#341D BEST WESTERN PONY SOLDIER MOTOR
☐ INN
1233 N. Central      (206) 852-7224
Kent, WA 98031      Hydropool MH

#342A GRAND CENTRAL SAUNA & HOT
☐ TUB CO.
2620 2nd Avenue    (206)447-9444
Seattle, WA 98121       PR

One of a chain of urban locations, established by Grand Central, a pioneer in the private room rent-a-tub business. Open all year.

Private-space hot pools using chlorine-treated tap water are for rent to the public by the hour. 23 indoor wood tubs are maintained at temperatures from 102° to 104°. Each unit contains a sauna. Visa and MasterCard are accepted.

Phone for rates, reservations and directions.

#342B ALEXIS HOTEL
☐ 1007 1st Ave.       (206) 624-4844
Seattle, WA 98104  In-room hydropools MH

#342C SEATTLE SHERATON HOTEL & TOWERS
☐ 6th & Pike Sts.      (206) 621-9000
Seattle, WA 98111  In-room hydropools MH

#342D BEST WESTERN EXECUTIVE INN
☐ 200 Taylor Ave. N.   (206) 628-9444
Seattle, WA 98109  In-room hydropools MH

#342E WARWICK HOTEL
☐ Fourth and Lenora   (206) 625-6700
Seattle, WA 98121    Hydropool MH

#342F RODESIDE LODGE
☐ 12501 Aurora Ave.   (206) 364-7771
Seattle, WA 98133    Hydropool MH

| #342G | HOLIDAY INN CROWNE PLAZA | |
| □ | 1113 6th Ave. | (206) 464-1980 |
| | Seattle, WA 98101 | Hydropool MH |

| #342H | FOUR SEASONS OLYMPIC HOTEL | |
| □ | 411 University St. | (206) 621-1700 |
| | Seattle, WA 98101 | Hydropool MH |

| #342I | BEST WESTERN LOYAL INN | |
| □ | 2301 8th Ave. | (206) 682-0200 |
| | Seattle, WA 98121 | Hydropool MH |

| #342J | VANCE AIRPORT INN | |
| □ | 18220 Pacific Hwy S. | (206) 246-5535 |
| | Seattle, WA 98188 | Hydropool MH |

| #342K | SEATTLE MARRIOTT SEA-TAC AIRPORT | |
| □ | 3201 S. 176th St. | (206) 241-2000 |
| | Seattle, WA 98188 | Hydropool MH |

| #342L | SEATTLE AIRPORT HILTON | |
| □ | 17620 Pacific Hwy S. | (206) 244-4800 |
| | Seattle, WA 98188 | Hydropool MH |

| #342M | DOUBLETREE PLAZA HOTEL | |
| □ | 16500 Southcenter Pkwy. | (206) 575-8220 |
| | Seattle, WA 98188 | Hydropool MH |

| #342N | THE WESTIN HOTEL | |
| □ | 1900 5th Ave. | (206) 624-7400 |
| | Seattle, WA 98101 | Hydropool MH |

| #342O | APPLE INN | |
| □ | 20651 Military Rd. S. | (206) 824-9902 |
| | Seattle, WA 98188 | Hydropool MH |

| #342P | GEISHA INN | |
| □ | 9613 Aurora Ave. | (206) 524-8880 |
| | Seattle, WA 98103 | Hydropool MH |

| #342Q | TUKWILA SILVER CLOUD MOTEL | |
| □ | 13050 48th Ave. S. | (206) 241-2200 |
| | Seattle, WA 98168 | Hydropool MH |

| #342R | SKYWAY MOTEL | |
| □ | 20045 Pacific Hwy S. | (206) 878-3310 |
| | Seattle, WA 98188 | Hydropool MH |

| #342S | QUALITY INN AT SEA-TAC | |
| □ | 3000 S. 176th St. | (206) 246-9110 |
| | Seattle, WA 98188 | Hydropool MH |

| #343A | BELLEVUE HILTON | |
| □ | 100 112th Ave. N.E. | (206) 455-3330 |
| | Bellevue, WA 98004 | Hydropool MH |

| #343B | TRAILER INNS | |
| □ | near I-90 & I-405 | (206) 747-9181 |
| | Bellevue, WA 98009 | Hydropool CRV |

| #343C | AQUA BARN RANCH CAMPGROUND | |
| □ | on Hwy 169 | (206) 255-4618 |
| | Renton, WA 98055 | Hydropool CRV |

| #344A | HOLIDAY INN—ISSAQUAH | |
| □ | 1801 12th Ave. N.W. | (206) 392-6421 |
| | Issaquah, WA 98027 | Hydropool MH |

## #344B FRATERNITY SNOQUALMIE

□ P.O. Box 985           (206)392-NUDE
   Seattle, WA 98111          PR + CRV

Long-established nudist park occupying a hillside fruit orchard surrounded by evergreens. Elevation 500 ft. Open all year.

The outdoor hydrojet pool is maintained at 104° on weekends only. The outdoor swimming pool is solar heated, ranging from 80° in the summer to 50° in the winter. The wading pool is filled only in the summer. All pools use well water treated with chlorine. There is also a wood-fired sauna.

Clothing is not permitted in the pools or sauna.

Overnight camping and RV hook-ups are available on the premises. It is four miles to a cafe, store, service stations and motel. No credit cards.

This is a membership organization not open to the public for drop-in visits, but prospective members may be issued a guest pass by prior arrangement. Telephone or write for information or directions.

▲ *Fraternity Snoqualmie:* The pool may not have natural mineral water, but, to a skinny-dipper, the absence of swim suits is a plus.

## #345 GOLDMEYER HOT SPRINGS

■ P.O. Box 1292     (206) 888-4653
North Bend, WA 98045     PR + CRV

Very remote and beautiful mountain hot springs being developed and managed by a volunteer organization. Prior reservations are required. Elevation 1,800 ft. Open all year.

Natural mineral water flows out of several springs and an old horizontal mine shaft at temperatures up to 150°. A dam has been built across the mouth of the shaft, creating a combination steam bath and soaking pools, with water temperatures ranging up to 109°. Outdoor soaking pools are planned at nearby springs. Ask for the status of construction when making reservations. Bathing suits are optional.

The springs are a ½ mile hike from the nearest parking, and overnight camping is available on the premises. It is 28 miles to all other services. MasterCard and Visa are accepted.

Access roads vary in quality from Forest Service Class A to Class D—not suitable for trailers, motor homes and low clearance vehicles. Ask for a current report on weather conditions when phoning for reservations and directions.

You can support the work of this organization by sending tax-deductible contributions to Goldmeyer Hot Springs Northwest Wilderness Programs, 202 N. 85th, Seattle, WA 98103.

*Goldmeyer Hot Springs:* A tumbling mountain stream is part of the wilderness atmosphere at this cave-mouth rock and cement pool.

## #349 LAKE ASSOCIATES

☐ P.O. Box 277     (206) 793-0286
Sultan, WA 98294     PR + MH + CRV

Unusually spacious nudist park with its own 7½-acre lake, waterfall and evergreen forest. Elevation 800 ft. Open all year.

Two outdoor hydrojet pools using chlorine-treated artesian well water are maintained within a range of 97° to 104°. The spring-fed lake warms to 80° in the summer and freezes over in the winter. There is also a coin-operated electrically heated sauna. Clothing is prohibited in pool, sauna and lake, and is optional elsewhere.

Rental trailers, laundry facilities overnight camping and RV hook-ups are available on the premises. It is six miles to a cafe, store, service station and motel. No credit cards are accepted.

This is a membership organization not open to the public for drop-in visits, but interested visitors may be issued a guest pass by prior arrangement. Telephone or write for information and directions.

| #346A | OVERLAKE SILVER CLOUD MOTEL | | |
|---|---|---|---|
| ☐ | 15304 N.E. 21st St. | (206) 746-8200 | |
| | Redmond, WA 98052 | Hydropool | MH |

| #346B | BEST WESTERN ARNOLD'S MOTOR INN | | |
|---|---|---|---|
| ☐ | 12223 N.E. 116th St. | (206) 822-2300 | |
| | Kirkland, WA 98033 | Hydropool | MH |

| #346C | TOTEM LAKE SILVER CLOUD MOTEL | | |
|---|---|---|---|
| ☐ | 12202 N.E. 124th St. | (206) 821-8300 | |
| | Kirkland, WA 98034 | Hydropool | MH |

| #346D | SEATTLE NORTH RV PARK | | |
|---|---|---|---|
| ☐ | on 15th Ave. N.E. | (206) 481-1972 | |
| | Bothell, WA 98011 | Hydropool | CRV |

| #347A | BEST WESTERN LANDMARK INN | | |
|---|---|---|---|
| ☐ | 4300 200th St. S.W. | (206) 775-7447 | |
| | Lynnwood, WA 98036 | Hydropool | MH |

| #347B | BEST WESTERN HOTEL LYNNWOOD | | |
|---|---|---|---|
| ☐ | 5621 196th St. S.W. | (206) 771-1777 | |
| | Lynnwood, WA 98036 | Hydropool | MH |

| #348 | SPORTSMAN SKYKOMISH RESORT | | |
|---|---|---|---|
| ☐ | on US 2 | (206) 793-0522 | |
| | Gold Bar, WA 98251 | Hydropool | CRV |

| #350A | HOLIDAY INN | | |
|---|---|---|---|
| ☐ | 101 128th St. S.W. | (206) 745-2555 | |
| | Everett, WA 98204 | Hydropool | MH |

| #350B | RAMADA EVERETT PACIFIC | | |
|---|---|---|---|
| ☐ | 3105 Pine St. | (206) 339-3333 | |
| | Everett, WA 98204 | Hydropool | MH |

| #350C | NORTHWEST MOTOR INN | | |
|---|---|---|---|
| ☐ | 9602 19th Ave. S.E. | (206) 337-9090 | |
| | Everett, WA 98204 | Hydropool | MH |

| #351 | KOA—BURLINGTON CASCADE | | |
|---|---|---|---|
| ☐ | on old Hwy 99 | (206) 724-5511 | |
| | Burlington, WA 98233 | Hydropool | CRV |

| #352A | PARK MOTEL | | |
|---|---|---|---|
| ☐ | 101 N. Samish Way | (206) 733-8280 | |
| | Bellingham, WA 98225 | Hydropool | MH |

| #352B | COACHMAN INN | | |
|---|---|---|---|
| ☐ | 120 Samish Way | (206) 671-9000 | |
| | Bellingham, WA 98225 | Hydropool | MH |

*Doe Bay Village Resort:* This hot-pool deck area gives the illusion of being up in a tree house, overlooking Rosario Strait and the lush greenery of the San Juan Islands.

| #352C | HOLIDAY INN | |
|---|---|---|
| ☐ | 714 Lakeway Dr. | (206) 671-1011 |
| | Bellingham, WA 98225 | Hydropool MH |

| #352D | BEST WESTERN HERITAGE INN | |
|---|---|---|
| ☐ | 151 E. McLeod Rd. | (206) 647-1912 |
| | Bellingham, WA 98226 | Hydropool MH |

| #353 | ISLANDS MOTEL | |
|---|---|---|
| ☐ | 3401 Commercial Ave. | (206) 293-4644 |
| | Anacortes, WA 98221 | Hydropool MH |

| #354 | ISLANDER LOPEZ | |
|---|---|---|
| ☐ | on Fisherman's Bay | (206) 468-2283 |
| | Lopez Island, WA 98261 | Hydropool MH |

| #355 | ISLAND LODGE | |
|---|---|---|
| ☐ | 1016 Guard St. | (206) 378-2000 |
| | Friday Harbor, WA 98250 | Hydropool MH |

| #356 | DEER HARBOR RESORT AND MARINA | |
|---|---|---|
| ☐ | On Orcas Island | (206) 376-4420 |
| | Deer Harbor, WA 98243 | Hydropool MH |

| #357 | ROSARIO RESORT HOTEL | |
|---|---|---|
| ☐ | On Orcas Island | (206) 376-2222 |
| | Eastsound, WA 98245 | Hydropool MH |

## #358   DOE BAY VILLAGE RESORT
**Orcas Island Star Route 86**

**(206) 376-2291**

**Olga, WA 98279**     **PR + MH + CRV**

Fantastic combination of running stream, waterfall, ocean view, hot mineral-water pools, cabins, RV spaces, youth hostel, vegetarian restaurant and a general clothing-optional policy. Ideal for a casual, natural retreat. Elevation sea level. Open all year.

Natural mineral water is pumped out of a well at 105° and is piped to two outdoor pools, where it is treated with chlorine. Each pool is large enough for a dozen people, and one of them has hydrojets. Both are maintained at 104° to 106°, and a smaller cold pool is maintained at 70° to 80°. There is also a wood-fired sauna large enough for 20 people. The pools and sauna are available to the public as well as to registered guests. Bathing suits are optional.

Massage, vegetarian meals, cabins, overnight camping, RV hook-ups and a youth hostel are available on the premises. It is seven miles to a store and service station. Visa, MasterCard and American Express are accepted.

Directions: Take the Anacortes Ferry to the San Juan Islands and get off at Orcas Island. Go north on horseshoe highway through Eastshore to the resort at the east end of the island.

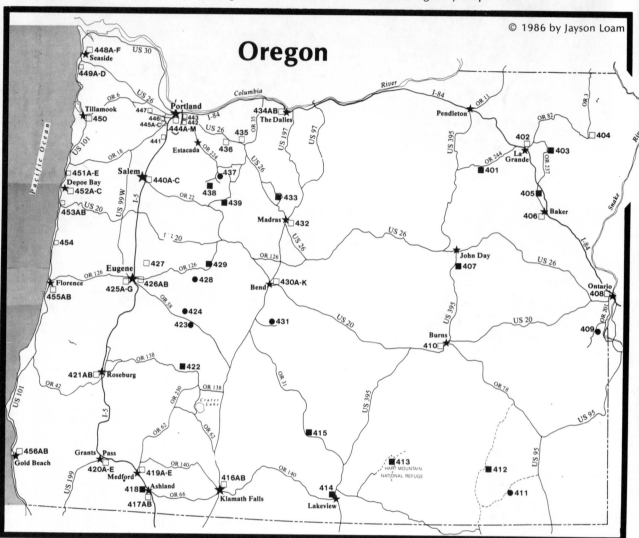

© 1986 by Jayson Loam

# Oregon

## MAP AND DIRECTORY SYMBOLS

● Unimproved natural mineral water pool
■ Improved natural mineral water pool
□ Gas-heated tap or well water pool

———— Paved highway
– ‑ – ‑ – Unpaved road
·····‥····· Hiking route

PR = Tubs or pools for rent by hour, day or treatment

MH = Rooms, cabins or dormitory spaces for rent by day, week or month

CRV = Camping or vehicle parking spaces, some with hookups,
for rent by day, week, month or year

▲ *Lehman Hot Springs:* After being closed for many years, this famous Eastern Oregon resort is again open and expanding its facilities.

➤ *Cove Swimming Pool:* Although the 86° water temperature is not exactly "hot", it is fine for a town plunge, especially with no chlorine.

## #401  LEHMAN HOT SPRINGS

■ P.O. Box 247             (503) 427-3613
Ukiah, OR 97880           PR + CRV

Historic major hot spring being developed into a large destination resort, nestled in a timbered setting of the beautiful Blue Mountains. Elevation 4,300 ft. Open all year.

Natural mineral water flows out of several springs at temperatures up to 167°, and is mixed with cold creek water before being piped to a series of outdoor pools. The first pool ranges from 112° to 115°, the second pool ranges from 107° to 110° and the swimming pool ranges from 85° to 90° in the summer and from 90° to 96° in the winter. All pools operate on a flow-through basis and no chemical treatment is necessary. The pools are available to the public as well as to registered guests. Bathing suits are required.

Locker rooms, cafe, camping and RV hook-ups are available on the premises. Saddle horses, hiking trails, fishing, hunting, cross country skiing and snow-mobiling are available nearby. A store, service station and motel are within 18 miles. Visa and MasterCard are accepted.

Developments in the future include plans for a large RV park, therapy pools, massage, store, garden golf, motel, lodge, stables and restaurant. Phone for status of construction.

Directions: From Ukiah on OR 244, go 18 miles east, watch for signs and go one mile south to resort.

## #402  BEST WESTERN PONY SOLDIER MOTOR INN

□ Rte. 4, Box 4009          (503) 963-4154
La Grande, OR 97850        Hydropool  MH

## #403  COVE SWIMMING POOL

■ Rte. 1, Box 36            (503) 586-4890
Cove, OR 97824            PR + CRV

Rural community plunge and picnic grounds in the foothills of the Wallowa Mountains. Elevation 3,200 ft. Open May 1 through Labor Day.

Natural mineral water flows out of a spring at 86° directly into and through an outdoor swimming pool. No chlorine is added. Bathing suits are required.

Picnic grounds and overnight parking are available on the premises. It is eight miles to a cafe, store, service station and RV hook-ups, and 15 miles to a motel. No credit cards are accepted.

Directions: On OR 237 go 16 miles east of the town of La Grande.

59

#404  WILDERNESS INN
□  301 W. North St.
Enterprise, OR 97828     (503) 426-4535
Hydropool MH

#405  **RADIUM HOT SPRINGS**
■  P.O. Box 220
**Haines, OR 97833**     (503) 856-3609
PR + CRV

Community plunge, picnic grounds and RV park surrounded by the flat agricultural lands of the Baker Valley. Elevation 3,300 ft. Open June 1 through Labor Day.

Natural mineral water flows out of the spring at 135°. The outdoor swimming pool is chlorine-treated and maintained at 90° to 95°. The buildings are heated with geothermal energy. Bathing suits are required.

Picnic grounds and overnight RV spaces are available on the premises. It is one mile to a cafe, store and service station, seven miles to a motel and 12 miles to RV hook-ups. No credit cards are accepted.

Directions: On US 30 go one mile north of the town of Haines.

▲  *Radium Hot Springs:* According to the owner, this sign eliminated his trespasser problem.

▼  This aerial view of *Radium Hot Springs,* with UFO invitation, decorates a wall in the owner's home.

▲ *Snively Hot Springs:* This river-edge soaking pool escapes spring washouts because the river is controlled by an upstream dam.

---

| #406 ☐ | EL DORADO<br>695 E. Campbell St.<br>Baker, OR 97814 | (503) 523-6494<br>Hydropool MH |
|---|---|---|

### #407  J BAR L GUEST RANCH
**I Z Route** **(503) 575-2517**
**Canyon City, OR 97820** **PR + MH + CRV**

Renovated guest ranch with hot springs adjoining Strawberry Mountain Wilderness. Elevation 4,500 ft. Open all year.

Natural mineral water flows out of several springs with temperatures ranging up to 120° and is piped to an outdoor swimming pool which ranges from 70° to 90°, depending on weather conditions. Swimming pool is open to the public as well as to registered guests. Bathing suits are required.

Future plans include reconstructed bath houses and an additional pool. Phone for status of construction.

Sauna, locker rooms, picnic area, cabins, overnight camping and RV hook-ups are available on the premises. Hiking trails, fishing and hunting are available nearby. A cafe, store and service station are located within ten miles. Visa and MasterCard are accepted.

Directions: Drive 10 miles south of John Day on US 395. Turn left on FS 15 and turn immediately left into ranch.

| #408 ☐ | COLONIAL MOTOR INN<br>761 Tapadera Ave.<br>Ontario, OR 97914 | (503) 889-9615<br>Hydropool MH |
|---|---|---|

### #409  SNIVELY HOT SPRINGS
■ **Southwest of the town of Owyhee**
**non-commercial**

Easily accessible primitive hot spring on the river's edge in the Owyhee River canyon. Elevation 2,400 ft. Open all year.

Natural mineral water flows out of several springs and a concrete standpipe at temperatures of more than 150°, and then flows toward the river, where volunteers have built several rock-and-sand soaking pools. The temperature in the pools is controlled by varying the amount of cold river water permitted to enter. The pools are visible from the road, so bathing suits are advisable.

There are no services available on the premises except for a large parking area on which overnight parking is not prohibited. It is 10 miles to a cafe, store and service station and 18 miles to a motel and RV hook-ups. Owyhee Lake offers excellent fishing 11 miles south of this hot spring.

Directions: From the town of Owyhee, on OR 201, follow signs west toward Owyhee State Park. When the road enters Owyhee Canyon look for a large metal water pipe running up a steep slope on the west side of the road. 1.4 miles beyond that metal pipe, look on the other side of the road for a low concrete standpipe from which steaming water is flowing.

Source map: USGS *Owyhee Dam, Oregon.*

61

#410　　COMFORT INN
□　　　999 Oregon Ave.　　　(503) 573-5295
　　　　Burns, OR 97720　　　Hydropool  MH

## #411　WHITEHORSE RANCH HOT SPRING
### Southeast of Alvord Desert
**non-commercial**

A very remote primitive hot spring requiring about 28 miles of unpaved road travel in southeastern corner of Oregon. Elevation 3,500 ft. Open all year.

Natural mineral water flows out of a spring at 114° into a small volunteer-built soaking pool which ranges in temperature from 104° to 112°. The overflow runs into a larger second pool which ranges in temperature from 70° to 90°, depending on air temperature and wind conditions. The apparent local custom is clothing optional.

There are no services on the premises but there is plenty of level space on which overnight parking is not prohibited. It is 45 miles to all services.

Directions: From Burns Junction on US 95, go 21 miles south on US 95, then turn west on a gravel road and go 21 miles to Whitehorse Ranch. Continue five miles past the ranch, go east on a dirt road for .4 mile, then south for 1.4 miles, then west around a butte to the spring. There are no USGS quad maps for the area.

## #412　ALVORD HOT SPRINGS　(see map)
### Northeast of Denio Junction(NV)
**non-commercial**

Semi-improved hot spring on the western edge of the Alvord Desert. Elevation 4,000 ft. Open all year.

Natural mineral water flows out of a spring at 120°, through a ditch to two cement soaking pools, one of them enclosed by sheets of bullet-riddled corrugated metal. Temperature in each pool is controlled by diverting the 120° inflow whenever desired. The apparent local custom is clothing optional.

There are no services available on the premises but there is an abundance of space along the edge of the road where overnight parking is not prohibited. It is 25 miles to all services.

Source map: USGS *Alvord Hot Springs, Oregon.*

◀ *Whitehorse Ranch Hot Spring:* This spot is about as far from the city as you can get.

▼ *Hart Mountain Hot Spring:* The wall provides privacy and wind protection but kills the view.

## #413　HART MOUNTAIN HOT SPRING
　　　　　　　　　　　　　　　　**(see map)**
### North of the town of Adel
**non-commercial**

Semi-improved hot spring, enclosed by roofless cement block wall, surrounded by miles of barren plateau within the Hart Mountain National Antelope Refuge. Elevation 6,000 ft. Open all year.

Natural mineral water flows out of a spring at 98°. The edge of the spring has been cemented to create a soaking pool which maintains that temperature. There is no posted clothing policy, which leaves it up to the mutual consent of those present.

There are no services available on the premises, but there is an abundance of level ground on which overnight parking is not prohibited. It is 20 miles to a cafe and store, and 40 miles to all other services.

Source map: *Hart Mountain National Antelope Refuge.*

▲ *Alvord Hot Springs:* This is a favorite stop for sand sailors who navigate the windy, level Alvord Desert.

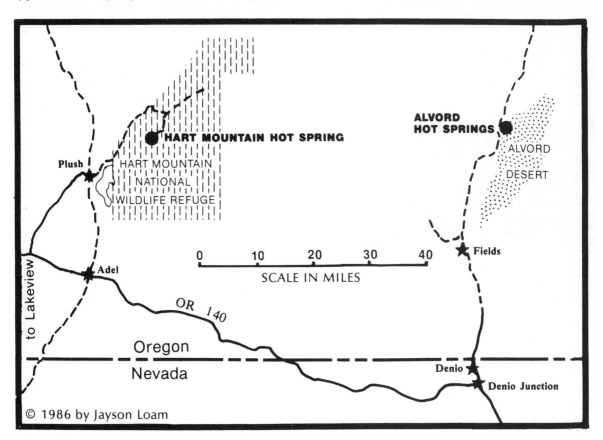

HART MOUNTAIN HOT SPRING

ALVORD HOT SPRINGS

ALVORD DESERT

Plush

HART MOUNTAIN NATIONAL WILDLIFE REFUGE

0    10    20    30    40
SCALE IN MILES

Fields

Adel

OR 140

to Lakeview

Oregon

Nevada

Denio

Denio Junction

© 1986 by Jayson Loam

63

*Hunter's Hot Spring Resort:* This geyser is hardly as large as Yellowstone's Old Faithful, but no one has to wait more than two minutes.

## #414 HUNTER'S HOT SPRING RESORT

P.O. Box 911      (503) 947-2127
Lakeview, OR 97630

Historic spa in the process of a major expansion and tasteful remodeling into a destination resort. Located in rolling southern Oregon hills two miles north of Lakeview. Elevation 4,200 ft. Open all year.

Natural mineral water flows out of several springs at temperatures up to 203°, into cooling ponds, from which it is piped to the pool and to a heat exchanger for the hot-water system in the buildings. Natural mineral water also erupts out of a geothermal geyser every one minute and 20 seconds into two large cooling ponds. An outdoor swimming pool is maintained at approximately 100° on a flow-through system with a minimum of chlorine treatment. Pool use is limited to registered guests, and bathing suits are required.

A restaurant, store, service station, overnight camping and motel rooms are available on the premises. Pickup service to a private airport four miles away is also available. Golf, hunting and fishing are available in the area. Visa and MasterCard are accepted.

Location: Two miles north of the town of Lakeview on US 395.

Note: Expansion plans include a health club, supervised physical therapy, several major museum buildings, a new lodge and a full hook-up RV park. Phone or write ahead for current brochure and status of construction.

## #415 SUMMER LAKE HOT SPRINGS

(503) 943-3931
Summer Lake, OR 97640      PR + CRV

Small indoor plunge in the wide open spaces south of Summer Lake. Elevation 4,200 ft. Open all year.

Natural mineral water flows out of a spring at 118° and cools as it is piped to the pool building. Water temperature in the indoor pool is maintained at 102° in the winter and 100° in the summer on a continuous flow-through basis, which requires no chemical treatment of the water. Bathing suits are required.

Dressing rooms, overnight camping and RV hook-ups are available on the premises. It is six miles to all other services. No credit cards.

Location: Six miles northwest of the town of Paisley on OR 31. Watch for sign on north side of road.

| #416A | OREGON MOTEL 8 | |
|---|---|---|
| | Rte. 5, Box 1348 | (503) 883-3431 |
| | Klamath Falls, OR 97601 | Hydropool MH |

| #416B | MALLARD CAMPGROUND | |
|---|---|---|
| | on US 97 | (503) 882-0482 |
| | Klamath Falls, OR 97601 | Hydropool CRV |

▲ *Jackson Hot Springs:* Thanks to geothermal heat this swimming pool is open all winter.

▼ *Summer Lake Hot Springs:* This spring has enough flow to avoid pool chlorination.

#### #417A ASHLAND HILLS INN
☐ 2525 Ashland St.  (503) 482-8310
Ashland, OR 97520  Hydropool MH

#### #417B ROMEO INN
☐ 295 Idaho St.  (503) 488-0884
Ashland, OR 97520  Hydropool MH

## #418 JACKSON HOT SPRINGS
■ 2253 Hwy 99 N.  (503) 482-3776
Ashland, OR 97520  PR + MH + CRV

Older resort with public plunge, indoor soaking tubs, picnic grounds and RV park. Elevation 1,800 ft. Open all year.

Natural mineral water flows out of a spring at 86°, directly into an outdoor swimming pool which is treated with chlorine and maintains a temperature of 84°. There are two indoor individual soaking tubs large enough for two persons each, in which additionally heated natural mineral water may be controlled up to 110°. These tubs are drained and cleaned after each use so no chemical treatment of the water is necessary. Bathing suits are required except in private rooms.

Locker rooms, picnic grounds, cabins, overnight camping and RV hook-ups are available on the premises. There is a cafe within two blocks, and a store and service station within two miles. Visa and MasterCard are accepted.

Location: On US 99, two miles north of Ashland.

#### #419A BEST WESTERN PONY SOLDIER MOTOR INN
☐ 2340 Crater Lake Hwy  (503) 779-2011
Medford, OR 97502  Hydropool MH

#### #419B BEST WESTERN THUNDERBIRD LODGE
☐ 1015 S. Riverside Ave.  (503) 773-8266
Medford, OR 97501  Hydropool MH

#### #419C HORIZON MOTOR INN
☐ 1150 E. Barnett Rd.  (503) 779-5085
Medford, OR 97504  Hydropool MH

#### #419D SHILO INN—MEDFORD
☐ 2111 Biddle Rd.  (503) 770-5151
Medford, OR 97501  Hydropool MH

#### #419E WINDMILL INN
☐ 1950 Biddle Rd.  (503) 779-0050
Medford, OR 97501  Hydropool MH

### #420A CEDAR CREST HOT TUB RENTALS

☐ 227 N.E. Hillcrest Dr.  (503) 476-8444
Grants Pass, OR 97526  PR

Clean and spacious rent-a-tub establishment located near the K-Mart plaza.

Private-space hot pools, using chlorine-treated tap water, are for rent to the public by the hour. Four indoor fiberglass hydrojet tubs are maintained at 102° to 104°. No credit cards are accepted.

Phone for rates, reservations and directions.

### #420B RODEWAY INN

☐ 111 Agnes Ave.  (503) 476-1117
Grants Pass, OR 97526
In-room hydropools  MH

### #420C BEST WESTERN RIVERSIDE MOTEL

☐ 971 S.E. Sixth St.  (503) 476-6873
Grants Pass, OR 97526  Hydropool  MH

### #420D SHILO INN—GRANTS PASS

☐ 1880 N.W. Sixth St.  (503) 479-8391
Grants Pass, OR 97526  Hydropool  MH

### #420E ROYAL VUE MOTOR HOTEL

☐ 110 N.E. Morgan Lane  (503) 479-5381
Grants Pass, OR 97526  Hydropool  MH

### #421A BEST WESTERN GARDEN VILLA MOTEL ANNEX

☐ 511 S.E. Stephens St.  (503) 673-6625
Roseburg, OR 97470  Hydropool  MH

### #421B WINDMILL INN

☐ 1450 Mulholland Dr.  (503) 673-0901
Roseburg, OR 97470  Hydropool  MH

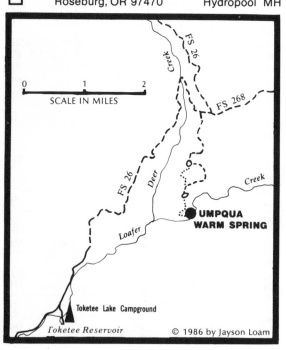

0  1  2
SCALE IN MILES

FS 26

Creek

FS 268

FS 26

Deer

Creek

UMPQUA WARM SPRING

Loafer

Toketee Lake Campground

Toketee Reservoir

© 1986 by Jayson Loam

▲ *Cedar Crest Hot Tub Rentals:* Water purity and temperature are checked often each day.

### #422 UMPQUA WARM SPRING (see map)
**Northwest of Crater Lake**

■ **non-commercial**

Popular, small, semi-improved hot spring on a wooded bluff overlooking Loafer Creek. Located in Umpqua National Forest at the end of a fairly steep one-mile hike. Elevation 2,800 ft. Open all year.

Natural mineral water flows out of a spring at 108°, directly into a sheltered 6' by 6' pool which volunteers have carved out of the spring-built tufa mound. There are no posted clothing requirements, and the location is quite remote, so a clothing-optional custom would be expected. However, the location is so popular, especially on summer weekends, that it is advisable to take a bathing suit with you. You may have to wait your turn to share a rather crowded pool.

There are no services available on the premises but there is a level area approximately one mile from the pools where overnight parking is not prohibited. It is five miles to a Forest Service campground and 25 miles to all other services.

Directions: One mile southeast of the steel bridge over Deer Creek, on FS 268 northeast of Toketee Lake, turn south onto an unmarked, unmaintained dirt road and go 1.6 miles to the upper parking area. Just .2 mile before reaching this parking area the road will run under some power lines for .3 mile. The road continuing on to the lower parking area is so poor that only 4-wheel-drive rigs should attempt it. Instead, look for a path at the lower edge of the upper parking area and hike downhill for 650 yards to the lower section of the road, plus another 300 yards on that road to the lower parking area. A cement marker indicates the starting point for a steep but well-maintained trail (¼ mile) down to the spring.

Source map: *Umpqua National Forest.*

*Umpqua Warm Spring:* The pool, and its rustic shelter, are perched well up into the trees, more than 100 feet above Loafer Creek. The location is so popular that the tiny pool will often have wall-to-wall bodies.

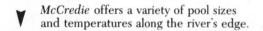
*McCredie Hot Springs:* Clothed and unclothed soakers co-exist here with minimum friction.

*McCredie* offers a variety of pool sizes and temperatures along the river's edge.

## #423   MCCREDIE HOT SPRINGS
### East of the town of Oakridge
**non-commercial**

Easily accessible primitive hot springs with a strong skinny-dipping tradition, located on the north bank of Salt Creek in the Willamette National Forest. Elevation 2,000 ft. Open all year.

Natural mineral water flows out of several springs at 120°, and is channeled into a series of shallow, volunteer-built rock-and-mud pools, where the water cools as it flows toward the creek. Despite the proximity to a main highway the apparent local custom is clothing optional.

There are no services available on the premises, but there is a large level area nearby in which overnight parking is not prohibited. It is less than one mile to a Forest Service campground, and 11 miles to all other services.

Directions: From the town of Oakridge, on OR 58, go approximately 11 miles east, past Blue Pool Campground. At 0.1 mile past mile marker 45, turn right (south) into large parking area between road and creek. Walk to upstream (east) end of parking area and follow well-worn path 40 yards to springs.

*Meditation Pool Warm Spring:* The gentle tumbling sound of Wall Creek, a few feet away, is just enough for quiet centering.

On a crisp and sunny morning *McCredie* is enveloped by an enjoyable, mystical mist.

## #424    MEDITATION POOL (WALL CREEK) WARM SPRING
### Northeast of the town of Oakridge
#### non-commercial

Idyllic primitive warm spring on the wooded banks of Wall Creek, at the end of a short, easy trail in the Willamette National Forest. Elevation 2,200 ft. Open all year.

Natural mineral water flows up through the gravel bottom of a volunteer-built rock-and-sand pool at 98°. The pool temperature ranges up to 96°, depending on air temperature and wind conditions. While the water is not hot enough for therapy soaking, it is ideal for effortless lolling. The apparent local custom is clothing optional.

There are no services available on the premises. It is five miles from the trailhead to a Forest Service campground and nine miles to all other services.

Directions: On OR 58, in the town of Oakridge, at the "city center" highway sign, turn north on Rose St., over the train tracks. At First St. turn east and keep going as that street becomes FS 24. Approximately 10 miles from Oakridge on FS 24, turn north on FS 1934 for ½ mile and watch for trailhead sign on west side of road. There is no name or number given for the trail at the trailhead area. Follow a well-worn path along Wall Creek for 600 yards to creekside pool.

Source map: *Willamette National Forest.*

69

### #425A  ONSEN HOT TUB RENTALS

☐  1883 Garden Ave.      (503) 345-9048
   Eugene, OR 97403           PR

Well-maintained, enclosed-pool rent-a-tub establishment, located near the University of Oregon.

Private space hydrojet pools, using chlorine-treated tap water, are for rent to the public by the hour. Fourteen fiberglass tubs, in open-roof enclosed spaces, are maintained at 102°. Each unit includes a covered dressing area. Visa and MasterCard are accepted.

Phone for rates, reservations and directions.

### #425B  EMERALD PARK AND
###          RIVER ROAD POOL

☐  1499 Lake Dr.        (503) 688-4052
   Eugene, OR 97404           PR

Two spotless outdoor hydrojet pools included in a public recreation complex near downtown Eugene. Open all year.

Large tiled pools, using chlorine-treated tap water, are available for free use by the public, except when reserved for special group use. Water temperature is maintained at 104° in the winter and 102° in the summer. The complex includes an outdoor wading pool and a large indoor swimming pool, as well as a fitness center with weight equipment. One of the hydrojet pools has a roof, and both of them are within a grassy, fenced patio area adjoining the indoor pool. Bathing suits are required. No credit cards are accepted.

Phone to find out the hours when the hydrojet pools are available to the public.

▲ *Onsen Hot Tub Rentals:* Oregon residents enjoy these outdoor pools, rain or shine.

▼ *Emerald Park and River Road Pool:* This is one of the first community-owned hot pool units.

▲ *Springfield Spas:* Urban rent-a-tubs, such as this one, offer a combination of comfort, convenience and total personal privacy.

| #425C | HOLIDAY INN OF EUGENE | |
| :-- | :-- | :-- |
| ☐ | 225 Coburg Rd. | (503) 342-5181 |
| | Eugene, OR 97401 | Hydropool  MH |

| #425D | VALLEY RIVER INN | |
| :-- | :-- | :-- |
| ☐ | 1000 Valley River Way | (503) 687-0123 |
| | Eugene, OR 97401 | Health Club  MH |

| #425E | THE EUGENE HILTON | |
| :-- | :-- | :-- |
| ☐ | 66 E. 6th Ave. | (503) 342-2000 |
| | Eugene, OR 97401 | Hydropool  MH |

| #425F | BEST WESTERN NEW OREGON MOTEL | |
| :-- | :-- | :-- |
| ☐ | 1655 Franklin Blvd. | (503) 683-3669 |
| | Eugene, OR 97440 | Hydropool  MH |

| #425G | SHERWOOD FOREST—KOA | |
| :-- | :-- | :-- |
| ☐ | on Oregon Ave. | (503) 895-4110 |
| | Eugene, OR 97401 | Hydropool  CRV |

| #426A | SPRINGFIELD SPAS | |
| :-- | :-- | :-- |
| ☐ | 1100 Main St. | (503) 741-1777 |
| | Springfield, OR 97477 | PR |

Well-maintained suburban rent-a-tub establishment, located on the main street.

Private-space hydrojet pools, using chlorine-treated tap water, are for rent to the public by the hour. Eight fiberglass tubs, in open-roof enclosed spaces, are maintained at 102°. Each unit includes a covered dressing area. No credit cards are accepted.

Phone for rates, reservations and directions.

| #426B | RED LION MOTOR INN | |
| :-- | :-- | :-- |
| ☐ | 3280 Gateway Rd. | (503) 726-8181 |
| | Springfield, OR 97477 | Hydropool  MH |

| #427 | WILLAMETANS | |
| :-- | :-- | :-- |
| ☐ | P.O. Box 1054 | (503) 933-9955 |
| | Eugene, OR 97401 | PR + MH + CRV |

Large, well-equipped nudist park in the forested foothills east of Eugene. Elevation 1,200 ft. Open all year.

One indoor hydrojet pool, using chlorine-treated tap water, is maintained at 102°. The outdoor swimming pool is maintained at 78° in the summer and is not heated in the winter. There is also a coin-operated sauna. Clothing is prohibited in the pools and sauna, and is optional elsewhere.

Overnight camping and RV hook-ups are available on the premises. It is five miles to all other services. Visa is accepted for payment of ground fees.

Note: This is a membership organization not open to the public for drop-in visits, but interested visitors may be issued a guest pass by prior arrangement. Telephone or write for information and directions.

▲ *Willametans:* While the urban rent-a-tub sites in or near Eugene put their hot pools outside, this nudist pool is indoors, out of the weather.

71

### #428 TERWILLIGER (COUGAR RESERVOIR) HOT SPRINGS (see map)
**Southeast of the town of Blue River**
**non-commercial**

A lovely series of user-friendly log-and-stone soaking pools in a picturesque forest canyon at the end of an easy ¼ mile trail in Willamette National Forest. Elevation 3,000 ft. Open all year.

Natural mineral water flows out of a spring at 112°, directly into the first of a series of volunteer-built pools, each of which is a few degrees cooler than the one above. An organized group of volunteers has also built access steps and railings, and provides a full-time resident caretaker to protect and maintain the location. The apparent local custom is clothing optional.

There are no services available on the premises. There is a walk-in campground within ½ mile, and overnight parking is not prohibited in the roadside space near the trailhead. It is four miles to a Forest Service campground and eight miles to all other services.

Directions: From OR 126, approximately five miles east of Blue River, turn south on FS 19 along the west side of Cougar Reservoir. The unmarked hot-springs trailhead is on the west side of the road, 0.3 mile south of Boone Creek. A large parking area is on the east side of the road, 0.1 mile beyond the trailhead.

Reference map: *Willamette National Forest.* (hot springs not shown)

▲ *Terwilliger (Cougar Reservoir) Hot Springs:* One of the most beautiful multi-pool springs.

▶ At *Terwilliger* the fresh water creek (on left) dwindles to a trickle during a dry summer.

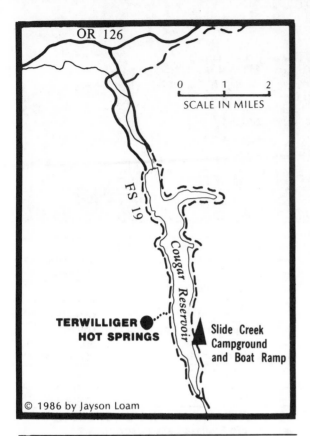

© 1986 by Jayson Loam

## #429 BELKNAP HOT SPRINGS

P.O. Box 1 (503) 822-3535
McKenzie Bridge, OR 97413    RV + MH

Modern riverside resort, with in-room jet tubs and a RV park, surrounded by the lush greenery of Willamette National Forest. Elevation 1,700 ft. Open all year.

Natural mineral water flows out of a spring at 196°, and is piped into a combination reservoir and heat exchanger, where heat is extracted for space heating and for the hot-water supply in the lodge and the RV park. The cooled mineral water is piped to outdoor pools at the lodge and the RV park. Both pools are treated with the chlorine and maintained at a temperature of 102° in the winter and 93° in the summer. Six lodge rooms have indoor hydrojet tubs controllable up to 110°. These tubs are drained and cleaned after each use so no chemical treatment of the water is needed. The use of the pools is limited to registered guests of the lodge and the RV park. Bathing suits are required except in private rooms.

Rooms, overnight camping and RV hook-ups are available on the premises. It is six miles to all other services. Visa and MasterCard are accepted.

Location: On OR 126, 6 miles east of the town of McKenzie Bridge. Follow signs.

▲ *Belknap Hot Springs:* Scalding hot mineral water is piped across the river through the pipes visible beyond the far edge of pool area.

*Dig Your Own Hot Springs:* The magic place to dig is just below the treeless rock slide on the far side of Paulina Lake.

#### #430A THE SPA HOUSE

950 S. Hwy 97 (3rd St.)

(503) 389-0246

Bend, OR 97702   PR

Spacious rent-a-tub establishment, with tasteful wood-paneled rooms, located on main highway.

Private-space hydrojet pools, using chlorine-treated tap water, are for rent to the public by the hour. Water temperature is maintained at 104°. One of the two indoor pool rooms has a fireplace, there are two enclosed outdoor pools, and two of the units also have a sauna. No credit cards are accepted.

Phone for rates, reservations and directions.

#### #430B BEND RIVERSIDE

P.O. Box 151   (503) 382-3802

Bend, OR 97709   Hydropool MH

#### #430C HOLIDAY MOTEL

880 S.E. 3rd St.   (503) 382-4620

Bend, OR 97702   Hydropool MH

#### #430D SPORTSMAN'S MOTEL

3705 US 97 N.   (503) 382-2211

Bend, OR 97701   Hydropool MH

#### #430E DUNES MOTEL

1515 N.E. 3rd St.   (503) 382-6811

Bend, OR 97701   Hydropool MH

#### #430F WESTWARD HO MOTEL

904 S.E. 3rd St.   (503) 382-2111

Bend, OR 97702   Hydropool MH

#### #430G SUNRIVER RESORT

Sunriver   (503) 593-1221

Bend, OR 97702   Hydropool MH

#### #430H RIVERHOUSE MOTOR INN

3075 N. Hwy 97   (503) 389-3111

Bend, OR 97701   Hydropool MH

#### #430I RED LION MOTEL

849 N.E. Third St.   (503) 382-8384

Bend, OR 97701   Hydropool MH

#### #430J INN OF THE SEVENTH MOUNTAIN

P.O. Box 1207   (503) 382-8711

Bend, OR 97709   Hydropool MH

#### #430K BEST WESTERN ENTRADA LODGE

P.O. Box 975   (503) 382-4080

Bend, Or 97709   Hydropool MH

#### #431 DIG YOUR OWN HOT SPRINGS

c/o Paulina Lake Resort, Box 7

(503) 536-2240

La Pine, OR 97739   non-commercial

Unique underground geothermal flow which may by tapped by digging a hole in the lakeshore gravel. Located at Paulina Lake, in Newberry Crater, south of the city of Bend. Elevation 6,300 ft. Open all year.

Natural mineral water does not flow out of the ground, but rather flows up at the northeast edge of the lake, joining the lake water without emerging on the surface. When the lake level is just right, a hole dug in the lake-edge gravel will fill with water ranging up to 110°. Access is via a 2½ mile trail or, in the summer, by boat. There are no posted clothing requirements, leaving it up to the mutual consent of those present.

Boat rental, cabins, cafe, store and gas pumps are available at Paulina Lake Resort, and overnight camping is available nearby. Fishing, hiking, skiing and snowmobiling are also available in the area. No credit cards are accepted.

Phone Paulina Lake Resort to find out if the lake level is right, and to get information on boat rental rates.

Directions: On US 97, approximately 20 miles south of Bend, follow signs east to Paulina Lake.

#### #432 SONNY'S MOTEL

1539 S.W. US 97   (503) 475-7217

Madras, OR 97741   Hydropool MH

### #433　KAH-NEE-TA VACATION RESORT VILLAGE

■

P.O. Box K　　　　　　　(503) 553-1112
Warm Springs, OR 97761　PR + MH + CRV

A modern resort owned and operated by the Confederated Tribes of the Warm Springs Indian Reservation. In these foothills on the east side of the Cascade Mountains, the sun shines 340 days a year. Elevation 1,500 ft. Open all year.

Natural mineral water flows out of a spring at 140° and is piped to the bathhouse and swimming pool. The large outdoor swimming pool is chlorinated and maintained at a temperature of 95°. The men's and women's bathhouses each contain five tiled Roman tubs in which the soaking temperature is individually controlled up to 110°, and are drained and filled after each use. Pools and bathhouses are available to the public as well as to registered guests. Bathing suits are required in public areas.

Massage, dressing rooms, restaurant, cabins, teepees, overnight camping, RV hook-ups and miniature golf are available on the premises. Resort hotel and golf course nearby. It is 11 miles to a store and service station. Visa, MasterCard, American Express, Diner's Club and Carte Blanche are accepted.

Directions: From US 26, in Warm Springs, follow signs 11 miles northeast to resort.

*Kah-Nee-Ta Vacation Resort Village:* Visitors have a choice of conventional cabins or the canvas teepees visible in the background.

| #434A | PORTAGE INN | |
|---|---|---|
| ☐ | 3223 Frontage Rd. | (503) 298-5502 |
| | The Dalles, OR 97058 | Hydropool MH |
| #434B | ECONO LODGE | |
| ☐ | 2500 W. 6th | (503) 296-1191 |
| | The Dalles, OR 97058 | Hydropool MH |
| #435 | TIMBERLINE LODGE | |
| ☐ | Off US 26 | (503) 272-3311 |
| | Government Camp, OR 97028 | |
| | | Hydropool MH |
| #436 | RIPPLING RIVER RESORT | |
| ☐ | 6810 E. Fairway Rd. | (503) 622-3101 |
| | Welches, OR 97067 | Hydropool MH |

## #437   AUSTIN HOT SPRINGS   (see map)
### Southeast of the town of Estacada
#### non-commercial

One of the rare primitive hot springs that are adjacent to a paved highway. Located in the tall timber of Mt. Hood National Forest. Elevation 1,800 ft. Open all year.

Natural mineral water flows out of several springs on both sides of the Clackamas River, with temperatures up to 160°. Along the north side of the river volunteers have built a series of shallow rock-and-sand pools in which river water and mineral water mix to provide safe soaking temperatures. No clothing policy is posted but bathing suits are usually worn because the area is popular and easily visible from the road.

The grounds, including rest rooms and picnic area, are owned and maintained by the Portland Gas & Electric Co. There are no services available and overnight parking is prohibited. It is three miles to a Forest Service campground and 28 miles to all other services.

Source map: *Mt. Hood National Forest.*

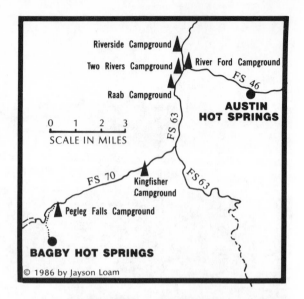

© 1986 by Jayson Loam

The soaking pools at *Austin Hot Springs* are clearly in the "use only as directed" class.

*Austin Hot Springs:* These soakers have a comfortable mix of river water and scalding water as is seen flowing on the other bank.

## #438   BAGBY HOT SPRINGS   (see map)
### Southeast of the town of Estacada
### non-commercial

One of the best. A well-planned rustic facility featuring hand-hewn cedar-log tubs, with hot water supplied through a 150-ft. log flume. A lush rain forest and tumbling mountain streams make the 1½-mile access path enjoyable in its own right. Elevation 2,200 ft. Open all year.

Natural mineral water flows out of two springs at 135°, supplying a large cedar tub on a deck in the family area and two bathhouses in the adult area. The fully roofed bathhouse is a replica of the one that burned down in 1979, offering five hewn-cedar tubs in private rooms. The open-sided half-roof bathhouse offers a single communal space containing three hewn tubs and a round cedar tub. A flume diversion gate at each tub brings in more hot water whenever desired, and all tubs are drained and cleaned daily, so no chemical treatment of the water is necessary. There are no posted clothing requirements, and the apparent local custom in the communal bathhouse is clothing optional. All of the facilities on this special-management five-acre leasehold are made possible by the work of Friends of Bagby, Inc., a nonprofit corporation formed to work with the Forest Service to restore, preserve and provide ongoing maintenance for the area. You can support this pioneering organization by sending tax-deductible contributions to Friends of Bagby, Inc., P.O. Box 15116, Portland, OR 97215.

There is a picnic area on the premises, but no overnight camping is permitted. There is a Forest Service campground within one mile of the springs trailhead. All other services are available 32 miles away in Estacada.

Source map: *Mt. Hood National Forest.*

▲ *Bagby Hot Springs:* The volunteer group at Bagby has accepted the responsibility of giving all the tubs a daily scrubbing.

▼ All the *Bagby Hot Springs* tubs have natural-wood-trough supply systems for mineral-water.

**#439**    **BREITENBUSH COMMUNITY**
          **HEALING \* RETREAT \***
          **CONFERENCE CENTER**

■      **P.O. Box 578**          **(503) 854-3501**
         **Detroit, OR 97342**         **PR + MH**

A rustic older resort being renovated by a residential holistic community on the banks of the Breitenbush River, surrounded by the Willamette National Forest. Elevation 2,000 ft. Open all year.

Natural mineral water flows out of springs and artesian wells at temperatures up to 180°. There are four roofed-over outdoor hydrojet pools in which the temperature of chlorine-treated water can be controlled from 96° to 110°. There are three outdoor foot baths in the meadow which operate on a flow-through basis and average a temperature of 100°, depending on weather conditions. The steam-bath building is supplied with 180° water direct from an adjoining well. Plans to renovate the swimming pool are pending. Phone ahead for status of construction. The pools are available to the public as well as to registered guests but prior reservations are required! Bathing suits are required in the pool area from 9 A.M. to noon, optional thereafter.

Massage (by reservation), vegetarian meals, cabins, seminars and conferences are available on the premises. It is 11 miles to a store, service station and phone, three miles to overnight camping and 70 miles to RV hook-ups. No credit cards are accepted.

The resort is located 11 miles northeast of Detroit. Phone for rates, reservations and directions.

### BREITENBUSH COMMUNITY
#### HEALING – RETREAT CONFERENCE CENTER
## BY RESERVATION ONLY
## (503) 854-3501
### NEAREST PHONE
### 10 MILES IN DETROIT ➞

▲   *Breitenbush Community Healing ° Retreat ° Conference Center:* No drop-in visitors, please.

▼   At *Breitenbush* the combination of colorful tile and lush greenery seems just right.

► *Four Seasons Hot Tubbing:* This newer facility features shiny acrylic tubs and the extra convenience of a toilet in each dressing room.

**#440A** ☐ CHUMAREE COMFORTEL
3301 Market St., N.E.　　　(503) 370-7888
Salem, OR 97303　In-room hydropools MH

**#440B** ☐ BEST WESTERN PACIFIC HWY INN
4526 Portland Rd., N.E.　　(503) 390-3200
Salem, OR 97303　　　　　　Hydropool MH

**#440C** ☐ BEST WESTERN NEW KINGS INN
3658 Market St.　　　　　　(503) 581-1559
Salem, OR 97301　　　　　　Hydropool MH

**#441** ☐ HOLIDAY INN—SOUTH
25425 S.W. Boones Ferry Rd.　(503) 682-2211
Wilsonville, OR 97070　　　　Hydropool MH

**#442** ☐ MONARCH MOTOR INN
12566 S.E. 93rd St.　　　　　(503) 652-1515
Clackamas, OR 97015
In-room hydropools MH

**#443** ☐ FOUR SEASONS HOT TUBBING
19059 S.E. Division　　　　　(503) 666-3411
Gresham, OR 97030　　　　　　　　　PR

Attractive suburban rent-a-tub facility featuring enclosed outdoor tubs. Open all year.

Private-space hot pools using chlorine-treated tap water are for rent to the public by the hour. Six enclosed outdoor fiberglass hydrojet pools are maintained at a temperature of 104°. Each unit includes indoor dressing room, shower and toilet. Visa and MasterCard are accepted.

Phone for rates, reservations and directions.

**#444A** ☐ OPEN AIR HOT TUBBING
11126 N.E. Halsey　　　　　(503) 257-8117
Portland, OR 97220　　　　　　　　PR

Unique suburban rent-a-tub featuring open-roofed wood patios. Open all year.

Private-space hot pools using chlorine-treated tap water are for rent to the public by the hour. Six enclosed outdoor fiberglass hydrojet pools are maintained at temperatures ranging from 102° to 104°. Each unit has an outdoor water spray over the pool and indoor dressing room with shower and toilet. Three of the units can be combined to accommodate a party of 24. There is a sauna in one unit and an open-air tanning salon. Visa and MasterCard are accepted.

Phone for rates, reservations and directions.

## #444B  THE FAMILY HOT TUB

☐   4747 S.E. Hawthorne    (503) 239-TUBS
    Portland, OR 97215          PR

Small neighborhood rent-a-tub facility, on a main street in the east-side suburbs. Open all year.

Private-space hot pools using chlorine-treated tap water are for rent to the public by the hour. Three indoor fiberglass hydrojet pools are maintained at a temperature of 104°. One of the rooms also has a sauna. No credit cards are accepted.

Phone for rates, reservations and directions.

## #444C  JUST FOR THE HEALTH OF IT

☐   610 S.W. 12th Ave.     (503) 243-2584
    Portland, OR 97205          PR

Modern, spacious rent-a-tub establishment in the downtown area. Open all year.

Private-space hot pools using chlorine-treated tap water are for rent to the public by the hour. Fifteen indoor fiberglass hydrojet pools are maintained at a temperature of 104°. Each unit includes a sauna. The facilities also include a tanning unit. Visa and MasterCard are accepted.

Phone for rates, reservations and directions.

▲ *The Family Hot Tub:* This indoor facility features pool-edge tile and wood paneling.

▲ *Just For The Health Of It:* Each unit has a rest area as well as a private sauna.

| #444D | RED LION INN—LLOYD CENTER | | |
|---|---|---|---|
| ☐ | 1000 N.E. Multnomah St. | (503) 281-6111 | |
| | Portland, OR 97232 | In-room hydropools | MH |
| #444E | CHUMAREE COMFORTEL | | |
| ☐ | 8247 N.E. Sandy Blvd. | (503) 256-4111 | |
| | Portland, OR 97220 | In-room hydropools | MH |
| #444F | HOLIDAY INN—AIRPORT | | |
| ☐ | 8439 N.E. Columbia Blvd. | (503) 256-5000 | |
| | Portland, OR 97220 | Hydropool | MH |
| #444G | NENDEL'S MOTOR INN—PORTLAND AIRPORT | | |
| ☐ | 7101 N.E. 82nd Ave. | (503) 255-6722 | |
| | Portland, OR 97220 | Hydropool | MH |
| #444H | RED LION MOTOR INN—JANTZEN BEACH | | |
| ☐ | 909 N. Hayden Island Dr. | (503) 283-4466 | |
| | Portland, OR 97217 | Hydropool | MH |
| #444I | PORTLAND MARRIOTT | | |
| ☐ | 1401 S.W. Front Ave. | (503) 226-7600 | |
| | Portland, OR 97201 | Hydropool | MH |
| #444J | COSMOPOLITAN AIRTEL | | |
| ☐ | 622 N.E. 82nd Ave. | (503) 255-6511 | |
| | Portland, OR 97220 | Hydropool | MH |
| #444K | BEST WESTERN KINGS WAY INN | | |
| ☐ | 420 N.E. Holiday St. | (503) 233-6331 | |
| | Portland, OR 97232 | Hydropool | MH |
| #444L | SHERATON INN—PORTLAND AIRPORT | | |
| ☐ | 8235 N.E. Airport Way | (503) 281-2500 | |
| | Portland, OR 97218 | Hydropool | MH |
| #444M | BEST WESTERN FLAMINGO | | |
| ☐ | 9727 N.E. Sandy Blvd. | (503) 255-1400 | |
| | Portland, OR 97220 | Hydropool | MH |

| | | |
|---|---|---|
| #445A | R-INN | |
| ☐ | 7300 S.W. Hazelfern Rd. | (503) 620-3460 |
| | Tigard, OR 97223   In-room hydropools  MH | |

| | | |
|---|---|---|
| #445B | BEST WESTERN VIP'S MOTOR INN | |
| ☐ | 17993 S.W. Lower Boones Ferry Rd. | |
| | | (503) 620-2030 |
| | Tigard, OR 97223   In-room hydropools  MH | |

## #446   ELITE TUBBING AND TANNING

☐ 4240 S.W. 110th   (503) 641-7727
Beaverton, OR 97005   PR

Private rent-a-tub suites in a remodeled house across from Beaverton's Montgomery Ward Store. Open all year.

Private-space hot pools using chlorine-treated tap water are for rent to the public by the hour. Six indoor fiberglass hydrojet pools are maintained at a temperature of 103°. Each suite includes a shower and toilet. Facilities include tanning equipment.

Massage is available on the premises.

Visa and MasterCard are accepted.

Phone for rates, reservations and directions.

| | | |
|---|---|---|
| #447 | BEST WESTERN HALLMARK INN | |
| ☐ | 3700 N.E. Cornell Rd. | (503) 648-3500 |
| | Hillsboro, OR 97124 | |
| | In-room hydropools  MH | |

| | | |
|---|---|---|
| #448A | SHILO INN | |
| ☐ | 30 N. Prom | (503) 738-9571 |
| | Seaside, OR 97138 | Hydropool  MH |

| | | |
|---|---|---|
| #448B | EBB TIDE MOTEL | |
| ☐ | 300 N. Prom | (503) 738-8371 |
| | Seaside, OR 97138 | Hydropool  MH |

| | | |
|---|---|---|
| #448C | HI-TIDE MOTEL | |
| ☐ | 30 Ave. G | (503) 738-8414 |
| | Seaside, OR 97138 | Hydropool  MH |

| | | |
|---|---|---|
| #448D | ECONO LODGE—SEASIDE | |
| ☐ | 441 2nd Ave. | (503) 738-9581 |
| | Seaside, OR 97138 | Hydropool  MH |

| | | |
|---|---|---|
| #448E | SUNDOWNER MOTOR INN | |
| ☐ | 125 Ocean Way | (502) 738-8301 |
| | Seaside, OR 97138 | Hydropool  MH |

| | | |
|---|---|---|
| #448F | BEST WESTERN SEASHORE RESORT MOTEL | |
| ☐ | 60 N. Promenade | (503) 738-6368 |
| | Seaside, OR 97138 | Hydropool  MH |

| | | |
|---|---|---|
| #449A | TOLOVANA INN | |
| ☐ | P.O. Box 165, Tolovana Park | (503) 436-2211 |
| | Cannon Beach, OR 97145 | Hydropool  MH |

| | | |
|---|---|---|
| #449B | BEST WESTERN SURFSAND HOTEL | |
| ☐ | P.O. Box 219 | (503) 436-2274 |
| | Cannon Beach, OR 97110 | Hydropool  MH |

| | | |
|---|---|---|
| #449C | NEW SURFVIEW RESORT MOTEL | |
| ☐ | 1400 S. Hemlock | (503) 436-1566 |
| | Cannon Beach, OR 97110 | Hydropool  MH |

| | | |
|---|---|---|
| #449D | LAND'S END MOTEL | |
| ☐ | P.O. Box 475 | (503) 436-2264 |
| | Cannon Beach, OR 97110 | Hydropool  MH |

| | | |
|---|---|---|
| #450 | BEST WESTERN MAR-CLAIR MOTEL | |
| ☐ | 11 Main Ave. | (503) 842-7571 |
| | Tillamook, OR 97141 | Hydropool  MH |

| | | |
|---|---|---|
| #451A | THE INN AT SPANISH HEAD | |
| ☐ | 4009 S. Hwy 101 | (503) 996-2161 |
| | Lincoln City, OR 97367 | Hydropool  MH |

| | | |
|---|---|---|
| #451B | SHILO INN | |
| ☐ | 1501 N.W. 40th St. | (503) 994-3655 |
| | Lincoln City, OR 97367 | Hydropool  MH |

| | | |
|---|---|---|
| #451C | SURFTIDE BEACH RESORT | |
| ☐ | 2945 N.W. Jetty Ave. | (503) 994-2191 |
| | Lincoln City, OR 97367 | Hydropool  MH |

| | | |
|---|---|---|
| #451D | SEA GYPSY MOTEL | |
| ☐ | 145 N.W. Inlet Ave. | (503) 994-5266 |
| | Lincoln City, OR 97367 | Hydropool  MH |

| | | |
|---|---|---|
| #451E | "D" SANDS MOTEL | |
| ☐ | 171 S.W. Highway 101 | (503) 994-5244 |
| | Lincoln City, OR 97367 | Hydropool  MH |

| | | |
|---|---|---|
| #452A | SURFRIDER | |
| ☐ | Star Rte. N Box 219 | (503) 764-2311 |
| | Depoe Bay, OR 97341 | Hydropool  MH |

| | | |
|---|---|---|
| #452B | INN AT OTTER CREST | |
| ☐ | P.O. Box 50 Otter Rock | (503) 765-2111 |
| | Depoe Bay, OR 97369 | Hydropool  MH |

| | | |
|---|---|---|
| #452C | HOLIDAY RV PARK | |
| ☐ | on US 101 | (503) 765-2302 |
| | Depoe Bay, OR 97341 | Hydropool  CRV |

| | | |
|---|---|---|
| #453A | EMBARCADERO RESORT HOTEL | |
| ☐ | 1000 S.E. Bay Blvd. | (503) 265-8521 |
| | Newport, OR 97365 | Hydropool  MH |

| | | |
|---|---|---|
| #453B | NEWPORT HILTON AT AGATE BEACH | |
| ☐ | 3019 N. Coast Hwy | (503) 265-9411 |
| | Newport, OR 97365 | Hydropool  MH |

| | | |
|---|---|---|
| #454 | SHAMROCK LODGETTES | |
| ☐ | P.O. Box 346 | (503) 547-3312 |
| | Yachats, OR 97498   In-room hydropools  MH | |

| | | |
|---|---|---|
| #455A | DRIFTWOOD SHORES RESORT INN | |
| ☐ | 88416 First Ave. | (503) 997-8263 |
| | Florence, OR 97439 | Hydropool  MH |

| | | |
|---|---|---|
| #455B | LE CHATEAU MOTEL | |
| ☐ | P.O. Box 98 | (503) 997-3481 |
| | Florence, OR 97439 | Hydropool  MH |

| | | |
|---|---|---|
| #456A | INN OF THE BEACHCOMBER | |
| ☐ | 1250 S. Hwy 101 | (503) 247-6691 |
| | Gold Beach, OR 97444 | Hydropool  MH |

| | | |
|---|---|---|
| #456B | THE INN AT GOLD BEACH | |
| ☐ | 1435 S. Ellensberg | (503) 247-6606 |
| | Gold Beach, OR 97444 | Hydropool  MH |

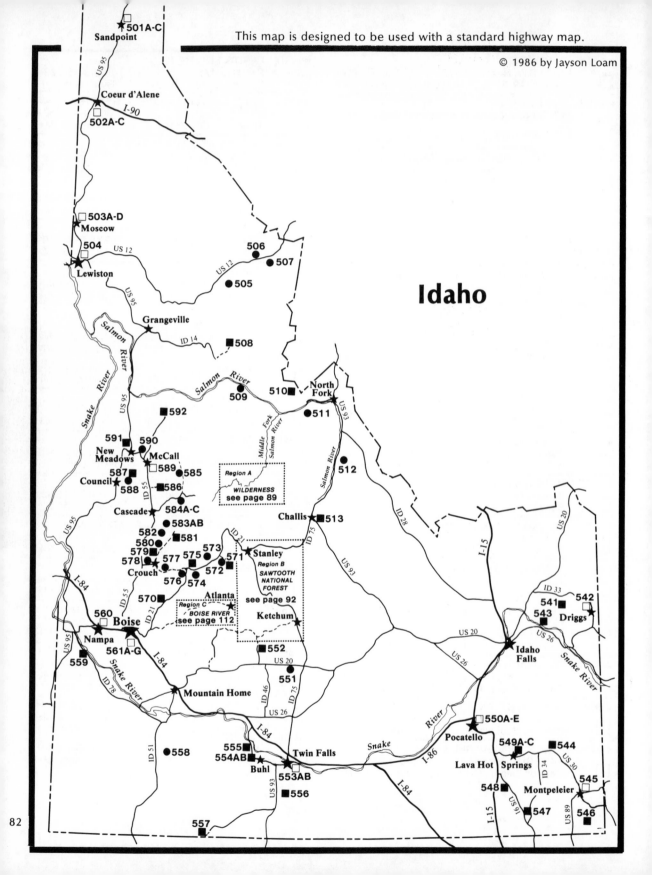

This map is designed to be used with a standard highway map.

© 1986 by Jayson Loam

Idaho

★ 501A-C
Sandpoint

Coeur d'Alene
□ 502A-C
I-90

□ 503A-D
Moscow

504
□ US 12
★ Lewiston

506
● 507
US 12

● 505

Grangeville
ID 14

■ 508

Salmon River

● 509
● 510
North Fork
US 93

● 511

■ 592

591
590
New Meadows
McCall
□ 589
● 585

587
Council
● 586
588
Cascade
■ 584A-C

● 512

Region A
WILDERNESS
see page 89

Challis
■ 513

● 583AB

582
■ 581
580
579
578  577  575  573  571
Crouch   576  574  572
570

Stanley
Region B
SAWTOOTH
NATIONAL
FOREST
see page 92

ID 28

560
Boise

Nampa
□ 561A-G

559

Atlanta

Region C
BOISE RIVER
see page 112

Ketchum

■ 552

541 ■ 542
543 Driggs

551

Mountain Home

US 20

US 26
Idaho Falls

Snake River

558

555
554AB
Buhl
□ 553AB

Twin Falls

Snake River

Pocatello
□ 550A-E

549A-C
Lava Hot Springs

■ 544

■ 556

■ 557

548

547

546

545
Montpeleier

82

## MAP AND DIRECTORY SYMBOLS

● **Unimproved natural mineral water pool**

■ **Improved natural mineral water pool**

☐ Gas-heated tap or well water pool

———————— Paved highway

- - ⌣ ⌒ - - Unpaved road

·····˙·˙·⁎·˙⁎·····  Hiking route

PR = Tubs or pools for rent by hour, day or treatment

MH = Rooms, cabins or dormitory spaces for rent by day, week or month

CRV = Camping or vehicle parking spaces, some with hookups,
for rent by day, week, month or year

---

#501A ☐ BEST WESTERN CONNIE'S MOTOR INN
325 Cedar St.     (208) 263-9581
Sandpoint, ID 83864     Hydropool MH

#501B ☐ QUALITY INN SANDPOINT
807 N. 5th     (208) 263-2111
Sandpoint, ID 83864     Hydropool MH

#501C ☐ EDGEWATER LODGE
56 Bridge St.     (208) 263-3194
Sandpoint, ID 83864     Health Club

#502A ☐ BEST WESTERN NORTH SHORE
N. Shore Plaza     (208) 664-9241
Coeur d'Alene, ID 83814     Hydropool MH

#502B ☐ GARDEN MOTEL
1808 Northwest Blvd.     (208) 664-2743
Coeur d'Alene, ID 83814     Hydropool MH

#502C ☐ FLAMINGO MOTEL
718 Sherman Ave.     (208) 664-2159
Coeur d'Alene, ID 83814     Hydropool MH

#503A ☐ SIT 'N SOAK
316 N. Main     (208) 882-5228
Moscow, ID 83843     PR

Combination tavern, cafe and rent-a-tub facility in downtown Moscow. Open all year.

Private-space pools using chlorine-treated tap water are for rent to the public by the hour. There are six enclosed outdoor tubs, in which the temperature is maintained at 104°. Visa and MasterCard are accepted.

Phone for rates, reservations and directions.

#503B ☐ BEST WESTERN UNIVERSITY INN
1516 Pullman Rd.     (208) 882-1611
Moscow, ID 83843     Hydropool MH

#503C ☐ CAVANAUGH'S MOTOR INN
645 Pullman Rd.     (208) 882-1611
Moscow, ID 83843     Hydropool MH

#503D ☐ MARK IV MOTOR INN
414 N. Main St.     (208) 882-7557
Moscow, ID 83843     Hydropool MH

#504 ☐ THREE RIVERS RESORT AND CAMPGROUND
on Selway Rd.     (208) 926-4430
Lewiston, ID 83501     Hydropool CRV

▲ *Sit 'N' Soak:* Glass containers are still prohibited but a bucket of suds is O.K.

## #505  STANLEY HOT SPRING
● **Northeast of the town of Lowell**
**non-commercial**

Several shallow pools in Rock Lake Creek canyon at the end of a rugged five-mile trail in the Selway-Bitterroot Wilderness. Elevation 4,500 ft. Open all year.

Natural mineral water flows out of a canyon-bank spring at 110° and into a series of volunteer-built rock-and-sand pools which range in temperature from 90° to 100°, depending on air temperature and wind conditions. The apparent local custom is clothing optional.

There are no services available on the premises. There is a Forest Service campground at the trailhead. All other services are 40 miles from the trailhead.

During the summer months an information service is provided at the Lochsa Historical Station, two miles west of the trailhead on US 12. Before attempting this trip, stop at the station for maps, wilderness regulations and information on current weather and trail conditions.

Source map: *Clearwater National Forest.*

## #506  WEIR CREEK HOT SPRINGS
● **Northeast of the town of Lowell**
**non-commercial**

Secluded primitive hot springs and creekside soaking pools reached via a sometimes difficult ½ mile path in Clearwater National Forest. Elevation 2,900 ft. Open all year.

Natural mineral water flows out of several springs at 117° and cools as it is channeled to volunteer-built rock-and-sand pools at the edge of the creek. Pool temperature is controlled by admitting cold creek water as needed. The apparent local custom is clothing-optional.

There are no services available on the premises. It is eight miles to a campground, 16 miles to a restaurant and motel, and 35 miles to all other services.

Directions: From the Colgate Licks Trail go five miles west on US 12 to the bridge over Weir Creek and an adjoining parking area. Follow an unmarked, unmaintained path up the west side of the creek for slightly less than ½ mile to the springs. Wherever it appears that the path has split, stay with the fork that keeps the creek in sight.

Source map: *Clearwater National Forest.*

▲ *Jerry Johnson Hot Springs:* These upper pools, overlooking a peaceful meadow, maintain a temperature of 106° without a creek water mix.

## #507  JERRY JOHNSON HOT SPRINGS
● **(see map)**
**Near US 12 in Clearwater National Forest**
**non-commercial**

Delightful series of user-friendly primitive hot springs at the end of an easy one-mile hike through a beautiful forest along the east bank of Warm Springs Creek. Elevation 4,000 ft. Open all year.

Odorless natural mineral water flows out of many fissures in the creek bank at 114° and also out of several other springs at temperatures up to 110°. Volunteers have constructed rock and mud soaking pools along the edge of the river and near the springs. The temperature within each pool is controlled by admitting cold creek water as needed or by diverting the hotter flow to let a pool cool down. The apparent local custom is clothing optional.

There are no services on the premises. Overnight camping is permitted but excessive vandalism may force the Forest Service to adopt a policy of day use only for this site. However, there are three uncrowded Forest Service campgrounds within five miles of the Jerry Johnson Hot Springs trailhead. It is ten miles to a cafe, service station and all other services.

Source map: *Clearwater National Forest.*

▲ This creekside geothermal outflow at *Jerry Johnson Hot Springs* is 115°, requiring a mix with cold stream water to be user friendly.

► This *Jerry Johnson* creek-edge pool is the final mixing place for hot mineral water after it has gone through four prior pools.

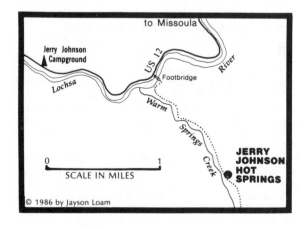

▲ This galvanized horse trough is part of the rustic charm of *Red River Hot Springs* resort.

▲ *Red River Hot Springs:* The restaurant area in the background overlooks the swimming pool and the soaking pool in the foreground.

## #508　RED RIVER HOT SPRINGS

■

**Elk City, ID 83525**　　**(208) 983-0452**
**PR + MH + CRV**

Friendly, remote, rustic resort featuring both public and private-space pools surrounded by tall timber in the Nezperce National Forest. Elevation 4,500 ft. Open all year.

Natural mineral water flows out of 10 springs at temperatures up to 130°. The chlorine-treated swimming pool temperature varies from 88° in the summer to 72° in the winter. The outdoor flow-through soaking pool is maintained at 104°, and requires no chemical treatment. There are also three claw-footed bathtubs located in private spaces which are drained and cleaned after each use. In a fourth private space there is an authentic galvanized horse trough which is surprisingly comfortable for a two-person soak. Pools are available to the public as well as to registered guests. Bathing suits are required in public areas.

Locker rooms, a cafe, store, rustic cabins and overnight camping are available on the premises. Hiking, fishing, cross-country skiing, snowmobiling, and horse trails are nearby. It is 30 miles to a service station and 150 miles to RV hook-ups. No credit cards are accepted.

Directions: From the town of Grangeville, take ID 14 to Elk City, then go 25 miles east to resort. The last 11 miles are on an easy gravel road.

## #509　BARTH HOT SPRINGS

●

**West of the town of North Fork**
**non-commercial**

A truly remote and unexpected claw-footed bathtub supplied by a hot spring in the "River Of No Return" section of the main Salmon River. Elevation 2,700 ft. Open all year.

Natural mineral water flows out of many small seeps at temperatures up to 140° and cools as it is gathered into a PVC pipe carrying it to the outdoor bathtub. There are no posted clothing requirements, which leaves that matter up to the mutual consent of those present.

There are no services available on the premises, nor are there any roads to this area. Access is by raft or jet boat. It is 65 miles by river to all services.

The Forest Service issues licenses to a limited number of outfitters who operate raft and boat trips on an individual seat and charter basis. For more information write to Idaho Outfitter's and Guides Association, Inc., Peck, Idaho, 83545.

Source map: Forest Service, *The Salmon, River of No Return.*

## #510　HORSE CREEK HOT SPRING

■

**Northwest of the town of North Fork**
**non-commercial**　　**(see map)**

Rock-lined primitive hot spring, enclosed by four walls, in a *remote* section of beautiful Salmon National Forest. Elevation 6,200 ft. Open all year.

Natural mineral water flows out of a spring at 97° directly into the pool, which is surrounded by a roofless bathhouse. The apparent local custom is clothing optional.

There is a picnic area, with tables and rest rooms, available at the springs. It is one mile to a campground, and 35 miles to all other services.

Directions: From the town of North Fork, go west on FS 030, then north on FS 038, then west and north on FS 044, then west and south on FS 065 to the spring.

Source map: *Salmon National Forest.*

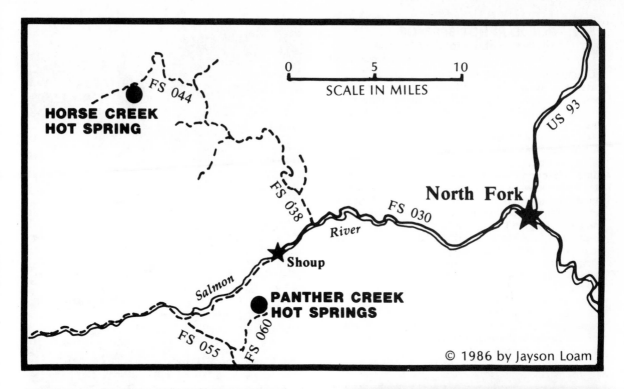

## #511 PANTHER CREEK HOT SPRINGS
### West of the town of North Fork
### non-commercial (see map)

Dozens of high-temperature geothermal outflows along Warm Springs Creek in a remote, rocky canyon in Salmon National Forest. Elevation 4,800 ft. Open all year.

Natural mineral water flows out of many small fissures in the rocks at more than 170° toward a series of volunteer-built rock pools along the bed of Panther Creek. In the winter these pools provide a variety of comfortable temperatures, but in the summer, after the snow has melted, Panther Creek does not carry enough surface water to cool the geothermal water, leaving the pools full of 150° water.

There are no services available on the premises. It is 33 miles to all services.

Source maps: *Salmon National Forest; USGS Shoup, Idaho-Montana.*

▲ *Horse Creek Hot Spring:* The pool enclosure provides privacy at the expense of the view.

### #512 GOLDBUG HOT SPRINGS
**Southwest of the town of Salmon**
**non-commercial**

Unusual underground mix of geothermal and creek water, emerging as warm cascades through shallow, rocky canyon pools, reached by a steep two-mile trail in Salmon National Forest. Elevation 5,000 ft. Open all year.

Natural mineral water flows out of several springs and also combines with creek water flowing under the rocky creek bed. Volunteers have added rock-and-sand dams to deepen the water-worn cascade pools where the combined water flow re-emerges. Temperatures in these cascade pools are determined by the rate of runoff in the canyon. Volunteers have also built a rock-and-sand pool fed by a small spring, resulting in temperatures in the range of 90° to 100°. The apparent local custom is clothing optional.

There are no services available on the premises, parking is available at the trailhead, and it is 19 miles to all other services.

Directions: On US 93, approximately 19 miles south of Salmon, look for mile marker 282. Go east on short gravel road to trailhead parking area. Cross Warm Springs Creek at the trailhead, and follow trail up the canyon to the springs.

▲ *Challis Hot Springs:* This pool needs no chemical treatment due to large flow-through.

▲ *Goldbug Hot Springs:* A rugged two-mile hike keeps the traffic to a minimum at this site.

### #513 CHALLIS HOT SPRINGS
| | |
|---|---|
| **H/C 63 Box 1779** | **(208) 879-4442** |
| **Challis, ID 83226** | **PR + CRV** |

Older community plunge and campground on the banks of the Salmon River. Elevation 5,000 ft. Pools open all year, campground open April 1 to November.

Natural mineral water flows from several springs at temperatures up to 127° and is piped to flow-through indoor and outdoor pools which require no chemical treatment. The temperature of the outdoor pool is maintained at approximately 90° and the temperature of the indoor pool ranges from 108° to 110°. Bathing suits are required.

Changing rooms, picnic areas, camping and RV hookups are available on the premises. All other services are available within seven miles. No credit cards are accepted.

Directions: From intersection of US 93 and ID 75 near Challis go southeast on US 93 and watch for signs to hot springs.

# Region A WILDERNESS

This is the region in which to totally escape urban noise pollution, because the only way to reach these springs is to hike or float in on a raft, or both. It is possible to plan a rugged backpack route which will take you to several hot springs over a two- or three-day period. It is equally possible to find packaged river-raft trips, featuring hot springs, which fly you to an upriver airstrip, carry all your food and gear, cook all your meals and even wash the dishes, while you sit back and enjoy unsurpassed beauty.

In any case, the first step is to consult with a ranger station in Challis National Forest or Salmon National Forest. For information on charter or single-seat raft trips, write to Idaho Outfitter's and Guides Association, Inc., Peck, ID 83545.

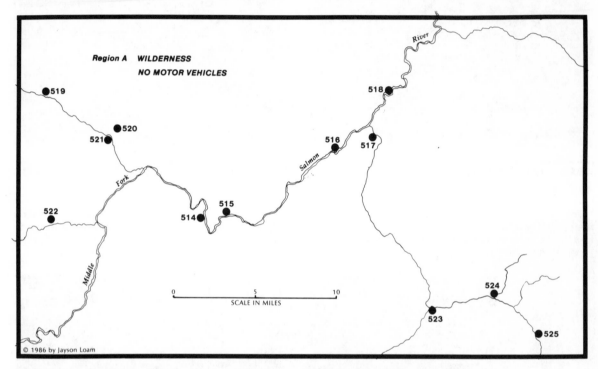

Region A   WILDERNESS
NO MOTOR VEHICLES

519
520
521
522
518
516
517
515
514
524
523
525

Salmon
River
Fork
Middle

0      5      10
SCALE IN MILES

© 1986 by Jayson Loam

## WILDERNESS HOT SPRINGS ACCESSIBLE BY RAFT

### #514   SUNFLOWER FLATS HOT SPRINGS
 ◄

Natural mineral water from a group of hot springs (109°) flows through some shallow cliff-top pools before dropping to the river's edge in the form of a hot waterfall.

## #515   HOOD RANCH HOT SPRINGS

The geothermal water from springs with temperatures up to 149° cools as it flows through pipes to a crude shower bath and soaking pool within 100 yards of the river.

## #516   LOWER LOON CREEK HOT SPRINGS

A large log soaking pool on the edge of Loon Creek is supplied by several springs with temperatures up to 120°. This pool does require a ¼-mile hike from the raft landing beach where the creek joins the river.

## #517 WHITEY COX HOT SPRINGS

A beautiful riverside meadow contains several classic natural soaking pools, supplied from nearby hot springs (131°) through channels where the water cools on the way.

## #518 HOSPITAL BAR HOT SPRINGS

Dozens of fissures in the riverbank rocks emit 115° geothermal water, which is collected for soaking in a few shallow pools next to a favorite landing spot for rafts.

## WILDERNESS HOT SPRINGS ACCESSIBLE BY TRAIL ONLY

**#519  KWIS KWIS HOT SPRINGS**

● Outflow temperature—156°.

**#520  MIDDLE FORK INDIAN CREEK HOT SPRINGS**

● Outflow temperature—162°.

**#521  INDIAN CREEK HOT SPRINGS**

● Outflow temperature—190°.

**#522  PISTOL CREEK HOT SPRINGS**

● Outflow temperature—115°.

**#523  OWEN CABIN HOT SPRINGS**

● Outflow temperature—133°.

**#524  FOSTER RANCH HOT SPRINGS**

● Outflow temperature—135°.

**#525  SHOWER BATH HOT SPRINGS**

● Outflow temperature—122°.

91

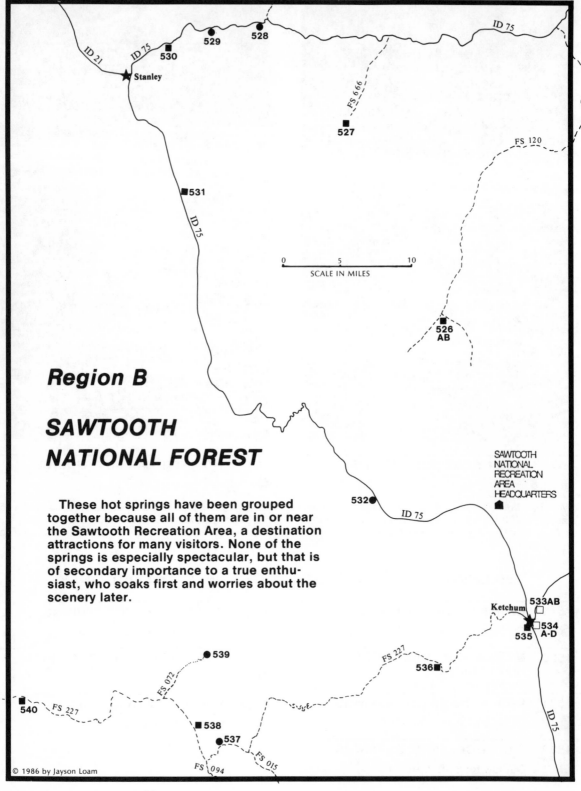

## Region B

## SAWTOOTH NATIONAL FOREST

These hot springs have been grouped together because all of them are in or near the Sawtooth Recreation Area, a destination attractions for many visitors. None of the springs is especially spectacular, but that is of secondary importance to a true enthusiast, who soaks first and worries about the scenery later.

© 1986 by Jayson Loam

92

### #526A LOWER BOWERY HOT SPRING
non-commercial

### #526B WEST PASS HOT SPRING
non-commercial
**Southeast of the town of Stanley**

Two semi-improved hot springs in the Sawtooth National Forest, temporarily unreachable by vehicle due to lack of legal right-of-way on access road. Elevation 7,000 ft. Open all year.

Natural mineral water flows out of two springs at approximately 125° and is piped to an outdoor fiberglass pool at Lower Bowery and to an outdoor bathtub at West Pass. Temperature in both pools is controlled by diverting the flow of hot water whenever desired.

Note: Personal inspection for more details was not possible due to road closure. The Forest Service staff is negotiating with the private-property owner involved to clear the right-of-way. Contact Sawtooth National Recreation Area Headquarters—8 miles north of Ketchum on ID 75—for the latest information.

Source map: *Challis National Forest.*

### #527 SLATE CREEK HOT SPRING
**East of the town of Stanley**
non-commercial

A single spring-fed cast-iron bathtub at the end of a 300-yard hike, in Sawtooth National Forest. Elevation 7,500 ft. Open all year.

Natural mineral water flows out of a spring at 122° and is piped to an open-air bathtub at the site of a demolished bathhouse. Tub-water temperature is controlled by diverting the flow of hot water when the desired soaking level has been reached. The apparent local custom is clothing optional.

There are no services available on the premises. It is 15 miles to all services.

Directions: From US 93, 1½ miles west of Holman Creek Campground, go south on FS 666 along Slate Creek for approximately six miles to the end of the gravel road. Follow path for the remaining 300 yards.

Source Map: *Sawtooth National Forest.*

### #528 SUNBEAM HOT SPRINGS
**East of the town of Stanley**
non-commercial

Several rock-and-sand pools on the edge of the Salmon River in Challis National Forest. Elevation 6,000 ft. Open all year.

Natural mineral water flows out of several springs on the north side of the road at temperatures up to 160°. The water flows under the road to several volunteer-built rock pools along the north bank of the river, where hot and cold water mix in a variety of temperatures. As all pools are easily visible from the road, bathing suits are advisable.

There are no services available on the premises. It is one mile to all services.

Location: Located on ID 75, one mile west of Sunbeam Resort, northeast of the town of Stanley.

Source map: *Challis National Forest.*

◄ *Sunbeam Hot Spring:* Scalding water pouring down the bank in the foreground has to be mixed with river water to be usable.

*Kem Hot Springs:* In the Sawtooth Recreation Area it is legal to camp in unmarked casual areas such as this riverside flat, just a few yards away from a fine, small primitive spring.

### #529 KEM HOT SPRINGS
**East of the town of Stanley**

non-commercial

Small primitive spring and soaking pools on the edge of the Salmon River in Challis National Forest. Elevation 6,000 ft. Open all year.

Natural mineral water flows out of a spring at 110° and cools as it flows through several volunteer-built rock-and-sand soaking pools along the edge of the river. Pool temperatures may be controlled by diverting the hot water or by bringing a bucket for adding cold river water. Because the spring is at the east end of a popular unofficial campground, bathing suits are advisable in the daytime until you check the situation out with your neighbors.

Except for the camping area, there are no services on the premises. It is six miles to all services.

Directions: On ID 75, 0.7 mile east of mile marker 197, turn off the highway toward the river and down a short gravel road into camping area.

Source map: *Sawtooth National Forest* (north half)

### #530 ELKHORN HOT SPRING
**East of the town of Stanley**

non-commercial

Small wood soaking box perched on the rocks between the road and the Salmon River in Challis National Forest. Elevation 6,100 ft. Open all year.

Natural mineral water flows out of a spring at 136° and is piped under the road to the soaking box. The temperature in the box is varied by diverting the flow of hot water and pouring in buckets of cold river water. Bathing suits are advisable as the location is visible from the road.

Directions: On ID 75, 0.7 mile east of mile marker 192, watch for a small turnout (two-car limit) on the side of the road toward the river. The box is visible from the turnout.

Source map: *Sawtooth National Forest* (north half).

### #531 IDAHO ROCKY MOUNTAIN RANCH
H/C 64 Box 9934      (208) 774-3544
Stanley, ID 83278      MH

Guest ranch with rustic authenticity and peaceful ambience nestled in the heart of the breathtaking Sawtooth National Recreation Area. Elevation 6,500 ft. Open mid-June through September.

Natural mineral water flows out of a spring at 106° and is piped to a flow-through outdoor swimming pool that is maintained at 103° to 105° and requires no chemical treatment. Pool is available to registered guests only. Bathing suits are required.

Dressing rooms, restaurant, rooms and cabins are available on the premises. Hiking, fishing, boating, and horse trails are available nearby. All other services are available within two miles. Visa and MasterCard are accepted.

Phone for rates, reservations and directions.

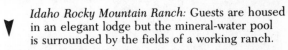

*Elkhorn Hot Spring:* A delivery boy to fetch cold river water is just what this father needed to cool the 136° water in the pipe.

*Idaho Rocky Mountain Ranch:* Guests are housed in an elegant lodge but the mineral-water pool is surrounded by the fields of a working ranch.

## #532 RUSSIAN JOHN HOT SPRING
### North of the town of Ketchum
**non-commercial**

Remains of an old sheepherder soaking pool on a slope 200 yards above the highway in Sawtooth National Forest. Elevation 6,900 ft. Open all year.

Natural mineral water flows out of a spring at 89° directly into a small clay-bottom pool, which maintains a temperature of no more than 86°. Despite the cool temperature, this pool is popular, so you might have to wait your turn. The apparent local custom is clothing optional.

There are no services available on the premises. It is 16 miles to all services.

Directions: On ID 75, 30 yards south of mile marker 146, turn west and then south to parking area.

▲ *Bald Mountain Hot Springs:* The entire motel is built around the four sides of the large pool.

◄ *Russian John Hot Spring:* This easy-access idyllic primitive spring has only one big drawback; you can't get warm in 86° water.

▼ *Warfield Hot Spring:* Volunteers maintain this isolated building in remarkably good condition.

| #533A | TAMARACK LODGE | |
|---|---|---|
| ☐ | 225 Walnut Ave. N. | (208) 726-3344 |
| | Sun Valley, ID 83353 | Hydropool MH |

| #533B | ELKHORN RESORT AT SUN VALLEY | |
|---|---|---|
| ☐ | P.O. Box 1067 | (208) 622-4511 |
| | Sun Valley, ID 83353 | Hydropool MH |

| #534A | STOVALL'S BEST WESTERN TYROLEAN LODGE | |
|---|---|---|
| ☐ | 308 3 Ave. S. | (208) 726-5336 |
| | Ketchum, ID 83340 | Hydropool MH |

| #534B | HEIDELBERG INN | |
|---|---|---|
| ☐ | Warm Springs Rd. | (208) 726-5361 |
| | Ketchum, ID 83353 | Hydropool MH |

| #534C | BEST WESTERN CHRISTIANIA LODGE | |
|---|---|---|
| ☐ | 651 Sun Valley Rd. | (208) 726-3351 |
| | Ketchum, ID 83340 | Hydropool MH |

| #534D | KOA-SUN VALLEY | |
|---|---|---|
| ☐ | on Hwy. 75 | (208) 726-3429 |
| | Ketchum, ID 83340 | Hydropool CRV |

## #535 BALD MOUNTAIN HOT SPRINGS
**151 S. Main St.**      **(208) 726-9963**
**Ketchum, ID 83340**      **PR + MH**

Historic motel with Olympic-size swimming pool and soaking pool, near the center of Ketchum. Elevation 6,100 ft. Open all year.

Natural mineral water flows out of Guyer Hot Spring at 158° and is piped three miles to the motel. The outdoor swimming pool, treated with chlorine, is open Memorial Day to Labor Day, and is maintained at 88° to 92°. The indoor soaking pool operates on a daily drain and flow-through basis, so no chemical treatment of the water is necessary, and pool temperature is controllable. The pools are available to the public as well as to registered guests. Bathing suits are required.

Motel room are available on the premises. It is two blocks to a cafe, store and service station, and one mile to overnight camping and RV hook-ups. Visa, MasterCard and Diners Club are accepted.

Phone for rates, reservations and directions.

## #536 WARFIELD HOT SPRING
### West of the town of Ketchum.
**non-commercial**

Funky old bathhouse in Warm Springs Canyon. Elevation 6,400 ft. Open all year.

Natural mineral water flows out of two springs at 97° and 102°, supplying two individual tubs in the bathhouse. Bathing suits are not required in tub rooms.

No services are available on the premises. It is 11 miles to services.

Location: Located on FS 227, 10.4 miles west along Warm Springs Road from ID 75 (Main St.) in Ketchum.

Source map: *Sawtooth National Forest.*

### #537 WORSWICK HOT SPRINGS
**West of the town of Ketchum**

**non-commercial**

Dozens of primitive springs send a large flow of geothermal water tumbling down several acres of rolling hillside in Sawtooth National Forest. Elevation 6,400 ft. Open all year.

Natural mineral water flows out of many springs at temperatures of more than 150°, supplying a series of volunteer-built rock-and-log pools in the drainage channels. The water cools as it flows, so the lower the

Worswick Hot Springs: On a chilly day the entire slope is dotted with steam plumes.

pool, the lower is the temperature you will find. The apparent local custom is clothing optional.

There are no services available on the premises. It is two miles to overnight camping and 14 miles to all other services.

Directions: From the intersection of FS 227 and FS 094, go 2.2 miles east on FS 227. Alternate route: From the town of Fairfield on US 20, go north on FS 094 to intersection with FS 227, then follow above directions.

Source map: *Sawtooth National Forest.*

### #538 PREIS HOT SPRING
**West of the town of Ketchum**

**non-commercial**

Small two-person soaking box near the side of the road in Sawtooth National Forest. Elevation 6,000 ft. Open all year.

Natural mineral water flows out of the spring at 94° directly into a small pool that has been given board sides large enough to accommodate two very friendly soakers. Bathing suits are advisable.

There are no services available on the premises. It is two miles to overnight camping and 14 miles to all other services.

Directions: From the intersection of FS 227 and FS 094, go 2.1 miles north on FS 227, and watch for spring 10 yards from east side of road. Alternate route: From the town of Fairfield, on US 20, go north on FS 094 to intersection with FS 227, then follow above directions.

Source map: *Sawtooth National Forest.*

### #539 SKILLERN HOT SPRINGS
**East of the town of Featherville**

**non-commercial**

Primitive hot spring on Big Smokey Creek, three miles by trail from Canyon Campground. Elevation 5,800. Open all year.

Natural mineral water flows out of a spring at more than 110°, supplying a volunteer-built rock pool at the edge of the creek. Pool temperature is controllable by varying the amount of cold creek water admitted. The local custom is clothing optional.

There are no services on the premises. It is three miles to the campground and trailhead, and 24 miles to all other services.

Directions: From Featherville go 21 miles east on FS 227. About 2 miles beyond South Fork Boise River turn north to Canyon Campground. Trailhead is at north end of campground. The trail fords the stream several times, and might not be passable during high water.

Source maps: *Sawtooth National Forest;* USGS *Sydney Butte* and *Paradise Peak, Idaho.*

▲ *Baumgartner Hot Springs:* This pool and tree-shaded camping spaces are very popular.

▼ The donor of the *Baumgartner* Campground is buried on the ground he loved and gave.

## #540 BAUMGARTNER HOT SPRINGS
### East of the town of Featherville
#### non-commercial

Well-maintained soaking pool in popular Baumgartner Campground in Sawtooth National Forest. Elevation 5,000 ft. Open all year.

Natural mineral water flows out of a spring at 105°, supplying the soaking pool on a flow-through (no-chlorine) basis, which maintains the pool temperature at 104°. Because of the pool's location in a campground, bathing suits are advisable.

Campground facilities are available on the premises. It is 11 miles to rooms, a restaurant, service station and grocery store, and 48 miles to RV hook-ups.

Location: On FS 227, 11 miles east of Featherville.

Source map: *Sawtooth National Forest.*

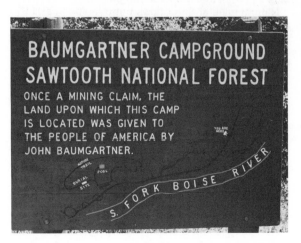

BAUMGARTNER CAMPGROUND
SAWTOOTH NATIONAL FOREST
ONCE A MINING CLAIM, THE
LAND UPON WHICH THIS CAMP
IS LOCATED WAS GIVEN TO
THE PEOPLE OF AMERICA BY
JOHN BAUMGARTNER.

YOU ARE HERE

S. FORK BOISE RIVER

99

*Green Canyon Hot Springs:* The new outdoor hydropool was designed to accommodate dozens of families at peak use. The original indoor swimming pool, with its snack bar and electronic games, continues to be a social center.

## #541   GREEN CANYON HOT SPRINGS
■
Box 96                     (208) 458-4454
**Newdale, ID 83436**           **PR + CRV**

Rural indoor plunge and RV park in a really *green* canyon. Elevation 6,000 ft. Open weekends all year plus mid-April to the end of September.

Natural mineral water flows out of a spring at 118° and is piped to two pools and a geothermal greenhouse. The indoor swimming pool is maintained at 90° to 95° and the outdoor hydrojet pool is maintained at 105°. Both pools are treated with chlorine and bathing suits are required.

Locker rooms, snack bar, picnic area and RV hook-ups are available on the premises. It is 21 miles to all other services.

No credit cards are accepted.

Directions: From the town of Driggs, go north and west 17 miles on ID 33. At Canyon Creek bridge, turn south and follow signs four miles to resort.

#542   BEST WESTERN TETON WEST INN
☐
476 N. Main St.            (208) 354-2363
Driggs, ID 83422          Hydropool  MH

## #543   HEISE HOT SPRINGS
■
Box 417                     (208) 538-7312
**Ririe, ID 83443**             **PR + CRV**

Modernized family-oriented resort with spacious, tree-shaded picnic and RV grounds on the north bank of the Snake River. Elevation 5,000 ft. Open all year except the month of November.

Natural mineral water flows out of a spring at 126° and is piped to an enclosed hydrojet pool which is maintained at 105°, with no chemical treatment required. Tap water, treated with chlorine and heated by geothermal heat exchangers, is used in the other pools. An outdoor soaking pool is maintained at 92° to 93°, the large swimming pool at 82° and the waterslide pick-up pool at 85°. Bathing suits are required in all areas.

Locker rooms, cafe, overnight camping, RV hook-ups, picnic area and golf course are available on the premises. It is five miles to a store, service station and motel. No credit cards are accepted.

Directions: From the town of Idaho Falls, go east 22 miles on US 26 and then follow signs four miles north across river to resort.

*Heise Hot Springs:* A giant water slide is the most recent addition to this large and popular resort near Idaho's eastern border.

*Soda (Hooper) Springs:* Free bubble water by the jugful is the attraction for this family.

## #544 SODA (HOOPER) SPRINGS
### North of the town of Soda Springs
#### non-commercial

Naturally carbonated cold-water spring surrounded by a tree-shaded picnic area. Elevation 5,200 ft. Open all year.

Natural mineral water flows out of the ground at 54° into an open pool where many people fill their jugs with supplies of "soda water," believed to be good for the digestion. The original source of local hot mineral water, "Steamboat Springs," was drowned many years ago under a new reservoir.

Directions: From US 30 in Soda Springs, take ID 34 north and watch for signs "Hooper Springs Park."

101

*Bear Lake Hot Springs:* A popular evening attraction in a seasonal recreation area.

*Riverdale Resort:* Daily drain and fill avoids chemical treatment of this large pool.

#### #545 BEST WESTERN CREST MOTEL
243 N. 4th Ave.    (208) 847-1782
Montpelier, ID 83254    Hydropool MH

#### #546 BEAR LAKE HOT SPRINGS
Box 75    (208) 945-2494
St. Charles, ID 83272    PR + CRV

Large pool building and campground on a remote section of lakeshore. Elevation 6,000 ft. Open May to September.

Natural mineral water flows out of a spring at 120° and is piped to two indoor pools, which are treated with chlorine. The swimming pool is maintained at 75° to 85°, the ten-person soaking pool at 110° to 115°. Bathing suits are required.

Locker rooms, cafe, overnight parking and a boat dock are on the premises. It is seven miles to a store, service station and motel No credit cards are accepted.

Directions: From US 89, on the north side of the town of St. Charles, follow signs across the north end of Bear Lake to the resort.

#### #547 RIVERDALE RESORT
Rte 2, Box 405    (208) 852-0266
Preston, ID 83263    PR + CRV

Completely new commercial development in a rural valley subdivision. Phone for status of additional construction. Elevation 4,000 ft. Open all year.

Natural mineral water is pumped from a geothermal well at 122°, then cooled with tap water as needed to maintain temperatures in various outdoor pools. All pools are drained daily, eliminating the need for chemical treatment of the water. The partly shaded hydrojet pool is maintained at 103° to 105°, and a large soaking pool is maintained at 96° to 100° in the summer and at 102° to 104° in the winter. The water-slide catch pool is maintained at approximately 80°. Bathing suits are required.

Locker rooms, massage by appointment, snack bar, overnight camping and RV hook-ups are available on the premises. It is less than six miles to a cafe, store, service station and motel. No credit cards are accepted.

Directions: From Preston, on US 91, go 6 miles north on ID 34 and watch for resort signs.

▲ *Downata Hot Springs:* Swinging from ring to ring is one of the most difficult, and popular, challenges at this major summertime resort.

► The superslide rules at *Downata Hot Springs* include encouragement as well as the usual list of prohibitions and warnings.

---

## #548    DOWNATA HOT SPRINGS

■ Route 1        (208) 897-5736
Downey, ID 83234     PR + CRV

Expanded older rural plunge and picnic grounds in the rolling hills of southeastern Idaho. Elevation 4,000 ft. Open May 1 to Labor Day.

Natural mineral water flows out of a spring at 112°, and is piped to outdoor pools treated with chlorine. The main swimming pool and the water-slide catch pool are maintained at 85° to 95°. Bathing suits are required.

Locker rooms, snack bar, picnic grounds, overnight camping, and miniature golf are available on the premises. It is three miles to a store, service station and motel. No credit cards are accepted.

Directions: On US 91, drive 3 miles south from the town of Downey and watch for resort signs.

LAVA HOT SPRINGS

LONG BEFORE WHITE MEN DISCOVERED THESE
SPRINGS, SEPT. 9, 1812, INDIANS GATHERED
HERE TO USE THE FREE HOT WATER.

Except where they found hot springs, pre–historic Indians had a hard time getting hot water. They wove water-tight baskets into which they put heated rocks. Here they had plenty of hot water for baths and for processing hides without going to all the work of heating baskets. This was one of their major campgrounds, especially in winter. After 1868, when they began to stay mostly on the Fort Hall Indian reservation, this spot lost its importance as a winter camp.

▲ *Lava Hot Springs:* This location rates a large Highway Department historical site sign, with text prepared by the Idaho Historical Society.

▼ *Lava Hot Springs Foundation:* Several years ago this Olympic-size swimming and diving complex was built to host Olympic Games trials, and then to be available to the public at low fees. Water-heating costs were eliminated by using hot-spring water and a heat exchanger.

## #549A  LAVA HOT SPRINGS FOUNDATION

■    P.O. Box 668          (208) 776-5221
     Lava Hot Springs, ID 83246          PR

Two attractive and well-maintained recreation areas operated by a self-supporting state agency in the town of Lava Hot Springs. Elevation 5,000 ft.

GEOTHERMAL POOLS: (East end of town; open all year) Natural mineral water flows out of the ground at 110° directly up through the gravel bottoms of two large, partly shaded soaking pools. No chemical treatment is necessary. Pool temperatures range down to 107° at the drain end of the lower soaking pool. The same water is pumped to two partly shaded hydrojet pools that maintain an average temperature of 106°. Bathing suits are required in all pools. Massage is available on the premises.

SWIMMING POOLS: (West end of town; open May 1 to Labor Day) Chlorinated city water is used in the TAC-size pool and in the Olympic-size pool. Hot mineral water, piped from the geothermal pools, is run through a heat exchanger to maintain the pool temperatures at 88°. The pool complex is surrounded by a large, level lawn. Bathing suits are required.

Locker room are available at both locations, and it is less than three blocks to all other services. No credit cards are accepted.

## #549B RIVERSIDE INN

■ 212 Portneuf Ave.     (208) 776-9906
Lava Hot Springs, ID 83246     PR + MH

A picturesque, historic hotel, once known as the *Elegant Grand,* visible on the main street between the two Lava Hot Springs Foundation locations. Elevation 5,400 ft. Open all year.

Natural mineral water is pumped out of a well at 118°, then piped to five soaking pools, which are drained and filled after each use, making chemical treatment unnecessary. Two rock-lined pools, each large enough for six people, are in one room, and three cement pools, each large enough for two people, are in another private room. Water temperature in each pool is controllable by mixing in cold tap water as desired. The pools are available to the public as well as to registered guests.

Hotel rooms are available on the premises. It is less than three blocks to all other services. Visa, MasterCard and American Express are accepted.

▲ The mineral-water soaking pools of the *Lava Hot Springs Foundation* are built on the springs.

## #549C HOME HOTEL AND MOTEL

■ 305 E. Main     (208) 776-5507
Lava Hot Springs, ID 83246     MH

Remodeled older hotel featuring hot mineral baths in all units, on the main street between the two Lava Hot Springs Foundation locations. Elevation 5,400 ft. Open all year.

Natural mineral water flows out of a spring at 121° and is piped to two-person tubs in all rooms. Temperature in each tub is controllable by the customer. The eight rooms in the hotel are non-smoking; the 13 rooms in the motel section permit smoking.

It is less than 3 blocks to a cafe, store, service station, overnight camping and RV hook-ups. No credit cards are accepted.

▲ *Indian Springs Natatorium:* Changing rooms around the pool edge are a convenience and a protection from the sometimes gusty winds.

| #550A ☐ | POCATELLO QUALITY INN 1555 Pocatello Creek Rd. Pocatello, ID 83201 | (208) 233-2200 Hydropool MH |
|---|---|---|
| #550B ☐ | BEST WESTERN COTTONTREE INN 1415 Bench Rd. Pocatello, ID 83201 | (208) 237-7650 Hydropool MH |
| #550C ☐ | HOLIDAY INN 1399 Bench Rd. Pocatello, ID 83201 | (208) 237-1400 Hydropool MH |
| #550D ☐ | LITTLETREE INN 133 W. Burnside Pocatello, ID 83201 | (208) 237-0020 Hydropool MH |
| #550E ☐ | OXBOW MOTOR INN 4333 Yellowstone Ave. Pocatello, ID 83202 | (208) 237-3100 Hydropool MH |

### #550F  INDIAN SPRINGS NATATORIUM

■ P.O. Box 366                    (208) 226-2174
American Falls, ID 83211          PR + CRV

Older rural picnic ground and plunge with RV accommodations. Elevation 5,200 ft. Open April 1 to Labor Day.

Natural mineral water flows out of a spring at 90° and is piped to an outdoor swimming pool, which maintains a temperature of 90° on a flow-through basis, requiring no chemical treatment of the water. Bathing suits are required.

Locker rooms, picnic area and full hook-up RV spaces are available on the premises. It is three miles to all other services. No credit cards are accepted.

Located on Idaho Route 37, three miles south of the city of American Falls.

### #551  HOT SPRINGS LANDING AT MAGIC RESERVOIR

● East of the town of Fairfield

**non-commercial**

Abandoned hot spring and small boat landing on the edge of near-empty reservoir. Elevation 5,100 ft. Open all year.

Natural mineral water flows out of an artesian well at more than 170° and runs along the ground into the reservoir. Volunteers have built small rock-and-mud pools, where the water has cooled to around 100°. Bathing suits are advisable.

No services are available on the premises, but there is a large level area on which overnight parking is not prohibited. It is 15 miles to services.

Directions: From Fairfield go 15 miles east on US 20. Look for signs, and turn south to reservoir.

▲ *Paradise Inn:* The spray is more than just a decoration; it is a full-time device for cooling 110° water to swimmable temperatures.

► Indoor soaking pool temperatures at *Paradise Inn* are controlled by adding as much hot spring water or cold tap water as desired.

▼ *Hot Springs Landing at Magic Reservoir:* Each time the reservoir fills, this pool is destroyed.

## #552 PARADISE INN

■ Rocky Bar Stage                     (208) 587-7931
   Mountain Home, ID 83647            MH

Small, private, family resort with limited public access, surrounded by Sawtooth National Forest. Elevation 4,500 ft. Open all year.

Natural mineral water flows out of a spring at 110° and is piped to an outdoor swimming pool and three large indoor private-space soaking pools. Chlorine is used in all pools. The temperature in the outdoor pool ranges from 75° to 90° and the temperature in the indoor pools is controllable. The pools are available to resort members and registered guests only. Bathing suits are required.

Changing rooms, restaurant and hotel rooms are available on the premises. It is one mile to overnight camping and six miles to all other services. Visa and MasterCard are accepted.

Phone for information on restrictions, rates, reservations and directions.

▲ *Banbury Hot Springs:* The log tethered in the middle of the pool is an indestructible toy which gets lots of action from teenagers.

| #553A ☐ | BEST WESTERN APOLLO MOTOR INN<br>296 Addison Ave. W.<br>Twin Falls, ID 83301 | (208) 733-2010<br>Hydropool MH |
|---|---|---|
| #553B ☐ | ANDERSON'S CAMP<br>on Tipperary Rd.<br>Twin Falls, ID 83301 | (208) 733-6756<br>Hydropool CRV |

## #554A BANBURY HOT SPRINGS
**■** **Rte. 3** **(208) 543-4098**
**Buhl, ID 83316** **PR + CRV**

Community plunge on the Snake River with soaking pools and spacious, tree-shaded area for picnics and overnight camping. Elevation 3,000 ft. Open weekends from Easter weekend to May 1; open every day from May 1 to Labor Day.

Natural mineral water flows out of a spring at 141°. The large outdoor chlorine-treated pool is maintained at temperatures ranging from 89° to 95°. The four indoor soaking pools and the three indoor hydrojet pools are in private rooms, and the temperatures of the pools are individually controlled. Each pool is drained and refilled after each use, requiring no chemical treatment of the water. Bathing suits are required in the outside pool.

Locker rooms, snack bar, gas pump, overnight camping, RV hook-ups, and a boat ramp and dock are located on the premises. It is four miles to a restaurant and 12 miles to a store, service station and motel. No credit cards are accepted.

Directions: From the town of Buhl, go ten miles north on US 30. Watch for sign and turn east 1½ miles to resort.

## #554B MIRACLE HOT SPRINGS
**■** **Route 3 Box 171** **(208) 543-6002**
**Buhl, ID 83316** **PR + CRV**

Older health spa surrounded by rolling agricultural land. Elevation 3,000 ft. Open all year (closed on Sundays).

Natural mineral water is pumped out of a well at 139° into an outdoor swimming pool and 15 roofless enclosed soaking pools, all of which operate on a flow-through basis, requiring no chemical treatment. The swimming pool is maintained at a temperature of 95° and the temperature in the individual pools is controllable. Bathing suits are required in public areas. All buildings and dressing rooms are supplied with geothermal heat.

Massage by appointment, locker rooms and overnight camping are available on the premises. A restaurant and RV hook-ups are available within three miles, and all other services are available within 10 miles. No credit cards are accepted.

Location: Located on US 30 ten miles north of the town of Buhl.

## #555 SLIGAR'S THOUSAND SPRINGS RESORT
**■** **Route 1, Box 90** **(208) 837-4987**
**Hagerman, ID 83332** **PR + CRV**

Indoor plunge with private-space hydrojet tubs and green; shaded RV park with a view of multiple waterfalls on cliffs across the Snake River. Elevation 2,900 ft. Open all year.

Natural mineral water flows out of a spring at 200° and is piped to an outdoor swimming pool, 15 indoor hydrojet pools large enough for eight people and one indoor hydrojet pool large enough for 20 people. The temperature in the swimming pool is maintained between 90° and 96°, while the temperature in the hydrojet pools is individually controllable. All the pools are chlorinated. Bathing suits are required in public areas.

Locker rooms, overnight camping and RV hook-ups are available on the premises. A restaurant is within one mile and all other services are within 10 miles. No credit cards are accepted.

Directions: On US 30, eight miles south of the town of Hagerman.

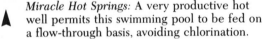

*Miracle Hot Springs:* A very productive hot well permits this swimming pool to be fed on a flow-through basis, avoiding chlorination.

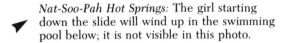

*Nat-Soo-Pah Hot Springs:* The girl starting down the slide will wind up in the swimming pool below; it is not visible in this photo.

*Sligar's Thousand Springs Resort:* This indoor pool also offers a tethered log as a challenge for would-be lumberjacks of any age or sex.

## #556   NAT-SOO-PAH HOT SPRINGS

| | |
|---|---|
| Route 1 | (208) 655-4337 |
| Hollister, ID 83301 | PR + CRV |

Clean and quiet community plunge with soaking pools and acres of tree-shaded grass for picnics and overnight camping. Located on the Snake River plain south of Twin Falls. Elevation 4,400 ft. Open May 1 to Labor Day.

Natural mineral water flows out of a spring at 98° and is piped to three outdoor pools. The swimming pool is maintained at 84° to 88°, using flow-through and some chlorine treatment. Part of the swimming pool flow-through is heated with a heat pump to supply the soaking pool, which is maintained at a temperature of 104° to 106°. The hydrojet pool, supplied by direct flow-through from the spring, maintains a temperature of 98° and requires no chemical treatment. There is also a small water slide at the side of the swimming pool. Bathing suits are required.

Locker rooms, snack bar, picnic area, overnight camping and RV hook-ups are available on the premises. It is four miles to a store and service station and 16 miles to a motel. No credit cards are accepted.

Directions: From US 93, ½ mile south of Hollister and ½ mile north of the Port of Entry, go east three miles on Nat-Soo-Pah Road, directly into the location.

## #557 MURPHY'S HOT SPRINGS

**Rogerson, ID 83302**

**(208) 857-2233**

**PR + MH + CRV**

"Western funky" pool, bathhouse, bar and RV park, in a remote section of the Jarbridge River Canyon. Elevation 5,100 ft. Open all year.

Natural mineral water flows out of two springs at 129° into an outdoor chlorine-treated pool and into three indoor flow-through soaking pools requiring no chemicals. The swimming pool is maintained at a temperature ranging from 80° to 90°. The large indoor pool, for use by six people, is maintained at 96°, and the two smaller, 2-person tubs, are maintained at 104° and 107°. Pools are open to the public in addition to registered guests. Bathing suits are required in the pool and public areas.

Dressing rooms, cafe, gas pump, cabins, overnight camping and RV hook-ups are available on the premises. It is 49 miles to a store and service station. No credit cards are accepted.

Directions: From Twin Falls go approximately 37 miles south on US 93. Watch for highway sign, and turn southwest ½ mile into Rogerson. At main intersection watch for Murphy Hot Springs highway sign and follow signs 49 miles to location. Only the last few miles are gravel.

▲ *Murphy's Hot Springs:* The meandering creek along the side of the pool is just right for this informal outpost of civilization.

◄ *Indian Bathtub:* The streaked panels on the right are tufa formations deposited and then eroded over a period of many centuries.

## #558 INDIAN BATHTUB    (see map)

**South of the town of Bruneau.**

**non-commercial**

Unimproved soaking pool in rugged cliffs with access over a very rough road and then down a steep cliff. Elevation 2,400 ft. Open all year.

Natural mineral water flows out of a rock formation at 93° into a canyon bottom, where centuries of erosion have scoured shallow pockets in the rock. Volunteers have added a rock dam to deepen the main sandy-bottom soaking pool, which maintains a temperature of 80° to 91°. The volume of hot-water flow has been decreased dramatically due to nearby irrigation pumping since the days when local Indian tribes prized this mineral-water oasis in an otherwise arid land. The apparent local custom is clothing optional.

No services are available on the premises except for a small amount of level parking area at the top of the cliff. It is 11 miles to a grocery store and service station and 26 miles to all other services. Source maps: USGS *Hot Spring, Idaho; Sugar Valley, Idaho.*

## #559  GIVENS HOT SPRINGS

■ Star Route Box 103      (208) 495-2433
Melba, ID 83641         PR + CRV

Rural plunge, picnic grounds and RV park on agricultural plateau above the Snake River. Elevation 3,000 ft. Open all year.

Natural mineral water flows out of an artesian spring at 120° and is piped to a chlorine-treated indoor swimming pool and six indoor private-space soaking pools which operate on a drain-and-fill basis, requiring no chemicals. The swimming pool is maintained at a temperature of 99° in the winter and 85° in the summer. The temperature in the tubs is individually controllable, temperatures ranging from 105° to 110°. Bathing suits are required in public areas.

Locker rooms, a snack bar, picnic grounds, a softball diamond and overnight camping are available on the premises. It is 11 miles to all other services. No credit cards are accepted.

Location: Located 11 miles southeast of the town of Marsing on ID 78.

▲ *Givens Hot Springs:* Swimming and diving lessons are a year-round activity in this heated building with the geothermal pool.

|  |  |  |
|---|---|---|
| #560 ☐ | SHILO INN<br>617 Nampa Blvd.<br>Nampa, ID 83651 | (208) 466-8993<br>Hydropool  MH |
| #561A ☐ | FLYING J MOTEL<br>8000 Overland Rd.<br>Boise, ID 83709 | (208) 322-4404<br>Hydropool  MH |
| #561B ☐ | RED LION MOTOR INN/RIVERSIDE<br>2900 Chinden Blvd.<br>Boise, ID 83714 | (208) 343-1871<br>Hydropool  MH |
| #561C ☐ | RODEWAY INN<br>1115 N. Curtis Rd.<br>Boise, ID 83706 | (208) 376-2700<br>Hydropool  MH |
| #561D ☐ | SHILO INN<br>3031 Main St.<br>Boise, ID 83702 | (208) 344-3521<br>Hydropool  MH |
| #561E ☐ | HOLIDAY INN<br>3300 Vista Ave.<br>Boise, ID 83705 | (208) 344-8365<br>Hydropool  MH |
| #561F ☐ | NENDELS MOTOR INN<br>1025 S. Capitol Blvd.<br>Boise, ID 83706 | (208) 344-7971<br>Hydropool  MH |
| #561G ☐ | BEST WESTERN AIRPORT MOTOR INN<br>2660 Airport Way<br>Boise, ID 83705 | (208) 384-5000<br>Hydropool  MH |

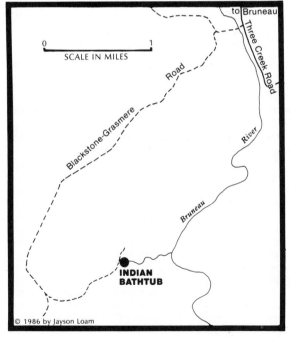

to Bruneau

Three Creek Road

0            1
SCALE IN MILES

Blackstone-Grasmere Road

River

Bruneau

● INDIAN BATHTUB

© 1986 by Jayson Loam

# Region C   BOISE RIVER — MIDDLE FORK

The common thread connecting these hot springs is a gravel road FS 268, which winds along the riverbank for 50 miles, often only one lane wide. Loaded logging trucks coming downstream have the inside lane, while upstream traffic must make do with turnouts on the edge toward the river— not recommended for trailers and motor homes. It is possible to reach Atlanta by taking FS 394, FS 327 and FS 268 from ID 21, 15 miles south of Lowman. Then, when you head downstream from Atlanta to Arrowroot Reservoir on FS 268, you will at least have the inside lane and will not be meeting any loaded logging trucks.

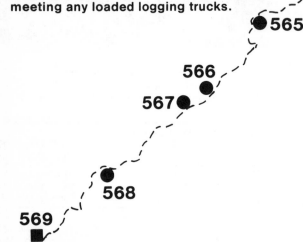

The hot springs below are listed in sequence, working downstream from Atlanta Hot Springs.

© 1986 by Jayson Loam

---

**#562   ATLANTA HOT SPRINGS   (see map)**
● North of the town of Atlanta

**non-commercial**

Primitive spring and a small rock-and-sand soaking pool on a wooded plateau in Boise National Forest. Elevation 5,400 ft. Open all year.

Natural mineral water flows out of a spring at 110° and cools as it travels to a nearby volunteer-built soaking pool. The pool temperature is approximately 100°, depending on air temperature and wind conditions. This site is easily visible from the nearby road, so bathing suits are advisable.

No services are available on the premises. It is ½ mile to a campground, one mile to cabins, cafe, service station and store, and 62 miles to RV hook-ups.

Source maps: *Boise National Forest; USGS Atlanta East* and *Atlanta West*.

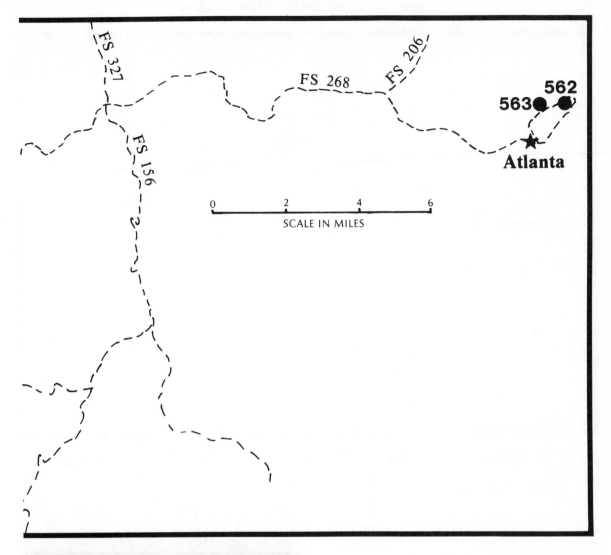

FS 327
FS 206
FS 268
FS 156

563 562

★ Atlanta

0      2      4      6
SCALE IN MILES

◄ *Atlanta Hot Springs:* Runoff from the hot pool flows to the larger cold pool visible across the road in the background.

113

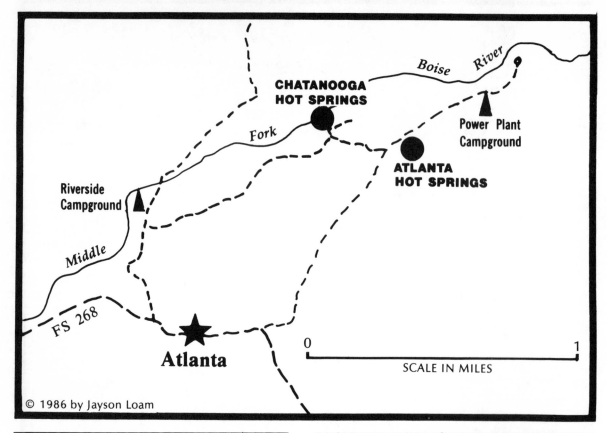

© 1986 by Jayson Loam

### #563 CHATANOOGA HOT SPRINGS
**(see map)**

**North of the town of Atlanta**
**non-commercial**

Large, comfortable, sand-bottom pool at the foot of a geothermal cliff surrounded by the tree-covered slopes of Boise National Forest. Elevation 5,400 ft. Open all year.

Natural mineral water flows out of fissures in a 100-ft. cliff at 120° and cools as it tumbles toward a volunteer-built rock-and-sand soaking pool, which retains a temperature of more than 100°. The apparent local custom is clothing optional.

There are no services available on the premises. It is ½ mile to a campground, one mile to a cafe, cabins, service station and store, and 62 miles to RV hook-ups.

Note: The pool is visible from the north edge of the unmarked parking area at the top of the cliff. Several well-worn, steep paths lead down to the pool. Source maps: *Boise National Forest*: USGS *Atlanta East* and *Atlanta West*.

### #564 DUTCH FRANK HOT SPRINGS
**non-commercial**

Scattered geothermal flows along 200 yards of riverbank. Located on the south bank of the river, immediately east of the Roaring River bridge.

### #565 NEINMEYER HOT SPRINGS
**non-commercial**

Several primitive hot springs on the south bank of the river, across from Neinmeyer Campground.

### #566 LOFTUS HOT SPRINGS
**non-commercial**

Small, volunteer-built soaking pool, with 100° water, ten yards from a small parking area on the north side of the road. It is located 0.2 mile east of the bridge over which the road crosses to the south side of the river.

### #567 SMITH CABIN HOT SPRINGS
**non-commercial**

Volunteer-built river's-edge pools on both sides of the river, 0.7 mile west of the above described bridge.

▲ *Dutch Frank Hot Springs:* No volunteers have tried to collect these flows into a pool.

◄ *Chatanooga Hot Springs:* This site, with its geothermal cascade, has one of the most dramatic settings along the Boise Middle Fork.

▼ *Loftus Hot Springs:* By excavating under a tufa layer, volunteers have created a shower bath as well as a soaking pool.

## #568 SHEEP CREEK BRIDGE HOT SPRINGS   non-commercial

Volunteer-built pool with rock screen, containing algae-laden water at temperatures up to 100°, depending on weather conditions. It is located 20 yards from the south end of the bridge over which the road returns to the north side of the river.

▲ *Twin Springs Resort:* This flow-through hot pool, and the tavern, have continued to operate through many decades of management changes.

◄ *Sheep Creek Bridge Hot Springs:* One of the plentiful, but seldom used, primitive hot springs along the Boise Middle Fork.

## #569 TWIN SPRINGS RESORT
**c/o Atlanta Stage       (208) 362-1006**
**Boise, ID 83708                        PR**

Informal rural tavern, soaking pool and commercial fish ponds on an historic mining claim along the east bank of the Middle Fork Boise River. Elevation 3,300 ft. Open all year.

Natural mineral water flows out of two springs at more than 180°, and is piped to an enclosed outdoor soaking pool and to several commercial tropical fish ponds. The soaking pool is maintained at 90° in the summer and 105° in the winter. Bathing suits are optional at the pool.

Fishing is available on the premises. It is one mile to overnight camping and 30 miles to all other services. No credit cards are accepted.

Note: Future building plans include a lodge with steam baths, an open-roof soaking pool and a restaurant. Phone ahead for information on the status of construction. Plans also include the expansion of fish ponds to produce stock for other commercial fish farmers.

Source map: *Boise National Forest.*

This funky old bathhouse at *Twin Springs Resort* has become a welcome landmark on a long and dusty road to and from Atlanta. A fancy new lodge just won't be the same.

The reliable and unlimited supply of hot water at *Twin Springs Resort* makes possible the year-round raising of fast-growing Australian fish for human consumption.

*Warm Springs Resort:* A popular all year resort with one of the largest flow-through (no chlorination) swimming pools in Idaho.

*Sawtooth Lodge:* This site is the farthest upstream on the South Fork of the Payette River at the gateway to the Sawtooth Range.

### #570   WARM SPRINGS RESORT

P.O. Box 28        (208) 345-5437
Idaho City, ID 86361    PR + MH + CRV

Rural plunge and RV park surrounded by Boise National Forest. Elevation 4,000 ft. Open all year.

Natural mineral water flows out of a spring at 110° and then through an outdoor swimming pool, maintained at a temperature of 94° to 97°. Chemical treatment of the water is not required. The pools is open to the public as well as to registered guests. Bathing suits are required.

Locker rooms, snack bar, cabins, overnight camping and RV hook-ups are available on the premises. A cafe, store and service station are located within two miles. No credit cards are accepted.

Location: On ID 21, 1½ miles south of Idaho City.

### #571   SAWTOOTH LODGE

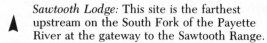

                     (208) 344-6685
Grandjean, ID 83637    PR + CRV + MH

Historic mountain resort in the Sawtooth Recreation Area. Elevation 5,100 ft. Open June through October.

Natural mineral water flows out of several springs with temperatures up to 150° and into an outdoor chlorinated swimming pool maintained at approximately 80°. The pool is available to the public as well as to registered guests. Bathing suits are required.

Dressing rooms, cafe, cabins, overnight camping, RV hook-ups and saddle horses are available on the premises. It is 28 miles to a store and service station. Visa and MasterCard are accepted.

Directions: From the town of Lowman, go 22 miles east on ID 21, then follow signs six miles on gravel road to lodge.

## #572    SACAJAWEA HOT SPRINGS
### West of the town of Grandjean.
#### non-commercial

Popular, large geothermal area on the north bank of the South Fork of the Payette River in Boise National Forest. Elevation 5,000 ft. Open all year.

Natural mineral water flows out of many springs at temperatures up to 108° and cools as it cascades into a series of volunteer-built rock pools along the river's edge. Because the pools are visible from the road, bathing suits are advisable.

There are no services available on the premises. It is one mile to a cafe, cabins, overnight camping and RV hook-ups, and 27 miles to a store and service station.

Directions: On the road to Grandjean, 0.6 mile east of Wapiti Creek bridge, look toward the river for the pools.

Source map: *Boise National Forest.*

*Sacajawea Hot Springs:* Here is the ideal solution for a vacationing family. Father is casting into a superb fishing stream, while mother and the children splash in a 100° soaking pool less than five yards away.

## #573 BONNEVILLE HOT SPRINGS
● West of the town of Grandjean
non-commercial

Popular semi-remote geothermal area on a tree-lined creek in Boise National Forest. Elevation 4,800 ft. Open all year.

Natural mineral water flows out of a multitude of springs with various temperatures up to 180°. Be careful not to step into any of the scalding-water runoff channels. There is one small wooden bathhouse with an individual tub supplied from a nearby spring at a temperature of 103°. Soakers drain the tub after each use. There are also many volunteer-built rock-and-sand soaking pools along the edge of the creek, where the geothermal water can be mixed with cold water. Bathing suits are advisable.

No services are available on the premises. It is ¼ mile to a campground, eight miles to a cafe, cabins and RV hook-ups, and 15 miles to a store and service station.

Directions: From the north edge of Bonneville Campground (formerly Warm Springs Campground) follow unmarked but well-worn path ¼ mile to geothermal area.

Source map: *Boise National Forest*.

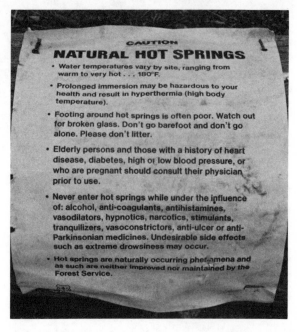

CAUTION
## NATURAL HOT SPRINGS
- Water temperatures vary by site, ranging from warm to very hot . . . 180°F.
- Prolonged immersion may be hazardous to your health and result in hyperthermia (high body temperature).
- Footing around hot springs is often poor. Watch out for broken glass. Don't go barefoot and don't go alone. Please don't litter.
- Elderly persons and those with a history of heart disease, diabetes, high or low blood pressure, or who are pregnant should consult their physician prior to use.
- Never enter hot springs while under the influence of: alcohol, anti-coagulants, antihistamines, vasodilators, hypnotics, narcotics, stimulants, tranquilizers, vasoconstrictors, anti-ulcer or anti-Parkinsonian medicines. Undesirable side effects such as extreme drowsiness may occur.
- Hot springs are naturally occurring phenomena and as such are neither improved nor maintained by the Forest Service.

▲ *Bonneville Hot Springs:* This Forest Service warning is in the middle of the path from Bonneville Campground to the hot springs area.

◄ The two channels for mixing *Bonneville Hot Springs* water and cold creek water are visible just upstream from the occupied soaking pool.

▼ Although this bathhouse at *Bonneville Hot Springs* gets some use, most visitors prefer to use the creekside pools and enjoy the view.

## #574   KIRKHAM HOT SPRINGS
### East of the town of Lowman
**non-commercial**

Popular geothermal area with many hot waterfalls and pools adjoining a National Forest campground on the South Fork of the Payette River. Elevation 4,200 ft. Open all year.

Natural mineral water flows out of many springs and fissures along the south bank of the river at temperatures up to 120°, and cools as it cascades toward the river. Volunteers have built several rock-and-sand soaking pools, in which temperatures can vary above or below 100°, depending on air temperature and wind conditions. Bathing suits are advisable, especially in the daytime.

Overnight camping is available on the adjoining campground. It is four miles to a cafe, store, service station and cabins, and 34 miles to RV hook-ups.

Directions: From the town of Lowman, go four miles east on ID 21 and watch for Kirkham Hot Springs Campground sign.

Source map: *Boise National Forest.*

◄ *Kirkham Hot Springs:* This easy-access campground is especially popular because it has natural hot showers and adjoining cold dips.

▼ For those who prefer a hot bath, *Kirkham* also offers a series of soaking pools just below a long stretch of natural hot showers.

## #576 PINE FLATS HOT SPRING
● West of the town of Lowman.

**non-commercial**

Spectacular geothermal cascade and cliffside soaking pool overlooking the South Fork of the Payette River in Boise National Forest. Elevation 4,100 ft. Open all year.

Natural mineral water flows from several springs on top of a one-hundred-foot cliff with temperatures up to 125°, cooling as it flows and tumbles over the rocks. There is one volunteer-built tarp-lined rock pool thirty feet above the river, immediately below a hot shower bath which averages 104°. Other rock pools at the foot of the cliff have lower temperatures. The apparent local custom is clothing optional.

The hot springs are located ⅓ mile from the Pine Flats Campground and Parking area. It is four miles to a cafe, store, service station and motel, and 27 miles to RV hook-ups.

Directions: From the west edge of Pine Flats Campground follow an unmarked but well-worn path ⅓ mile west down to and along a large riverbed rock-and-sand bar. Look for geothermal water cascading down the cliff onto the bar.

Source map: *Boise National Forest.*

▼ *Haven Lodge:* A central location for those who want to visit the primitive springs along the river but are not equipped for camping.

▲ *Pine Flats Hot Spring:* This unique soaking pool combines a sweeping view of the river with the sound of a 50′ geothermal cascade.

## #575 HAVEN LODGE
■ General Delivery (208) 259-3344
Lowman, ID 83637 PR + MH + CRV

Motel and RV park with swimming pool and soaking tub in Boise National Forest. Elevation 4,000 ft. Open all year.

Natural mineral water flows out of a spring at 148° and is piped to an outdoor chlorinated swimming pool and to an indoor drain-and-fill tub. The swimming pool is maintained at 80° to 90°. Soaking-tub temperature is controllable by each customer. The pool and tub are available to the public as well as to registered guests. Bathing suits are required in public areas.

Locker rooms, cafe, store, service station, cabins, overnight camping and RV hook-ups are available on the premises. No credit cards are accepted.

Location: On ID 21, 3½ miles east of the town of Lowman.

Source map: *Boise National Forest.*

## #578 DEER CREEK HOT SPRINGS
● **Near the town of Crouch**

**non-commercial**

Small volunteer-built soaking pool combining the flow from springs, a test well and a creek, in a gully 20 yards from a paved highway. Elevation 3,000 ft. Open all year.

Natural mineral water flows out of several springs, and out of an abandoned well casing at temperatures ranging up to 176°. Volunteers have built a shallow plastic-and-sand soaking pool on one side of the creek to mix the hot and cold water. There are no posted clothing requirements but the proximity to the highway makes bathing suits advisable.

There are no services available on the premises, but all services are available four miles away.

Directions: From the town of Crouch, go 4½ miles west toward the town of Banks, watching for a steep dirt road on the north side of the highway. Do not drive up the road—it deadends in just a few yards. Park in a turnout on the river side of the highway and walk back to the springs, which are just below the steep side road.

Source Map: *Boise National Forest.*

*Hot Springs Campground:* Vandalism and weather
▲ finished off the bathhouse, leaving the run-off for use in crude rivers-edge soaking pools.

► *Terrace Lakes Recreation Ranch:* For those who desire urban amenities in the mountains.

## #577 HOT SPRINGS CAMPGROUND
● **East of the town of Crouch**

**non-commercial**

The cement foundations of a long-gone bathhouse and some small volunteer-built soaking pools are intended to use some of the continuing hot-water flow. Located on a riverbank across the highway from a National Forest campground. Elevation 3,800 ft. Open all year.

Natural mineral water flows out of several springs at 105°, into volunteer-built shallow rock-and-sand pools near the south side of the highway. Bathing suits are advisable.

Overnight camping is available on the premises. All other services are available four miles away.

Directions: From the town of Crouch go four miles east toward Lowman. Look for Hot Springs campground one mile after entering Forest Service land.

Source map: *Boise National Forest.*

## #579 TERRACE LAKES RECREATIONAL RANCH
■ **Garden Valley, ID 83622    (208) 462-3250**

Private-membership recreation ranch in rolling foothills near Boise National Forest. Elevation 3,300 ft. Open all year.

Natural mineral water flows out of a spring at 176° and is piped to a chlorinated swimming pool maintained at temperatures ranging from 90° to 100°. All facilities are for the exclusive use of members and their guests. Bathing suits are required.

Golf, tennis, a restaurant and RV hook-ups are on the premises. It is four miles to a grocery store and service station, 18 miles to a campground and 40 miles to a motel.

Phone for rates, reservations and directions.

## #580 ROCKY CANYON (ROBERTS) HOT SPRING (see map)

**North of the town of Crouch**

**non-commercial**

Primitive hot spring on the Middle Fork of the Payette River in Boise National Forest. Elevation 4,000 ft. Open all year.

Natural mineral water flows out of a spring at 120°, then down a steep slope toward the river. To reach the spring you must ford the river, which might not be safe during high water. Volunteers have built a series of primitive rock pools, each cooler than the one above. All pools are visible from the road, so bathing suits are advisable.

There are no services available on the premises. It is ½ mile to a picnic area, one mile to a campground and 10 miles to all other services in Crouch.

Source map: *Boise National Forest.*

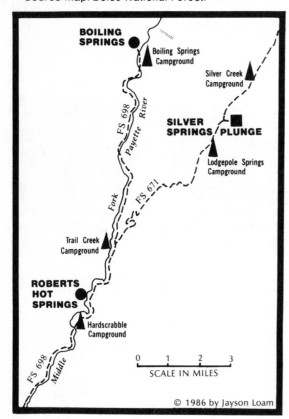

BOILING SPRINGS

Boiling Springs Campground

Silver Creek Campground

FS 698

Payette River

SILVER SPRINGS PLUNGE

Lodgepole Springs Campground

FS 671

Fork

Trail Creek Campground

ROBERTS HOT SPRINGS

Hardscrabble Campground

FS 698    Middle

0   1   2   3
SCALE IN MILES

© 1986 by Jayson Loam

## #581 SILVER SPRINGS PLUNGE (see map)

(208) 344-8688 (unit 1942)

**H/C 76 Box 2666**

**Garden Valley, ID 83622    PR+MH+CRV**

Remote mountain resort surrounded by Boise National Forest. Elevation 4,600 ft. Open May 1 through November 1.

Natural mineral water flows out of a spring at 109° and is piped to an outdoor swimming pool which is maintained at 84°. The pool operates on a flow-through basis and requires no chemical treatment. The pool is available to the public as well as to registered guests. Bathing suits are required.

Locker rooms, snack bar, rooms, cabins and overnight camping are available on the premises. It is 23 miles to a store, service station and RV hook-ups. No credit cards are accepted.

Directions: From the town of Crouch, go north 14 miles on FS 698, then bear northeast on FS 671 for nine miles to plunge.

Source map: *Boise National Forest.*

▼ *Silver Springs Plunge:* This popular resort now offers rooms in the lodge building visible on the far side of the flow-through pool.

## #582 BOILING SPRINGS (see map)
**North of the town of Crouch**

**non-commercial**

Large geothermal water flow on the Middle Fork of the Payette River in Boise National Forest. Elevation 4,200 ft. Open all year.

Natural mineral water flows out of a cliff at more than 130° into a pond adjacent to the Boiling Springs Guard Station. The water cools as it flows through a ditch to join the river. Summer volunteers usually build a rock-and-mud dam at the point where the water is cool enough for soaking. Because of the nearby campground, bathing suits are advisable.

No services are available on the premises. It is ¼ mile to a campground and 19 miles to all other services.

Directions: From the north edge of Boiling Springs Campground follow path ¼ mile to the Guard Station and spring.

Source map: *Boise National Forest.*

*Moon Dipper Hot Spring:* This equally lovely soaking pool is on the north bank of Dash Creek, 200 yards upstream from Pine Burl.

*Pine Burl Hot Spring:* This delightful pool is on the south bank of Dash Creek, just before it empties into the Payette Middle Fork.

## #583A MOON DIPPER HOT SPRING

## #583B PINE BURL HOT SPRING
**North of the town of Crouch**

**non-commercial**

Two remote and primitive hot springs on the bank of Dash Creek, very close together in Boise National Forest. Elevation 4,200 ft. Open all year.

Natural mineral water flows out of two springs at 120°, directly into volunteer-built rock soaking pools. Water temperature in the pools is controlled by mixing cold creek water with the hot water. The apparent local custom is clothing optional.

No services are available on the premises. It is a 1½-mile hike to overnight camping, and 21 miles to all other services.

Directions: From the Boiling Springs Guard Station (see #582) follow a well-used but unmarked path along the river, and ford the river twice during the 1½-mile hike, which could be dangerous during high water.

Source maps: *Boise National Forest;* USGS *Boiling Springs, Idaho.*

Note: There are several more primitive hot springs, with potential for volunteer-built soaking pools, further upstream from Moon Dipper and Pine Burl. However, all of them require that the river be forded many times, with a high risk of losing the faint unmarked path. Consult with a Boise National Forest ranger station before attempting to find any of these springs.

*Breit (Trail Creek) Hot Spring:* This is the view as seen from the large turnout parking area on the south side of the road.

## #584A BREIT (TRAIL CREEK) HOT SPRING
**(see map)**

● **West of Warm Lake**

**non-commercial**

Small scenic hot spring and soaking pool in a narrow canyon down a steep 60-yard path from a paved highway in Boise National Forest. Elevation 6,000 ft. Open all year.

Natural mineral water flows out of a fissure in the rocks at more than 115°. Volunteers have built a primitive rock-and-sand soaking pool on the edge of Trail Creek, where the hot and cold water can be mixed by controlling the amount of cold creek water admitted. The apparent local custom is clothing optional.

No services are available on the premises. It is two miles to a campground and 25 miles to all other services.

Directions: From the intersection of FS 22 and FS 474 west of Warm Lake go west 4½ miles and look for an especially large parking area on the south side of the road. From the west edge of this parking area the pool is visible at the bottom of Trail Creek canyon. There is no maintained trail, so be careful on the steep, scrambling path.

Source map: *Boise National Forest.*

## #584B MOLLY'S HOT SPRING    (see map)
● **West of Warm Lake**    **non-commercial**

Makeshift pools and bathtub perched on a steep geothermal hillside in Boise National Forest. Elevation 5,400 ft. Open all year.

Natural mineral water flows out of several springs at more than 120° and is gather by several pipes and hoses. The pool or tub temperature is controlled by diverting or combining the hotter and cooler flows. The apparent local custom is clothing optional.

No services are available on the premises. It is three miles to overnight camping and 25 miles to all other services.

Directions: From the intersection of FS 22 (paved) and FS 474 (gravel), go 1.7 miles south on FS 474 to intersection with road leading east toward Warm Lake. The road leading west from this intersection has been blocked to vehicle traffic but it is passable on foot. Follow the road 300 yards to an old vehicle bridge, cross the bridge and immediately turn right onto an unmarked path which leads 100 yards north to the geothermal area.

Source map: *Boise National Forest.*

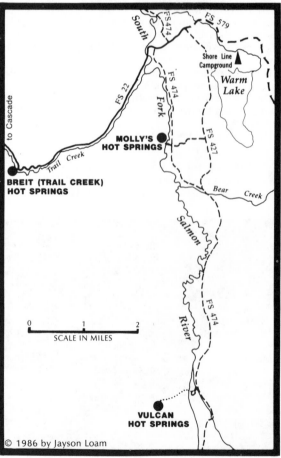

© 1986 by Jayson Loam

126

## #584C VULCAN HOT SPRINGS  (see map)
● **South of Warm Lake    non-commercial**

Once popular geothermal creek pool showing signs of neglect, in an insect-ravaged part of Boise National Forest. Elevation 5,600 ft. Open all year.

Natural mineral water flows out of many small bubbling springs at boiling temperature, creating a substantial hot creek, which gradually cools as it runs through the woods toward the South Fork of the Salmon River. Volunteers have built a log dam across this creek at the point where the water has cooled to approximately 105°. This dam has been partly wiped out by high water runoff, and the one-mile trail to it is no longer maintained. The apparent local custom is clothing optional.

An unmarked, unofficial camping area is located one mile south of Stolle Meadows at the head of the trail to the springs. It is six miles to a Forest Service campground and 32 miles to all other services.

Directions: At the west edge of the camping area is a log footbridge built by the Corps of Engineers. Cross this bridge and follow the path across two more log bridges. It is approximately one mile to the dam and pool.

Source maps: *Boise National Forest; USGS Warm Lake, Idaho.*

► *Sugah Hot Spring:* In addition to the superb location of this pool, note the small rock pool adjoining, where river water and hot pool runoff mix to make a temperate cool-water dip.

## #585  SUGAH HOT SPRING
● **North of Warm Lake    non-commercial**

A sweetie of a remote soaking pool for two, located on the edge of the South Fork of the Salmon River in Payette National Forest. Elevation 4,800 ft. Open all year.

Natural mineral water flows out of a spring at 115° and cools as it goes through makeshift pipes to the volunteer-built rock-and-masonry pool at river's edge. Pool temperature is controlled by diverting the hot water when not needed, and/or by adding a bucket of cold river water. The apparent local custom is clothing optional.

There are no services available on the premises. There is a campground within two miles, and it is 40 miles to all other service.

Directions: From the intersection of FS 22 (paved) and FS 474 (gravel) go north on FS 474 along the South Fork of the Salmon River for 16 miles. At 1.7 miles past Poverty Flats Campground there is a small (two car) turnout on the side of the road toward the river. Look for an unmarked steep path down to the pool.

Source maps: *Payette National Forest, Boise National Forest.*

## #586 GOLD FORK RETREAT (see map)
P.O. Box 522 (no phone)
Donnelly, ID 83615 PR

New ownership has made, and is planning, major changes at this popular location. During 1985 the log soaking pools and adjoining bathtubs were removed and the property closed to the public.

A five-year plan for future operation has been announced. In 1986 the site will be re-opened to the public with a single outdoor pool, where bathing suits will be required. Indoor pools and cabins with private pools are planned for subsequent years. Write ahead for information on the status of construction.

If there is insufficient time to inquire by mail and receive a reply, the adjoining map may be followed to the site and construction status determined by inspection.

## #587 WHITE LICKS HOT SPRINGS
(see map)
### West of the town of Donnelly
non-commercial

A large geothermal seep serving two small bathhouses in an unofficial camping area in a wooded area surrounded by Payette National Forest. Elevation 4,800 ft. Open all year.

Natural mineral water flows out of many small springs at temperatures up to 120°, supplying two small wood shacks, each containing a cement tub. Each tub is served by two plastic pipes, one bringing in 110° water, the other bringing in 80° water. The tub temperature is controlled by plugging up the pipe bringing in the temperature not desired. Soakers are expected to drain the tub after each use. Bathing suits are not required inside the bathhouses.

A picnic area and camping area are available on the premises. It is 16 miles to all other services.

Directions: From ID 55, in Donnelly, follow signs west toward Rainbow Point Campground. After crossing the bridge across Cascade Reservoir, follow FS 186 (gravel) as it starts north, curves west and then goes south. Watch for White Licks on the west side of FS 186, 3½ miles south of the intersection of FS 245 and FS 186.

Source map: *Payette National Forest.*

◄ *White Licks Hot Springs:* Although not a Forest Service campground, there is plenty of level ground for legal overnight parking

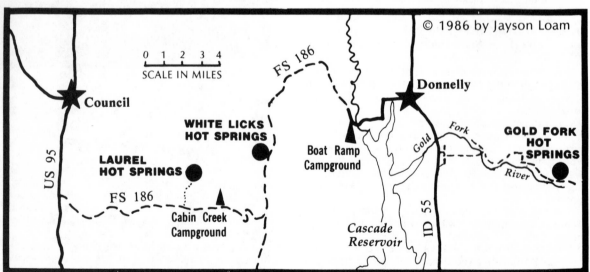

## #588 LAUREL HOT SPRINGS (see map)
**East of the town of Council**

**non-commercial**

Several primitive thermal springs in a steep, wooded canyon at the end of a rugged one-mile hike in Payette National Forest. Elevation 4,300 ft. Open all year.

Natural mineral water flows out of several springs at temperatures up to 120° into shallow volunteer-built rock-and-sand soaking pools along the bottom of Warm Springs Creek. The temperature in the pools is controlled by admitting cold creek water as desired. The local custom is clothing optional.

There are no services available on the premises. It is two miles to a campground and 23 miles to all other services.

Directions: From Cabin Creek Campground, on FS 186, go two miles west to Warm Springs Creek. Follow an unmarked path one mile north to springs.

Source Map: *Payette National Forest.*

► *Waterhole #1:* In one way these rent-a-tubs are better than the real thing; in winter the doors may be closed for cozy warm soaking.

▼ *Laurel Hot Springs:* This hot spring is seldom used; assume that you will have to be the volunteer who builds a soaking pool.

## #589 WATERHOLE #1
P.O. Box 676 (208) 634-7758
☐ Lake Fork, ID 83635 PR + CRV + MH

Tavern, lodge and unique hot tubs with a view of the mountains. Located five miles south of Mc Call.

Private-space hot pools using bromine-treated tap water are for rent to the public by the hour. There are six redwood hydrojet tubs in covered patios with one side openable toward a mountain view. Pool temperatures range from 102° to 108°. Each unit has an inside, heated dressing room.

A cafe, tavern, rooms and overnight camping are available on the premises. A store and service station are within five blocks, and RV hook-ups are within five miles. No credit cards are accepted.

Phone for rates, reservations and directions.

## #590 KRIGBAUM HOT SPRINGS
### East of the town of Meadows
#### non-commercial

Primitive hot spring and soaking pool on the east bank of Goose Creek, surrounded by Payette National Forest. Elevation 4,000 ft. Open all year.

Natural mineral water flows out of a spring at 102° and is piped to a volunteer-built rock-and-sand pool, where the temperatures range from 85° to 95°, depending on weather conditions. The apparent local custom is clothing optional.

There are no services available on the premises. It is two miles to a store, service station, overnight camping and RV hook-ups, and nine miles to a motel and restaurant.

Directions: On ID 55, go one mile east from Packer Johns Cabin State Park and turn north on gravel road along east bank of Goose Creek. Just before the road crosses a bridge over Goose Creek, park and hike 300 yards north along east bank to pool.

Source map: *Payette National Forest.*

◄ *Krigbaum Hot Springs:* This unfenced private-property spring goes through cycles of being destroyed and restored. Here is a good day.

▼ *Zim's Hot Springs:* Spray jets are used to cool incoming spring water to the right level for maintaining pool temperature.

▲ *Burgdorf Hot Springs:* This historic site, which has gone through many changes, is starting a phase of gradual rebuilding.

---

#### #591 ZIM'S HOT SPRINGS
■

P.O. Box 314      (208) 347-9447
New Meadows, ID 83654      PR + CRV

Older rural plunge and picnic grounds in an agricultural valley. Elevation 4,200 ft. Open all year.

Natural mineral water flows out of an artesian well at 151° and is cooled as it is sprayed into the chlorine-treated pools. The temperature in the outdoor swimming pool ranges from 90° to 100°, and in the outdoor soaking pool from 103° to 106°. Bathing suits are required.

Locker rooms, snacks, picnic area and overnight camping are available on the premises. A store, service station, motel and RV hook-ups are located within four miles. No credit cards are accepted.

Directions: From the town of New Meadows, take US 95 four miles north, then follow signs to plunge.

#### #592 BURGDORF HOT SPRINGS
■

Burgdorf, ID 83638      MH

Picturesque mountain-rustic resort, without electricity or telephone, surrounded by Payette National Forest. Elevation 6,000 ft. Open all year.

Natural mineral water flows out of spring at 112° directly into and through a sandy-bottom swimming pool which averages 100° and which requires no chemical treatment. There is also one indoor, claw-footed enamel bathtub, which is drained after each use. The pools are available only to registered guests. Bathing suits are required during the daytime.

Dressing rooms, a communal kitchen and cabins are available on the premises. Overnight camping is within ¼ mile. It is 30 miles to all other services. Hiking, skiing, snowmobiling and boating are nearby. No credit cards are accepted.

Directions: From ID 55, at the west end of McCall, take Warren Wagon Road 30 miles north to Burgdorf Junction, then follow signs two miles west to resort. For wintertime pick-up by snowmobile, write to the resort manager.

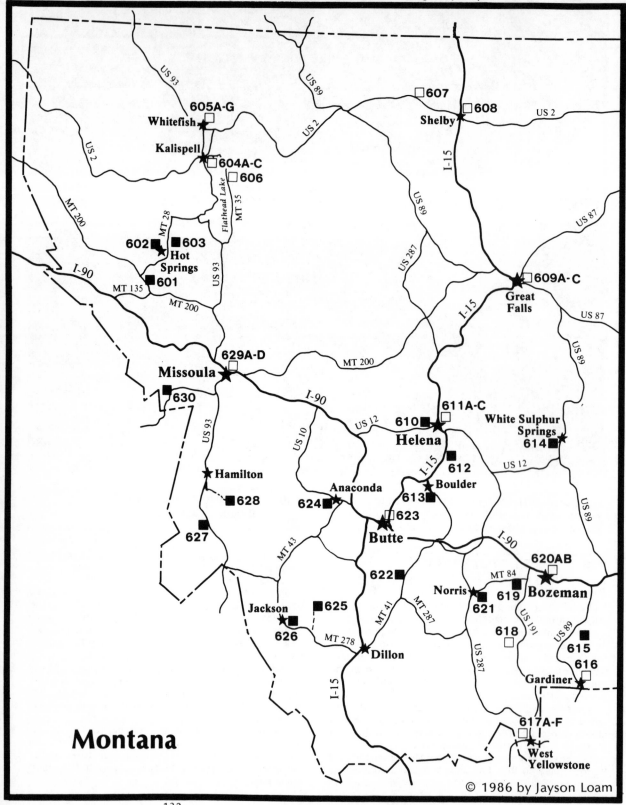

Montana

© 1986 by Jayson Loam

## MAP AND DIRECTORY SYMBOLS

● **Unimproved natural mineral water pool**        ——————— Paved highway
■ **Improved natural mineral water pool**          - ~ - ~ - Unpaved road
□ Gas-heated tap or well water pool              ....··.·..···.... Hiking route

PR = Tubs or pools for rent by hour, day or treatment

MH = Rooms, cabins or dormitory spaces for rent by day, week or month

CRV = Camping or vehicle parking spaces, some with hookups,
for rent by day, week, month or year

▲ *Quinn's Hot Springs:* Urban amenities and a fishing stream on the same land keep this resort busy all year.

#### #601   QUINN'S HOT SPRINGS
■
P.O. Box 12                      **(406) 826-3150**
**Paradise, MT 59856       PR + MH + CRV**

Complete family resort on the banks of the Clark Fork River. Elevation 2,700 ft. Open all year.

Natural mineral water flows out of a spring at 120°. The outdoor swimming pool is treated with chlorine and maintained at a temperature of 88°. The outdoor hydrojet pool is maintained at 100° and operates on a flow-through basis so that no chemical treatment of the water is needed. There are two indoor private-space fiberglass tubs, in which water temperature may be regulated by the customer. These pools are drained and refilled after each use, so that no chemical treatment is necessary. Pools are available to the public as well as to registered guests. Bathing suits are required except in private spaces.

Locker rooms, cafe, bar, store, service station, rooms and cabins, overnight camping, RV hook-ups and a fishing stream are available on the premises. MasterCard and Visa are accepted.

Location: On MT 135, three miles south of the junction with MT 200, which is east of St. Regis.

#### #602   SYMES HOTEL AND
####         MEDICINAL SPRINGS
■
**Hot Springs, MT 59845    (406) 741-2361**
**PR + MH**

Historic hotel with a long tradition of mineral water and other health treatments. Elevation 2,900 ft. Open all year.

Natural mineral water flows out of an artesian well at 80° to 90° and is heated as needed for use in soaking tubs. There are nine individual soaking tubs in the men's bathhouse and six in the women's bathhouse. There are also hotel rooms with mineral water piped to the room. Temperature is controllable within each tub, and no chemical treatment is added. Bathhouses are available to the public as well as to registered guests.

Locker rooms, hotel rooms and chiropractor services are available on the premises. It is two blocks to a cafe, store and service station and six blocks to overnight camping and RV hook-ups. No credit cards are accepted.

Directions: From MT 382 northeast of St. Regis, follow signs to the town of Hot Springs and then follow signs to the hotel.

▲ *Camp Aqua:* Give this site high marks for large family-size pools in bathroom-equipped suites.

## #603 CAMP AQUA
■ P.O. Box 592          (406) 741-3480
Hot Springs, MT 59845   PR + MH + CRV

Well-maintained family rent-a-tub establishment with overnight facilities, surrounded by rolling foothills. Elevation 4,000 ft. Open all year.

Natural mineral water flows out of an artesian well at 124° and is piped to a bathhouse building. There are six large indoor soaking pools in private rooms, each with steam bath, sauna, shower and toilet. Pool-water temperature is controllable by each customer up to 110°, and the pools are drained and refilled after each use, so no chemical treatment is needed. Bathing suits are not required in private rooms. Geothermal heat is used in all buildings.

Cabins, picnic area, overnight camping and RV hook-ups are available on the premises. It is six miles to all other services. No credit cards are accepted.

Directions: From MT 28, 2½ miles north of Hot Springs junction, follow signs two miles east on a gravel road to resort.

| #604A | THRIFTY SCOT MOTEL | |
|---|---|---|
| ☐ | 1830 Hwy 93 S. | (406) 755-3798 |
| | Kalispell, MT 59901 | Hydropool  MH |

| #604B | BEST WESTERN OUTLAW INN | |
|---|---|---|
| ☐ | 1701 Hwy 93 S. | (406) 755-6100 |
| | Kalispell, MT 59901 | Hydropool  MH |

| #604C | FOUR SEASONS MOTOR INN | |
|---|---|---|
| ☐ | 350 N. Main St. | (406) 755-6123 |
| | Kalispell, MT 59901 | Hydropool  MH |

| #605A | DUCK INN | |
|---|---|---|
| ☐ | 1305 Columbia Ave. | (406) 862-3825 |
| | Whitefish, MT 59937 | Hydropool  MH |

| #605B | MOUNTAIN HOLIDAY MOTEL | |
|---|---|---|
| ☐ | P.O. Box 302 | (406) 862-2548 |
| | Whitefish, MT 59937 | Hydropool  MH |

| #605C | VALLEY INN | |
|---|---|---|
| ☐ | P.O. Box 1570 | (406) 862-5515 |
| | Whitefish, MT 59937 | Hydropool  MH |

| #605D | VIKING LAKESHORE INN | |
|---|---|---|
| ☐ | 1360 Wisconsin | (406) 862-3547 |
| | Whitefish, MT 59937 | Hydropool  MH |

| #605E | KANDAHAR LODGE | |
|---|---|---|
| ☐ | P.O. Box 1659 | (406) 862-6098 |
| | Whitefish, MT 59937 | Hydropool  MH |

| #605F | GROUSE MOUNTAIN LODGE | |
|---|---|---|
| ☐ | 1205 Hwy 93 W. | (406) 862-351I |
| | Whitefish, MT 59937 | |
| | | In-room hydropools  MH |

| #605G | ALPINGLOW INN | |
|---|---|---|
| ☐ | P.O. Box 1670 | (406) 862-6996 |
| | Whitefish, MT 59937 | Hydropool  MH |

| #606 | TIMBERS MOTEL | |
|---|---|---|
| ☐ | P.O. Box 757 | (406) 837-6200 |
| | Bigfork, MT 59911 | Hydropool  MH |

| #607 | NORTHERN MOTOR INN | |
|---|---|---|
| ☐ | 609 W. Main St. | (406) 873-5662 |
| | Cut Bank, MT 59427 | Hydropool  MH |

| #608 | QUALITY INN | |
|---|---|---|
| ☐ | P.O. Box Z | (406) 434-5134 |
| | Shelby, MT 59474 | Hydropool  MH |

| #609A | HOLIDAY INN | |
|---|---|---|
| ☐ | 1411 10th Ave. | (406) 761-4600 |
| | Great Falls, MT 59405 | Hydropool  MH |

| #609B | BEST WESTERN HERITAGE INN | |
|---|---|---|
| ☐ | 1700 Fox Farm Rd. | (406) 761-1900 |
| | Great Falls, MT 59404 | Hydropool  MH |

| #609C | SHERATON GREAT FALLS | |
|---|---|---|
| ☐ | 400 Tenth Ave. S. | (406) 727-7200 |
| | Great Falls, MT 59405 | Hydropool  MH |

## #610 BROADWATER ATHLETIC CLUB
■ 4920 Hwy 12 W.        (406) 443-5777
Helena, MT 59601        PR

Large well-equipped health center on the outskirts of Helena. Elevation 5,000 ft. Open all year.

Natural mineral water flows out of a spring at 153° and is piped to several pools, where it is treated with bromine. The outdoor swimming pool is maintained at 93°, and the outdoor lap pool is maintained at 87°. The three indoor hydrojet pools—men's, women's and co-ed—are maintained at 104°. The men's and women's sections each contain a sauna and steambath. Facilities are available to the public as well as to members and guests. Bathing suits are required in public areas.

Locker rooms, massage by appointment, juice bar, weight room, racquet ball and running tracks (indoor and outdoor) are available on the premises. It is three miles to a cafe, store, service station and motel, and seven miles to overnight camping and RV hook-ups. Visa, MasterCard and American Express are accepted.

Location: On US 12, two miles west of Helena.

| #611A ☐ | SHILO INN<br>2020 Prospect Ave.<br>Helena, MT 59601 | (406) 442-0320<br>Hydropool MH |
|---|---|---|
| #611B ☐ | COACH HOUSE EAST<br>2101 E. 11th St.<br>Helena, MT 59601 | (406) 443-2300<br>Health Club MH |
| #611C ☐ | KOA—HELENA<br>on Montana Ave.<br>Helena, MT 59601 | (406) 458-5110<br>Hydropool CRV |

## #612 HILLBROOK NURSING HOME
**Clancy, MT 59634       (406) 933-8311**

Skilled intermediate nursing facility qualified for Medicare, VA and private patients. Elevation 5,000 ft. Open all year.

Natural mineral water flows out of a spring at 147° and is piped to the main building for use in hydrotherapy and for geothermal space heating. The indoor treatment tub is equipped with air jets and is drained and refilled after each use, so no chemical treatment is necessary. The facilities are available only to patients who have been admitted under a doctor's orders. An information brochure is available on request. No credit cards are accepted.

Directions: From I-15 south of Helena, take the Clancy exit, then go south one mile on frontage road.

▲ *Broadwater Athletic Club:* A hot spring was the beginning of this modern fitness center.

▼ *Boulder Hot Springs:* Yesterday's glories are struggling to meet today's health codes.

## #613 BOULDER HOT SPRINGS
**P.O. Box 649       (406) 225-4273**
**Boulder, MT 59632       PR + MH + CRV**

Historic 1880's resort in process of remodeling, at the foot of the Elkhorn Mountain Range. Elevation 5,000 ft. Open all year.

Natural mineral water flows out of a spring at 175° and is piped to outdoor and indoor pools, where it is treated with chlorine. The outdoor swimming pool is maintained at 80° to 100°. The two indoor plunges in the men's bathhouse are maintained at 90° and 106°, the plunge in the women's bathhouse at 104°. Pools are available to the public as well as to registered guests. Bathing suits are required in the outdoor pool in the daytime.

Locker rooms, massage, juice bar, rooms, hostel sleeping accommodations and overnight camping are available on the premises. Cross-country skiing is available nearby. It is three miles to cafe, store, service station and RV hook-ups.

No credit cards are accepted.

Directions: On I-15 south of Helena take Boulder exit and go south three miles on MT 69. Follow signs to resort.

## #614 SPA MOTEL
■ P.O. Box 370            (406) 547-3366
White Sulphur Springs, MT 59645

PR + MH

Remodeled older resort at the foot of the Castle Mountains. Elevation 5,100 ft. Open all year.

Natural mineral water flows out of a spring at 135° and is piped to two pools which operate on a flow-through basis, requiring no chemical treatment. The outdoor swimming pool is maintained at 94° in the summer and 104° in the winter. The indoor soaking pool is maintained at 106° to 108°. Bathing suits are required.

Rooms and picnic area are available on the premises. It is less than five blocks to all other services. Visa and MasterCard are accepted.

Location: On US 89 at the west end of White Sulphur Springs.

## #615 CHICO HOT SPRINGS
■ P.O. Box 127            (406) 333-4933
Pray, MT 59065

PR + MH

Large older resort surrounded by Gallatin National Forest. Elevation 5,000 ft. Open all year.

Natural mineral water flows out of several springs at 110°. The outdoor swimming pool is maintained at 90°, the enclosed soaking pool at 105°, and four private-space redwood hot tubs are at 105°. All pools operate on a flow-through basis so no chemical treatment is needed. Pools are available to the public as well as to registered guests. Bathing suits are required except in private spaces.

Changing rooms, restaurant, hotel rooms, saddle horses and a private trout lake are available on the premises. It is four miles to a store and service station and 15 miles to overnight camping and RV hook-ups. Visa and MasterCard are accepted.

Directions: From the town of Emigrant on US 89 south of Livingston, take MT 362 southeast for three miles. Follow signs to resort.

▲ In Montana, a saloon is called a saloon, so hot-tub rental fees are paid to the bartender, who is the keeper of the private space keys.

► *Chico Hot Springs:* These fine flow-through pools were recently supplemented by four private-space hot tubs in their own building.

**#616**    BEST WESTERN MAMMOTH HOT SPRINGS
☐    P.O. Box 646      (406) 848-7557
     Gardiner, MT 59030      Hydropool MH

**#617A**    CIRCLE R MOTEL
☐    321 W. Madison Ave.      (406) 646-7641
     West Yellowstone, MT 59758
     Hydropool MH

**#617B**    BEST WESTERN EXECUTIVE INN
☐    P.O. Box 1280      (406) 646-7681
     West Yellowstone, MT 59758
     Hydropool MH

**#617C**    BIG WESTERN PINE MOTEL
☐    234 Firehole Ave.      (406) 646-7622
     West Yellowstone, MT 59758
     Hydropool MH

**#617D**    STAGE COACH INN TRAVELODGE
☐    209 Madison Ave.      (406) 646-7381
     West Yellowstone, MT 59759
     Hydropool MH

**#617E**    TEEPEE MOTOR LODGE
☐    P.O. Box 519      (406) 646-7391
     West Yellowstone, MT 59758
     Hydropool MH

**#617F**    AMBASSADOR QUALITY INN
☐    P.O. Box 459      (406) 646-7365
     West Yellowstone, MT 59758
     Hydropool MH

**#618**    BEST WESTERN BUCK'S T-4 LODGE
☐    P.O. Box 895      (406) 995-4111
     Big Sky, MT 59716      Hydropool MH

## #619    BOZEMAN HOT SPRINGS
■    **133 Lower Rainbow Rd.**      **(406) 587-3030**
     **Bozeman, MT 59715**      **PR + RV**

Tree-shaded KOA campground with mineral water pools. Elevation 4,500 ft. Open all year. Pools closed from sundown Fridays to sundown Saturdays.

Natural mineral water flows out of a spring at 141° and is piped to an indoor-pool building. The swimming pool is maintained at 90° and adjoining soaking pools are maintained at temperatures ranging from 100° to 110°. There is also a 60° cold pool. All pools operate on a flow-through basis, including cold tap water for controlling temperatures, so no chemical treatment is needed. Pools are available to the public as well as to registered guests. Bathing suits are required.

Locker rooms, grocery store, laundromat, picnic area, RV hook-ups and tent-trailer rentals are available on the premises. It is one mile to a restaurant and service station, and eight miles to a motel. No credit cards are accepted.

Location: On US 191, eight miles southwest of the town of Bozeman.

▲   *Bozeman Hot Springs:* These multi-temperature pools help make this KOA campground popular.

**#620A**    LEWIS AND CLARK MOTEL
☐    824 W. Main St.      (406) 586-3341
     Bozeman, MT 59715      Hydropool MH

**#620B**    BEST WESTERN CITY CENTER MOTEL
☐    507 W. Main St.      (406) 587-3158
     Bozeman, MT 59715      Hydropool MH

## #621    BEAR TRAP HOT SPRINGS
■    **Box 24**      **(406) 685-3303**
     **Norris, MT 59745**      **PR + CRV**

Small RV park in foothills below Tobacco Root Mountains. Elevation 5,000 ft. Open all year.

Natural mineral water flows out of artesian springs at 128°. The outdoor soaking pool is maintained at 101° in the summer and 106° in the winter. The water contains no sulfur and no chemical treatment is added because the pool operates on a flow-through basis. The pool is available to the public as well as to registered guests. Bathing suits are required.

A store, picnic area, overnight camping and RV hook-ups are available on the premises. It is ¼ mile to a cafe and service station, and 10 miles to a motel. No credit cards are accepted.

Directions: From US 287 in the town of Norris, go ¼ mile east on MT 84.

*Fairmont Hot Springs:* Once a close relative to Canada's Fairmont Hot Springs, this site now struggles to maintain urban elegance.

*Barkell's Hot Springs:* In a good old Montana tradition this hot spring promoted the building of an indoor swimming pool with a connecting bar.

## #622 BARKELL'S HOT SPRINGS
**Silver Star, MT 59751     (406) 287-5621**
**PR + MH**

Community plunge with adjoining bar. Elevation 4,500 ft. Open all year.

Natural mineral water flows from a spring at 180° into a cooling pond. It is then piped to an indoor swimming pool, which is maintained at a temperature of 75° to 100° by the addition of cold tap water as needed. The pool is drained and refilled weekly so no chemical treatment is needed. Bathing suits are required.

Locker rooms and hunter's cabins are available on the premises. A store, service station, overnight camping and RV hook-ups are located within one mile. It is 10 miles to a motel and restaurant. No credit cards are accepted.

Location: On MT 41, ¼ mile south of the town of Silver Star.

## #623 BEST WESTERN COPPER KING INN
4655 Harrison Ave.     (406) 494-6666
Butte, MT 59701     Hydropool  MH

## #624 FAIRMONT HOT SPRINGS
**Anaconda, MT 59711     (406) 797-3241**
**PR + MH**

Large hotel-type resort and real-estate development in a wide valley. Elevation 5,300 ft. Open all year.

Natural mineral water flows out of a spring at 160° and is piped to a group of pools, where it is treated with chlorine. The indoor and outdoor swimming pools are maintained at 80° to 85°, the indoor and outdoor soaking pools 105°. There are also men's and women's saunas. Facilities are available to the public as well as to registered guests. Bathing suits are required.

Locker rooms, restaurant, rooms, mini zoo, tennis and golf are available on the premises. Overnight camping and RV hook-ups are available one block away to members of Coast-To-Coast. It is five miles to a store and service station. Visa, MasterCard and American Express are accepted.

Directions: From I-90, 12 miles west of Butte, take the Gregson-Fairmont exit and follow signs to the resort.

*Elkhorn Hot Springs:* This end-of-the-road resort looks and feels like it belongs way out in the woods, which is why it is such a fine headquarters for all-season exploring.

## #625 ELKHORN HOT SPRINGS

**P.O. Box 514**          **(406) 834-3434**
**Polaris, MT 59746**     **PR + MH + CRV**

Beautifully restored mountain resort, lodge, rustic cabins and all-season activities, situated among the tall trees of Elkhorn National Forest. Elevation 7,400 ft. Open all year.

Natural mineral water flows out of nine springs with temperatures ranging from 107° to 160°. The outdoor swimming pool is maintained at 88° to 95°, and the outdoor soaking pool is maintained at 95° to 104°. There are two co-ed Roman saunas maintained at 110°. All pools are drained and refilled weekly so no chemical treatment is needed. Pools are available to the public as well as to registered guests. Bathing suits are required.

Locker rooms, cafe, gasoline, tent spaces, picnic area, overnight camping and cabins are available on the premises. Hunting, fishing, backpacking, rock and mineral hunting, skiing and snowmobile trails are available nearby. Pick-up service is provided from the city of Butte by prior arrangement. No credit cards are accepted.

Directions: From I-15, three miles south of Dillon, take MT 278 west 27 miles to large sign, turn north and follow gravel road 13 miles to resort.

## #626 JACKSON HOT SPRINGS

**P.O. Box 808**          **(406) 834-3151**
**JACKSON, MT 59736**     **PR + MH + CRV**

Renovated lodge building and cabins on the main street of a small town. Elevation 6,400 ft. Open all year.

Natural mineral water flows out of a spring at 137° and is piped to cabins and an indoor pool. The indoor swimming pool is maintained at 98° to 100°, and operates on a flow-through basis, so no chemical treatment is necessary. Water temperatures in cabin bath tubs may be controlled by adding cold tap water as needed. The swimming pool is available to the public as well as to registered guests. Bathing suits are required.

Dressing rooms, restaurant, cabins, overnight camping and RV hook-ups are available on the premises. It is three blocks to a store and service station. No credit cards are accepted.

Location: On MT 278 in the town of Jackson.

*Medicine Hot Springs:* The addition of decks, tables, umbrellas and a hydrojet pool has tripled attendance at this fine summer resort.

## #627   MEDICINE HOT SPRINGS

Conner, MT 59827      (406) 821-3558
                                      PR + MH

Family-oriented, well-maintained resort surrounded by Bitterroot National Forest. Elevation 4,500 ft. Open April through September.

Natural mineral water flows from a spring at 155°. The outdoor swimming pool is maintained at 85° to 95°, the kiddie pool at 100°, and the outdoor fiberglass hydrojet pool at 104°. All pools operate on a flow-through basis so no chemical treatment is needed. There are also two indoor private spaces with individual tubs controllable up to 110°. These tubs are drained and refilled after each use, so no chemical treatment is needed. All pools are available to the public as well as to registered guests. Bathing suits are required except in private spaces.

Locker rooms, snack bar and housekeeping cabins are available on the premises. It is one block to overnight camping, one mile to RV hook-ups and three miles to a store and service station. No credit cards accepted.

Location: Just off US 93, 14 miles north of intersection with MT 43. Follow signs to resort.

*Sleeping Child Hot Springs:* A hot soak, a warm swim, a drink at the bar, and dinner can be had without walking more than 15 steps.

## #629A NEW LIFE FITNESS CLUB

☐    127 N. Higgins       (406) 721-5117
     Missoula, MT 59801           PR

Combination rent-a-tub establishment and fitness center in downtown Missoula.

Private-space pools, using bromine-treated tap water, are for rent to the public by the hour. There are four indoor hydrojet pools, in which the temperature is maintained at 103° to 105°. There are also two co-ed steam baths and two co-ed saunas. Bathing suits are not required in the saunas, steam baths or private spaces.

Locker rooms, weight rooms and massage are available on the premises. No credit cards are accepted.

Phone for rates, reservations and directions.

## #629B RESERVE STREET INN

☐    4825 Reserve St.      (406) 542-2122
     Missoula, MT 59802    Hydropool MH

## #629C SHERATON MISSOULA

☐    200 Pattee St.        (406) 721-8550
     Missoula, MT 59802    Hydropool MH

## #629D THUNDERBIRD MOTEL

☐    1009 E. Broadway    (406) 543-7251
     Missoula, MT 59802    Hydropool MH

## #630 LOLO HOT SPRINGS
### Lolo, MT 59847

■

Historic resort which went through bankruptcy and was closed while the new owners initiated an extensive remodeling program. Write or phone (through Lolo operator) for information on construction status and re-opening date.

▲  *Lolo Hot Springs:* Hopefully, it has been reborn.

## #628 SLEEPING CHILD HOT SPRINGS

■    P.O. Box 1468       (406) 363-6250
     Hamilton, MT 59840    PR + MH + CRV

A small resort designed to provide "rustic elegance," surrounded by Lolo National Forest. Elevation 5,400 ft. Open all year.

Natural mineral water flows from a spring at 125° and is piped to two outdoor soaking pools and one large outdoor swimming pool. The swimming pool is maintained at a temperature of 95° to 99°, and the soaking pools are maintained from 105° to 110°. All pools are flow-through so no chemical treatment is needed. There is also one co-ed sauna. Facilities are available to the public as well as to registered guests. Bathing suits are required.

Locker rooms, bar, restaurant, hotel rooms and overnight camping are available on the premises. Hiking, fishing, hunting and cross-country skiing are available nearby. A store, service station and RV hook-ups are located within 15 miles. MasterCard and Visa are accepted.

Directions: From the town of Hamilton, take US 93 south to MT 38, then go east to MT 501. Follow signs to resort. The last five miles are on gravel road.

# Wyoming

727 726
YELLOWSTONE
725
NATIONAL
PARK
724
723
722A-H
Jackson
720
721
US 89
719AB
Afton

701 702
Cody
US 20
US 310
US 14
WY 120
US 16
706
707A-E
Thermopolis
708AB
Dubois
US 26
709AB

703
Sheridan
Buffalo 704
I-90
705A-C
Gillette
US 16
I-25
WY 59
US 85

710A-C
Casper
I-25
Douglas 711
US 20
Lusk
712AB

US 20 US 26
US 287

US 26
713
Torrington
US 85

US 189
WY 28
US 191
US 287

Rock
Springs
717A-C
US 191

WY 130
Saratoga
716AB
I-80

715AB
Laramie

714AB
Cheyenne
I-25
US 85

US 30
I-80
718A-C
Evanston

WY 230

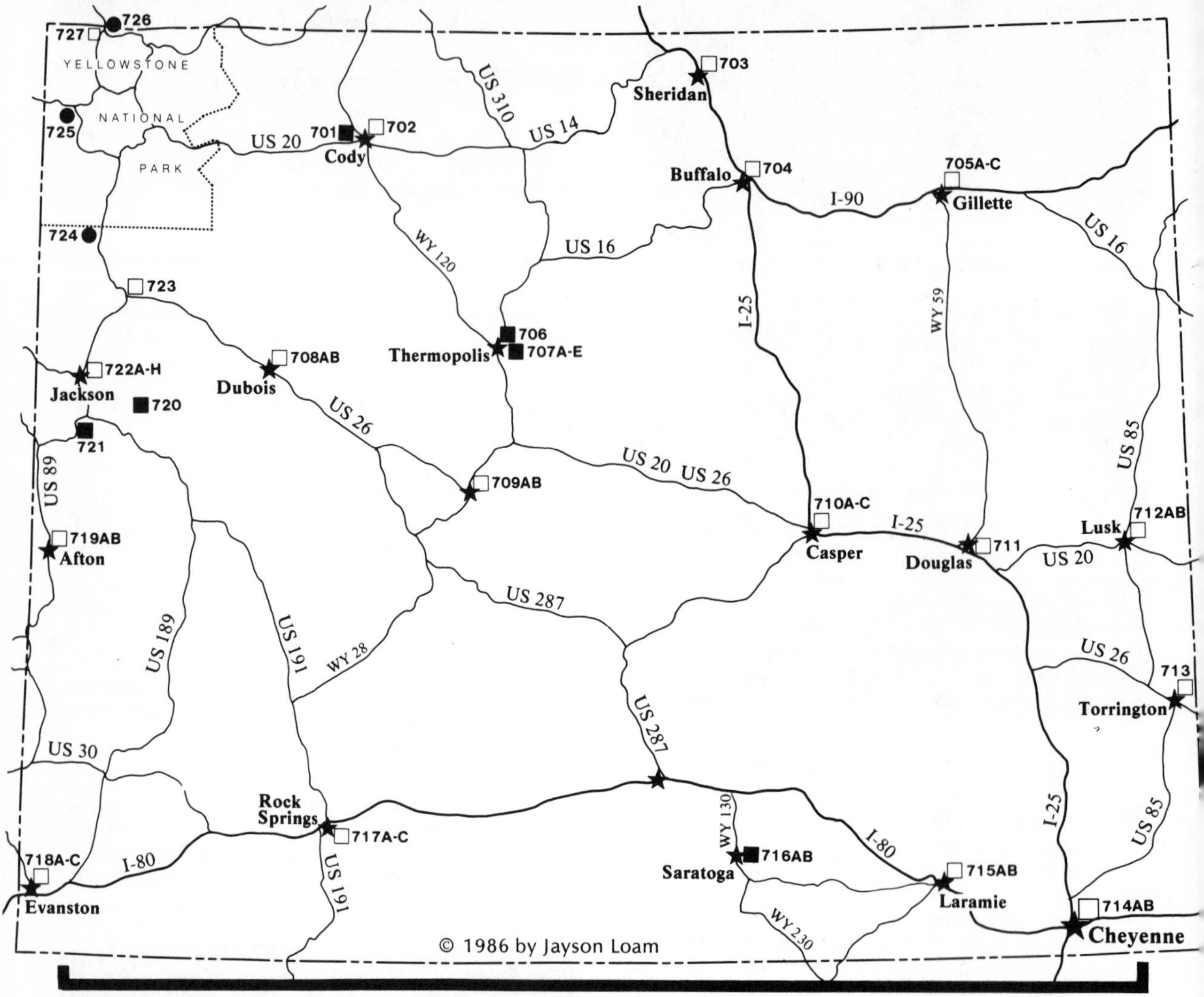

© 1986 by Jayson Loam

## MAP AND DIRECTORY SYMBOLS

● Unimproved natural mineral water pool          —————— Paved highway

■ Improved natural mineral water pool          – – – – Unpaved road

□ Gas-heated tap or well water pool          ·········· Hiking route

PR = Tubs or pools for rent by hour, day or treatment

MH = Rooms, cabins or dormitory spaces for rent by day, week or month

CRV = Camping or vehicle parking spaces, some with hookups,
      for rent by day, week, month or year

## #701　CODY ATHLETIC CLUB

■

    515 W. Yellowstone    **(303) 527-7131**
    Cody, WY 82414    **PR + MH**

Fully equipped health club and motel 31 miles east of Yellowstone National Park. Elevation 5,000 ft. Open all year.

Natural mineral water is pumped out of a well at 87° and piped to an outdoor swimming pool which maintains a temperature of 86°, without any chemical treatment. The enclosed hydrojet pool uses gas-heated tap water treated with chlorine, and is maintained at 105°. Bathing suits are required.

A co-ed steam bath, men's and women's exercise rooms, with a sauna in each, and racquetball courts are available on the premises. Motel rooms are also available. It is ½ mile to all other services. MasterCard and Visa are accepted.

Phone for rates, reservations and directions.

| #702 | WISE CHOICE INN | |
|---|---|---|
| ☐ | Northfork Star Route | (307) 587-5004 |
| | Cody, WY 82414 | Hydropool  MH |

▼  *Cody Athletic Club:* An elaborate health club and motel complex has been built up around this almost-hot spring. Unfortunately, the hot pool does not contain any mineral water.

▲  *Fountain Of Youth:* From the Sacajawea Well, scalding water runs into a cooling pond in foreground, then into the extensive main pool.

| #703 | HOLIDAY INN | |
|---|---|---|
| ☐ | 1809 Sugarland Dr. | (307) 672-8931 |
| | Sheridan, WY 82801 | Hydropool  MH |

| #704 | DEER PARK CAMPGROUND | |
|---|---|---|
| ☐ | on US 16 | (307) 684-5722 |
| | Buffalo, WY 82834 | Hydropool  CRV |

| #705A | PRIME RATE MOTEL | |
|---|---|---|
| ☐ | 2105 Rodgers Dr. | (307) 686-8600 |
| | Gillette, WY 82716 | Hydropool  MH |

| #705B | BEST WESTERN TOWER WEST LODGE | |
|---|---|---|
| ☐ | 109 N. US Hwy 14/16 | (307) 686-2210 |
| | Gillette, WY 82716 | Hydropool  MH |

| #705C | HOLIDAY INN | |
|---|---|---|
| ☐ | 2009 S. Hwy 59 | (307) 686-3000 |
| | Gillette, WY 82716 | Hydropool  MH |

## #706　FOUNTAIN OF YOUTH

■

    P.O. Box 711    **(307) 864-9977**
    Thermopolis, WY 82443    **PR + RV**

Well-kept RV park featuring a unique large soaking pool. Elevation 4,300 ft. Open all year.

Natural mineral water flows out of the historic Sacajawea Spring at the rate of over one million gallons per day. Some of this 130° water is channeled through a cooling pond into a 200 ft. long soaking pool where the temperatures vary from 106° at the inflow end to 99° at the outflow. The pool is available to the public as well as to registered guests. Bathing suits are required.

Restrooms, showers, overnight camping and RV hook-ups are available on the premises. It is two mile to all other services. No credit cards are accepted.

Location: On US 20 two miles north of the town of Thermopolis.

# HOT SPRINGS STATE PARK

**This square mile of land, with the Big Spring in the center, was presented to the State of Wyoming by the Federal Government after it had been purchased from the Shoshone and Arapahoe Indians in 1896. Elevation 4,300 ft. Open all year.**

**All of the establishments on the grounds are supplied with natural mineral water from the Big Spring, which flows out of the ground at 135°. Walkways have been provided through the large tufa terraces which have been built up by mineral deposits from the spring over the centuries. Facilities provided include a large tree-shaded picnic area in the center of the grounds.**

**All services not provided by an establishment within the State Park are available within ½ mile in the town of Thermopolis.**

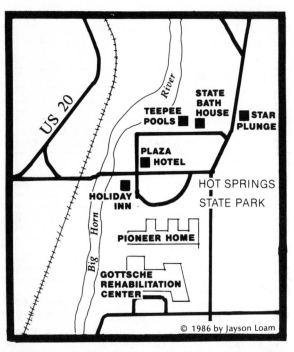

© 1986 by Jayson Loam

▲ *State Bath House:* Sparkling clean pools and bathhouses highlight this state-run facility.

## #707A  TEEPEE POOLS          (see map)

■   P.O. Box 750          (307) 864-9250
    Thermopolis, WY 82443          PR

The outdoor swimming pool is maintained at 87° to 93°, and the indoor swimming pool is maintained at 93° to 97°. The indoor soaking pool is maintained at 104°, and the indoor steam bath is maintained at 112° to 115°. All pools operate on a flow-through basis, so no chemical treatment is needed. Bathing suits are required.

Locker rooms and snack bar are available on the premises. No credit cards are accepted.

## #707B  STATE BATH HOUSE          (see map)

■   State Park          (307) 864-9902
    Thermopolis, WY 82443   non-commercial

The outdoor and indoor soaking pools are maintained at 104° to 108°. The temperature in 16 (eight men's and eight women's) individual soaking tubs is adjustable by the person using the tub. All pools are non-chlorinated flow-through mineral water. No charge is made for pool or tub use.

Changing rooms are available and bathing suits are required in the communal pools. There is a nominal charge for renting suits or towels. No credit cards are accepted.

144

▲ *Star Plunge:* This active commercial facility has recently replaced a risky toboggan ride with an outdoor super-slide installation.

▲ *Holiday Inn:* Only a giant corporate motel chain would install a tap-water swimming pool in a location with unlimited hot mineral water.

## #707C STAR PLUNGE

■ P.O. Box 627  (see map)
(307) 864-3771
Thermopolis, WY 82443  PR

The outdoor swimming pool is maintained at 92° to 96°, and the indoor swimming pool, including hydrojet section, is maintained at 96° to 98°. The waterslide pick-up pool is maintained at 86° and the co-ed steam bath is maintained at 115°. All pools are flow-through, requiring no chemical treatment. Bathing suits are required.

Locker rooms and snack bar are available on the premises. No credit cards are accepted.

## #707D PLAZA HOTEL AND APARTMENTS
(see map)

■ P.O. Box 671  (307) 864-2251
Thermopolis, WY 82443  PR + MH

An older resort building with men's and women's bathhouses. Each bathhouse has four individual mineral water tubs and two steam baths. Bathing suits are not required in bathhouses.

Hotel rooms, massage and sweat wraps are available on the premises. No credit cards are accepted.

## #707E HOLIDAY INN

■ P.O. Box 1323  (see map)
(307) 864-3131
Thermopolis, WY 82443  PR + MH

Conventional major motel with a unique adaptation of men's and women's bathhouses. Each bathhouse has private spaces for four individual soaking tubs, two saunas and two steam baths. These private spaces are rented to couples, even though they are in the men's and women's bathhouses.

The indoor soaking tubs are temperature controllable up to 110°, use natural mineral water, and are drained after each use, so no chemical treatment is needed. The outdoor hydrojet pool also uses natural mineral water, without chemical treatment, and is maintained at a temperature of 106°. The outdoor swimming pool uses gas-heated chlorine-treated tap water, and is maintained at a temperature of 78°. All pools and the athletic club facilities are available to the public as well as to registered guests. Bathing suits are required in all outdoor public areas.

Restaurant and motel rooms are available on the premises. Visa, MasterCard, American Express and Carte Blanche are accepted.

| #708A | SAGE MOTEL BUDGET HOST INN | |
|---|---|---|
| ☐ | P.O. Box 595 | (307) 455-2344 |
| | Dubois, WY 82513 | Hydropool  MH |

| #708B | THE RENDEZVOUS ON THE WIND RIVER | |
|---|---|---|
| ☐ | 1349 W. Ramshorn | (307) 455-2844 |
| | Dubois, WY 82513 | Hydropool  MH |

| #709A | HOLIDAY INN | |
|---|---|---|
| ☐ | on US 26 and WY 789 | (307) 856-8100 |
| | Riverton, WY 82501 | Hydropool  MH |

| #709B | BEST WESTERN TOMAHAWK MOTEL | |
|---|---|---|
| ☐ | 208 E. Main St. | (307) 856-9205 |
| | Riverton, WY 82501 | Hydropool  MH |

| #710A | HOLIDAY INN CASPER | |
|---|---|---|
| ☐ | 300 W. F ST. | (307) 235-2531 |
| | Casper, WY 82602 | Hydropool  MH |

| #710B | CASPER HILTON INN | |
|---|---|---|
| ☐ | I-25 and Ranch Road | (307) 266-6000 |
| | Casper, WY 82602 | Hydropool  MH |

| #710C | SHILO INN | |
|---|---|---|
| ☐ | P.O. Box 310 | (307) 237-1335 |
| | Evansville, WY 82636 | Hydropool  MH |

| #711 | HOLIDAY INN | |
|---|---|---|
| ☐ | 1450 Riverbend Dr. | (307) 358-9790 |
| | Douglas, WY 82633 | Hydropool  MH |

| #712A | BUDGET HOST TRAIL MOTEL | |
|---|---|---|
| ☐ | P.O. Box 1087 | (307) 334-2530 |
| | Lusk, WY 82225 | Hydropool  MH |

| #712B | COVERED WAGON MOTEL | |
|---|---|---|
| ☐ | P.O. Box 236 | (307) 334-2836 |
| | Lusk, WY 82225 | Hydropool  MH |

| #713 | BEST WESTERN KING'S INN | |
|---|---|---|
| ☐ | 1555 Main St. | (307) 532-4011 |
| | Torrington, WY 82240 | Hydropool  MH |

| #714A | HOLIDAY INN | |
|---|---|---|
| ☐ | 204 W. Fox Farm Rd. | (307) 638-4466 |
| | Cheyenne, WY 82001 | Hydropool  MH |

| #714B | BEST WESTERN HITCHING POST INN | |
|---|---|---|
| ☐ | 1700 W. Lincoln Way | (307) 638-3301 |
| | Cheyenne, WY 82001 | Hydropool  MH |

| #715A | BEST WESTERN FOSTER'S COUNTRY INN | |
|---|---|---|
| ☐ | 1561 Jackson St. | (307) 742-8371 |
| | Laramie, WY 82070 | Hydropool  MH |

| #715B | COMFORT INN | |
|---|---|---|
| ☐ | 1104 S. 3rd St. | (307) 742-3741 |
| | Laramie, WY 82070 | Hydropool  MH |

▲ *Saratoga Inn:* It is apparent that the management does not want anyone attempting to do any moonlight swimming in this pool.

## #716A THE SARATOGA INN

| ■ | P.O. Box 867 | (303) 326-5261 |
|---|---|---|
| | Saratoga, WY 82331 | MH |

Modest golf and tennis resort surrounded by rolling ranch country. Elevation 6,800 ft. Open all year.

Natural mineral water is pumped out of a spring at 114° and piped to an outdoor swimming pool, which is treated with chlorine and maintained at 100°. An outdoor rock soaking pool is built over another spring, and is maintained at 100° to 105°, with chlorine added as needed. Pool use is reserved for registered guests. Bathing suits are required.

Hotel rooms, restaurant, golf and tennis are available on the premises. It is four blocks to a store and service station and one mile to overnight camping and RV hook-ups. Visa, MasterCard and American Express are accepted.

Directions: From WY 130 in the town of Saratoga, go east on Bridge St. and follow signs four blocks to the resort.

## #716B HOBO POOL
### In the town of Saratoga
**(non-commercial)**

An improved by unfenced soaking pool, plus a fenced municipal swimming pool, located on the banks of the North Platte River. Elevation 6,800 ft. Open all year.

Natural mineral water flows out of the source spring at 115°. A large cement soaking pool (no charge) maintains a temperature of 100° to 110°, and volunteers have channeled the soaking pool run-off into shallow rock pools along the edge of the river. A daily charge is made for the use of the swimming pool, which is maintained at 90°. Bathing suits are required.

There are no services on the premises. It is three blocks to all services. No credit cards are accepted.

Directions: On WY 130, in the town of Saratoga, watch for HOBO POOL sign, then follow signs four blocks east to the pool.

▲ *Hobo Pool:* The town council has chosen to continue the free soak tradition at this pool.

▼ The town council does charge for use of this swimming pool built next to the *Hobo Pool.*

| | | |
|---|---|---|
| **#717A** | **AMERICAN FAMILY INN** | |
| ☐ | 1635 N. Elk St. | (307) 382-4217 |
| | Rock Springs, WY 82901 | Hydropool MH |
| **#717C** | **ROCK SPRINGS QUALITY INN** | |
| ☐ | 2518 Foothill Blvd. | (307) 362-9600 |
| | Rock Springs, WY 82901 | Hydropool MH |
| **#718A** | **SHERATON INN** | |
| ☐ | 1949 Hwy 30 W. | (307) 789-0785 |
| | Evanston, WY 82930 | Hydropool MH |
| **#718B** | **RODEWAY INN** | |
| ☐ | 261 Hwy 30 E. | (307) 789-0790 |
| | Evanston, WY 82930 | Hydropool MH |
| **#718C** | **TRAVEL CENTER INN** | |
| ☐ | 1936 Hwy 30 West | (307) 789-2810 |
| | Evanston, WY 82930 | Hydropool MH |
| **#719A** | **MOUNTAIN INN** | |
| ☐ | on US 89 | (307) 886-3156 |
| | Afton, WY 82110 | Hydropool MH |
| **#719B** | **BEST WESTERN HI COUNTRY INN** | |
| ☐ | P.O. Box 897 | (307) 886-3856 |
| | Afton, WY 83110 | Hydropool MH |

*Granite Creek Hot Springs:* For those who like the backwoods and mountain streams but prefer to soak in cement pools with someone in charge, this is the place to spend your days, and camp a short walk away.

If you can't imagine soaking after a snowstorm, go experience it at *Granite Creek Hot Springs*.

The CCC boys did a good job more than 50 years ago on this *Granite Hot Springs* pool.

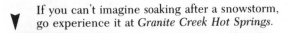

GRANITE HOT SPRINGS SWIMMING POOL

OPERATED UNDER SPECIAL USE PERMIT
BRIDGER-TETON NATIONAL FOREST

· POOL CONSTRUCTED IN 1933 BY ·
CIVILIAN CONSERVATION CORPS (CCC)

| AVERAGE YEARLY | WATER TEMP. |
|---|---|
| SNOWFALL 400" | SUMMER 93° |
| ELEVATION 6987 | WINTER 112° |

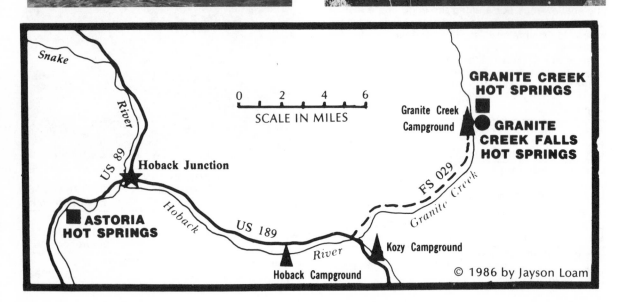

© 1986 by Jayson Loam

▲ *Granite Creek Falls Hot Spring:* This geothermal flow is just barely visible coming out of the rocks toward the right edge of the photo. A volunteer-built soaking pool is at the creek edge below the spring flow.

## #720   GRANITE CREEK HOT SPRINGS
(see map)

■ **East of Hoback Junction**                    **PR**

Part of a major bonanza for lovers of natural beauty and natural mineral water. Elevation 7,000 ft. Open all year, including the winter season, for those who have snow cats.

Natural mineral water flows out of a spring at 112° and tumbles directly into a large cement pool built by the CCC in the 1930's. Cold stream water is added as needed to maintain the pool temperature of 95° in the summer and 105° in the winter. The pool is drained and refilled each day so no chemical treatment is needed. Bathing suits are required.

Changing rooms and rest rooms are available on the premises, which are operated under a lease with the Forest Service. The site is closed, and gates locked, from 8 P.M. to 10 A.M. A large wooded creekside campground is ½ mile away. It is 10 miles to a cafe and motel and 22 miles to all other services.

Fifteen minutes by trail from this site is Granite Creek Falls Hot Spring. Natural mineral water flows out of a creek bank immediately below the falls at 130° and meanders through creekbed rocks, where volunteers have built soaking pools in which the hot and cold waters mix. These rock-and-sand pools must be rebuilt after each annual high water washout. Although the spring is partly visible from the road, the apparent local custom is clothing optional.

Allow no less than one full day and night to enjoy these two hot springs, the campground, and the beautiful scenery of Granite Creek Valley

## #721   ASTORIA MINERAL HOT SPRINGS
(see map)

■ **Star Route, Box 18**          **(307) 733-2659**
**Jackson, WY 83001**              **PR + CRV**

Large, well-kept RV resort on the south bank of the Snake River. Elevation 6,100 ft. Open May 1 to Oct. 1.

Natural mineral water flows out of a spring at 104° and is piped to an outdoor swimming pool which is treated with chlorine and maintained at a temperature of 84° to 92°. The pool is available to the public as well as to registered guests. Bathing suits are required.

Locker rooms, picnic area, tent spaces, RV hook-ups, grocery store, horse rentals and river raft trips are available on the premises. It is two miles to a cafe, service station and motel. No credit cards are accepted.

Location: On US 26, 17 miles south of the the town of Jackson.

▲ *Astoria Mineral Springs:* A very popular summer resort with a sweeping view of the Snake River.

▲ *Teton Hot Pots:* When the real thing is too cold or too far away, this is the way to go.

---

#### #722A TETON HOT POTS
☐ P.O. Box 3937      (307) 733-7831
    Jackson, WY 83001        PR

Informal and mellow rent-a-tub establishment near the center of town.

Redwood hot tubs, using chlorine-treated tap water, are for rent to the public by the hour. There are two indoor private-space tubs and one outdoor private-space tub, plus one large indoor communal tub. All tubs are equipped with hydrojets and maintained at 104°. The communal tub space and one of the private spaces are equipped with a cold plunge pool, and there is a sauna in the communal area in addition to the sauna in one of the private spaces. Clothing is required only in the public areas.

Dressing rooms and a juice bar are available on the premises. It is less than five blocks to a cafe, store, service station and motel, and one mile to overnight camping and RV hook-ups. MasterCard and Visa are accepted.

Location: The street address is 365 N. Cache (US 89), three blocks north of the town square center.

| #722B | THE 49'ER INN | |
|---|---|---|
| ☐ | 330 W. Pearl | (307) 733-7550 |
| | Jackson, WY 83001 | Hydropool MH |

| #722C | SPRING CREEK RANCH | |
|---|---|---|
| ☐ | P.O. Box 3154 | (307) 733-8833 |
| | Jackson, WY 83001 | Hydropool MH |

| #722D | WAGON WHEEL VILLAGE | |
|---|---|---|
| ☐ | 435 N. Cache St. | (307) 733-2357 |
| | Jackson, WY 83001 | Hydropool MH |

| #722D | JACKSON HOLE RACQUET CLUB RESORT | |
|---|---|---|
| ☐ | Box 362A Star Route | (307) 733-3990 |
| | Jackson, WY 83001 | Health Club MH |

| #722E | AMERICANA SNOW KING RESORT | |
|---|---|---|
| ☐ | 400 Snow King Dr. | (307) 733-5200 |
| | Jackson, WY 83001 | Hydropool MH |

| #722F | ALPENHOF | |
|---|---|---|
| ☐ | P.O. Box 288 | (307) 733-3242 |
| | Teton Village, WY 83026 | Hydropool MH |

| #722G | SOJOURNER INN | |
|---|---|---|
| ☐ | P.O. Box 328 | (307) 733-3657 |
| | Teton Village, WY 83025 | Hydropool MH |

| #722H | THE INN AT JACKSON HOLE | |
|---|---|---|
| ☐ | P.O. Box 328 | (307) 733-2311 |
| | Teton Village, WY 83025 | Hydropool MH |

| #723 | TOGWOTEE MOUNTAIN LODGE | |
|---|---|---|
| ☐ | P.O. Box 91 | (307) 543-2847 |
| | Moran, WY 83013 | Hydropool MH |

#### #724 HUCKLEBERRY HOT SPRINGS
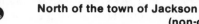 North of the town of Jackson
                     (non-commercial)

Large group of primitive hot springs along the north bank of Polecat Creek, near the south entrance to Yellowstone National Park. The site includes the remains of a resort dismantled by order of Teton National Park, which administers this area. Elevation 6,800 ft. Open all year.

Natural mineral water flows out of many springs at temperatures up to 130°, cooling as it follows various channels to the creek.

Volunteers have built small rock-and-mud soaking pools at several places where the water is in the 100° to 105° range. Bathing suits are advisable, especially in the daytime.

There are no services available on the premises. There is a commercial campground within one mile, and all other services within five miles.

Note: This location is in transition from a commercial campground with swimming pool to some form of daytime use which does not include the now-bulldozed swimming pool. Park Service future plans call for a parking area near the springs and "interpretive nature trails" through the area. There is no way to predict how future Park Service action may affect the volunteer-built pools described above.

Directions: From US 89, two miles south of the Yellowstone Park boundary, go west on the Flagg Ranch Campground road for one mile, across a bridge, and bear right on the road into Huckleberry. If the Huckleberry road is blocked off at the intersection with Flagg-Ashton road, park and walk in ½ mile on the old paved road to Huckleberry.

Look for some volunteer-built pools among the hot springs on the slopes west of the destroyed swimming pool and adjoining large geothermal pond. Another soaking pool is on the north bank of Polecat Creek, ¼ mile west of the north end of the bridge which is crossed by the Huckleberry road.

If the old road to Huckleberry is not available for either driving or hiking, there is an alternate route, requiring no bridges, via the horse trail that goes north and west from its starting point across from the entrance to Flagg Ranch Campground.

*Huckleberry Hot Springs:* While the Park Service is trying to decide what to do with the area, volunteers have built creek-edge soaking pools such as this. Hopefully, they will not be banned.

Just below the tree is another volunteer-built soaking pool using *Huckleberry Hot Springs* water. Perhaps the Park Service will decide to connect the volunteer-built pools with trails.

## #726  BOILING RIVER
● ⚠  **In Yellowstone National Park**

**non-commercial**

Turbulent confluence of hot mineral water and cold river water along the west bank of the Gardiner River, just below Park Headquarters at Mammoth Hot Spring. Elevation 5,500 ft. Open all year, during daylight hours only.

Natural mineral water flows out of a very large spring at 140°, travels 30 yards through an open channel, and tumbles down the south bank of the Gardiner River. Volunteers have rearranged some rocks in the river to control the flow of cold water into an eddy pocket, where the hot and cold water churn into a swirling mixture which varies from 50° to 110°. (The Chief Ranger wants it known that those volunteers were breaking officially posted Park regulations when they rearranged the rocks in the river, and that anyone caught in the act will be cited and prosecuted.)

No services are available at this location. Refer to the NPS Yellowstone Park map for the location of services.

Directions: On the North Entrance Road, between Mammoth Hot Spring and the town of Gardiner, look for the 45th Parallel sign on the east side of the road. Turn into the parking lot behind that sign and hike ½ mile upstream to where Boiling River cascades over the riverbank.

## #725  MADISON CAMPGROUND WARM SPRING
● ⚠  **in Yellowstone National Park**

**non-commercial**

Shallow, mud-bottom ditch near a campground inside the west boundary of Yellowstone National Park. Elevation 6,800 ft. Open all year.

Natural mineral water, combined with underground river water, bubbles up through a mud flat on the north bank of the Firehole River, just south of the campground. Volunteers have built a small sod dam across a narrow channel in order to accumulate enough 100° water to be 18″ deep. (The Chief Ranger wants it known the those volunteers were breaking officially posted park regulations when they built that dam, and that anyone caught in the act will be cited and prosecuted.)

Bathing suits are required.

No services are available at the pool. Refer to the NPS Yellowstone Park map for the location of all services.

Directions: Park on Loop G in Madison Campground and walk 100 yards south toward the Firehole River.

## #727 MAMMOTH HOT SPRINGS HOTEL AND CABINS

☐ ► Mammoth Hot Springs     (307) 344-7910
Yellowstone National Park, WY 82190    MH

Four fiberglass hydrojet pools, filled with chlorinated, electrically heated tap water, behind high board fences adjoining four small cabins. Elevation 6,200 ft. Open all year.

These pools are not available for public use by the hour or the day. During the winter they are available for communal use by registered guests in the hotel. Bathing suits are required. During the summer they are for the private use of the registered guests in each of the four cabins.

Phone for information about temperatures, restrictions, rates and reservations.

---

### STONEWALL AT YELLOWSTONE

To a hot springs enthusiast, Yellowstone National Park is a classic example of bueaucratic famine in the midst of natural abundance. Thousands of citizens approach Yellowstone each year with the expectation that they will be able to soak, at least once, in that magic mineral water. Unfortunately, Park Regulations originally intended to protect natural features from human traffic damage are being stretched to frustrate and/or prevent nearly every kind of human use of geothermal water.

A basic Park Regulation prohibits bathing in, or other use of geothermal springs, *and their run-off streams,* until after the geothermal water has mixed with surface water in a creek or river. This regulation is vigorously defended by the Park Service as being essential to the safe operation of the Park, and the protection of delicate algae formations around hot springs. The intent of this Regulation is obviously worthy of respect and support, but the administration of the Regulation leaves much to be desired.

In view of the fact that human use of all geothermal springs, and their run-off streams, is prohibited, it would seem appropriate for the Park Service to make a point of helping visitors find and enjoy those geothermal/surface water mixtures where human use is both legal and safe. Unfortunately, that is not the situation.

There are just three places in Yellowstone where geothermal and surface waters mix at temperatures tolerable for humans:

1. Midway Geyser Basin Bridge. Although this location was (and is) a legal geothermal/surface water mix, human use was prohibited several years ago by the Park Service on the grounds that the bathers were "too much of a distraction."

2. Madison Campground (see preceding page).

3. Boiling River (see preceding page).

Neither the Madison Campground soaking ditch nor the Boiling River spring appears on the official Yellowstone National Park map, nor are there any identifying signs on the nearby roads, nor are they included in any guided tours. Only if you own a book like this are you aware that they exist and where they can be found.

During a personal interview, the Chief Ranger was asked if the Park Service had any plans, was conducting any studies, or had any interest whatsoever, in finding or providing visitors with legal and safe opportunities to put their bodies in Yellowstone mineral water. The answer to all questions was a categorical "No!".

This Park Service refusal to give any consideration to the needs of visitors who prefer to obey all laws, and who also want a hot soak, was a very strong incentive to include in these pages complete directions to several moderate-temperature hot springs within Yellowstone, even though human use would be completely illegal and potentially dangerous. We chose to stick to our policy of including only legal locations, knowing that any fearless hot-spring buff could choose to make use of other sources, such as Wyoming Geothermal Energy Department maps and employees of commercial operating companies within Yellowstone.

Can an individual citizen do anything about the stonewall at Yellowstone? Probably not, but here are two suggestions which might have an accumulative effect over time:

1. Write to TW Services, Yellowstone National Park, WY 82190, complimenting them on taking the initiative to install four hot tubs at Mammoth Hot Springs Hotel, suggesting that they at least try to get some natural mineral water into those tubs, and encouraging them to serve the public by adding more soaking opportunities within Yellowstone National Park.

2. When you visit Yellowstone, take this book into any Ranger Station, open it to the section on Olympic National Park (state of Washington), and ask when Yellowstone National Park will start to offer visitors a similar opportunity for such an enjoyable (and revenue-producing) human use of geothermal water. Who knows, the idea might be recognized as a brilliant solution to a crippling budget crunch?

# Colorado

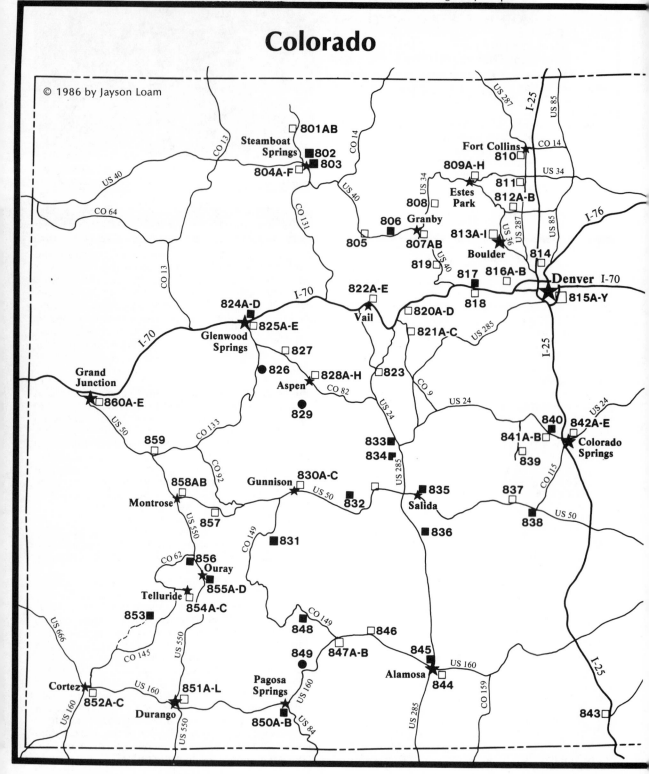

© 1986 by Jayson Loam

801AB

Steamboat
Springs  802
803

804A-F

Fort Collins
810

809A-H

811

CO 14

812A-B

808

Estes
Park

806  Granby

805

813A-I

807AB  Boulder

819

814

817  816A-B

822A-E

Denver  I-70

820A-D

818  815A-Y

Vail

824A-D

825A-E

821A-C

Glenwood
Springs

827  823

826

828A-H

Aspen  CO 82

840  842A-E

829

841A-B

833  839  Colorado
Springs

860A-E

834

Grand
Junction

859

830A-C

837

858AB

Gunnison  832  835

Salida

838

Montrose

857  836

831

856
Ouray

855A-D

Telluride

854A-C

853

848  CO 149

846

849

845

847A-B

Alamosa

Cortez

852A-C

851A-L

Pagosa
Springs

844

Durango

850A-B

843

154

*Strawberry Park Hot Springs:* Thanks to ingenious channeling of creek and geothermal water, multi-temperature pools are available.

| | | |
|---|---|---|
| **#801A** ☐ | THE HOME RANCH<br>P.O. Box KA<br>Clark, CO 80428 | (303) 879-1780<br>In-room hydropools  MH |
| **#801B** ☐ | GLEN EDEN RANCH FOUR SEASON RESORT<br>P.O. Box 867A<br>Clark, CO 80428 | (303) 879-3906<br>Hydropool  MH |

### #802 STRAWBERRY PARK HOT SPRINGS
■ P.O. Box 773332      (303) 879-7568
Steamboat Springs, CO 80477
PR + MH + CRV

New ownership is demonstrating how to retain a maximum of primitive naturalness while improving the services for a wide variety of modern hot-spring enthusiasts. Elevation 7,500 ft. Open all year.

Natural mineral water flows out of many hillside fissures at 165° and is channeled into a series of creek-bank rock-and-masonry pools, where it is combined with creek water to provide a range of soaking temperatures. There is also a private-space hydrojet tub which is maintained at a temperature of 104° to 106°. There is a wood-burning sauna available near the pools. Continuous flow-through in all pools eliminates the need for chemical treatment. Bathing suits are required in the creek-bed pool area during the day on Sunday, Tuesday, Thursday, Friday and Saturday, and are optional at other times and places.

Locker rooms, massage by appointment, cabins, overnight camping and catered private parties are available on the premises. By prior reservation there are also saddle-horse trips, cross-country skiing and snow-cat trips to and from the site. It is seven miles to all other services. Visa and MasterCard are accepted

Directions: From US 40 in the town of Steamboat Springs, go north on 7th St. and follow signs seven miles to location. Phone for rates, reservations and snow-cat transportation in the winter.

PAYING CUSTOMERS ONLY PAST THIS POINT

### #803 STEAMBOAT SPRINGS HEALTH AND RECREATION

**P.O. Box 1211**  (303) 879-1828
**Steamboat Springs, CO 80477**  PR

Large community plunge, hot pool, water slide and sauna near the city center. Elevation 6,700 ft. Open all year.

Natural mineral water flows out of a spring at 104° and is piped to three pools which are treated with chlorine. The enclosed soaking pool is maintained at a temperature of 100°, the water slide pick-up pool at 100° and the outdoor swimming pool at 80°. Bathing suits are required, including in the co-ed sauna.

Locker rooms, snack bar, exercise classes and tennis courts are available on the premises. It is three blocks to a cafe, store, service station and motel, and two miles to overnight camping and RV hook-ups. Visa and MasterCard are accepted.

Location: On the north side of US 40, on the east edge of the city of Steamboat Springs.

---

**#804A SHERATON VILLAGE HOTEL**
□ P.O. Box 774808  (303) 879-2220
Steamboat Springs, CO 80477

Hydropool MH

---

**#804B FOUR SEASONS AT STEAMBOAT**
□ 2315 Apres Ski Way  (303) 879-4445
Steamboat Springs, CO 80487

Hydropool MH

---

**#804C HARBOR HOTEL AND CONDOMINIUMS**
□ 703 Lincoln Ave.  (303) 879-1522
Steamboat Springs, CO 80477

Hydropool MH

---

**#804D HOLIDAY INN**
□ 3190 S. Lincoln  (303) 879-2250
Steamboat Springs, CO 80477

Hydropool MH

---

**#804E THE LODGE AT STEAMBOAT**
□ P.O. Box 6460  (303) 879-6000
Steamboat Springs, CO 80499

Hydropool MH

---

**#804F THE RANCH AT STEAMBOAT**
□ One Ranch Road  (303) 879-3000
Steamboat Springs, CO 80477

Hydropool MH

| #805 | LATIGO RANCH | |
|---|---|---|
| ☐ | P.O. Box 237A | (303) 724-3596 |
| | Kremmling, CO 80459 | Hydropool MH |

▲ *Hot Sulphur Springs:* Although there is no obvious sulphur smell to the water, the name may be a handicap for this aging resort.

## #806  HOT SULPHUR SPRINGS

■ **P.O. Box 175**  **(303) 725-3306**
**Hot Sulphur Springs, CO 80451**
**PR + MH + CRV**

Older resort on a main highway through the Rocky Mountains. Elevation 7,600 ft. Open all year.

Natural mineral water flows out of a spring at 112° and is piped to a variety of pools. The outdoor swimming pool is treated with chlorine and maintained at 85°. The outdoor soaking pool is maintained at 100° on a flow-through basis, which eliminates the need for chemical treatment. There are two indoor pools in private spaces rented by the hour, and there are two indoor pools in separate men's and women's bath houses. Temperatures in these pools are controllable up to 110°. Bathing suits are required except in indoor pools.

Locker rooms, rooms, tent spaces and picnic area are available on the premises. It is three blocks to a cafe, store and service station and 75 miles to RV hook-ups. No credit cards are accepted.

Directions: From US 40 in the town of Hot Sulphur Springs, follow signs north across river to resort.

| #807A | C LAZY U RANCH | |
|---|---|---|
| ☐ | P.O. Box 378 | (303) 887-3344 |
| | Granby, CO 80445 | Hydropool MH |

| #807B | YMCA OF THE ROCKIES | |
|---|---|---|
| | SNOW MOUNTAIN RANCH | |
| ☐ | 1 mile south of US 40 | (303) 887-2152 |
| | Granby, CO 80446 | Hydropool CRV |

| #808 | DRIFTWOOD LODGE | |
|---|---|---|
| ☐ | P.O. Box 609A | (303) 627-3654 |
| | Grand Lake, CO 80447 | Hydropool MH |

| #809A | TYROL MOTOR INN | |
|---|---|---|
| ☐ | 1240 Big Thompson Ave. | (303) 586-3382 |
| | Estes Park, CO 80517 | Hydropool MH |

| #809B | HOLIDAY INN | |
|---|---|---|
| ☐ | 101 S. St. Vrain | (303) 586-2332 |
| | Estes Park, CO 80517 | Hydropool MH |

| #809C | COMFORT INN | |
|---|---|---|
| ☐ | 1450 Big Thompson Ave. | (303) 586-2358 |
| | Estes Park. CO 80517 | Hydropool MH |

| #809D | FOUR WINDS MOTOR LODGE | |
|---|---|---|
| ☐ | P.O. Box 3460A | (303) 586-3313 |
| | Estes Park, CO 80517 | Hydropool MH |

| #809E | SILVER SADDLE MOTOR LODGE | |
|---|---|---|
| ☐ | Box 1747 AAA | (303) 586-4476 |
| | Estes Park, CO 80510 | Hydropool MH |

| #809F | SUNNYSIDE KNOLL MOTEL & CABINS | |
|---|---|---|
| ☐ | P.O. Box 794A | (303) 586-5759 |
| | Estes Park, CO 80510 | Hydropool MH |

| #809G | TIMBERLANE MOTOR LODGE | |
|---|---|---|
| ☐ | P.O. Box 387 | (303) 586-3137 |
| | Estes Park, CO 80510 | Hydropool MH |

| #809H | BEST WESTERN ESTES VILLAGE | |
|---|---|---|
| | MOTOR INN | |
| ☐ | 1040 Big Thompson Ave. | (303) 586-5338 |
| | Estes Park, CO 80517 | Hydropool MH |

| #810 | HOLIDAY INN OF FORT COLLINS | |
|---|---|---|
| ☐ | 3836 E. Mulberry | (303) 484-4660 |
| | Fort Collins, CO 80524 | Hydropool MH |

| #811 | BEST WESTERN COACH HOUSE | |
|---|---|---|
| | MOTOR INN | |
| ☐ | 5542 E. Hwy 34 | (303) 667-7810 |
| | Loveland, CO 80537 | Hydropool MH |

| #812A | BEST WESTERN CENTENNIAL INN | |
|---|---|---|
| ☐ | I-25 and CO 119 | (303) 776-8700 |
| | Longmont, CO 80501 | Hydropool MH |

| #812B | PLAZA HOTEL | |
|---|---|---|
| ☐ | P.O. Box 1937 | (303) 776-2000 |
| | Longmont, CO 80501 | Hydropool MH |

*First Resort:* Resting area, shower and full bath are part of each spacious rental unit.

## #813A FIRST RESORT

☐

4645 Broadway       (303) 449-6713
Boulder, CO 80302          PR

An ordinary motel building brilliantly remodeled to provide indoor and outdoor hot pools, a restaurant, massage rooms and meeting space/tub rooms capable of accommodating groups of 50. Elevation 5,400 ft. Open all year, 24 hours a day.

Private-space pools using tap water treated by ultraviolet radiation are for rent to the public by the hour. Twelve motel units have been converted into hot-pool units, four with the pool indoors and eight with the pool in an adjoining private patio. The temperature in all pools is maintained at 104°. Every unit has its own indoor shower, sink, toilet and rest space. Two units also have steam baths and two other units have saunas.

Massage and a restaurant are available on the premises. Visa and MasterCard are accepted.

Future plans include the construction of a central flower garden with communal soaking pools and the establishment of a seminar/workshop/conference program designed to enhance both physical and psychological health. Phone for status of construction and to request a copy of the current seminar/workshop schedule.

Phone for rates, reservations and directions.

## #813B TIME OUT BATHS

☐

805 Pearl St.       (303)442-TUBS
Boulder, CO 80302          PR

The first private-space rent-a-tub facility in Boulder, featuring both indoor and outdoor hydrojet pools.

Private-space pools using bromine-treated tap water are for rent to the public by the hour. There are three rooftop redwood tubs, in private enclosures, and two indoor cedar tubs in private rooms. Water temperatures are maintained at 104° to 105°. Hourly, monthly and communal tub rates are available.

Massage, sauna, sun-tan booth and flotation tanks are available on the premises.

Phone for rates, reservations and directions.

| #813C | THE BROKER INN | |
|---|---|---|
| ☐ | 555 30th St. | (303) 444-3330 |
| | Boulder, CO 80303 | Hydropool MH |

| #813D | ARAPAHOE LODGE | |
|---|---|---|
| ☐ | 2020 Arapahoe | (303) 449-7550 |
| | Boulder, CO 80302 | Hydropool MH |

| #813E | BEST WESTERN BOULDER INN | |
|---|---|---|
| ☐ | 770 28th St. | (303) 449-3800 |
| | Boulder, CO 80303 | Hydropool MH |

| #813F | BEST WESTERN GOLDEN BLUFF MOTOR INN | |
|---|---|---|
| ☐ | 1725 28th St. | (303) 442-7450 |
| | Boulder, CO 80302 | Hydropool MH |

| #813G | THE HILTON HARVEST HOUSE | |
|---|---|---|
| ☐ | 1345 28th St. | (303) 443-3850 |
| | Boulder, CO 80302 | Hydropool MH |

▲ *Time Out Tubbery:* Of the several types of hot-tub enclosures offered by this urban rent-a-tub facility, this curved fiberglass panel dome is the one most often requested.

▲ At *Time Out Tubbery* wooden hot tubs, with decking and skylights, are also available for rent by the hour or longer time periods.

▼ *Time Out Baths:* This pioneering Boulder rent-a-tub location offers both indoor tubs and rooftop communal tubs such as this one.

| #813H ☐ | HOLIDAY INN 800 28th St. Boulder, CO 80303 | (303) 443-3322 Hydropool MH |
|---|---|---|
| #813I ☐ | WAGON WHEEL MOTEL AND CAMPGROUND on CO 118 Boulder, CO 80303 | (303) 444-6882 Hydropool MH + CRV |
| #814 ☐ | SHERATON GRAYSTONE CASTLE 83 E. 120th Ave. Thorton, CO 80233 | (303) 451-1002 In-room hydropools MH |
| #815A ☐ | TIME OUT TUBBERY 6465 Leetsdale Denver, CO 80222 | (303) 399-7625 PR |

A pioneering rent-a-tub facility, offering a variety of private-space settings, in the southwest part of Denver.

Private-space pools using bromine-treated tap water are for rent to the public by the hour. Seven indoor hydrojet pools have skylights or windows, and seven outdoor hydrojet pools are in enclosed private patios adjoining private rooms. Two larger hydrojet pools are in modular fiberglass domes, with the top panels removed in the summer.

Pool temperatures are maintained in the range of 102° to 106°.

Massage and colonics are available on the premises. MasterCard and Visa are accepted.

Phone for rates, reservations and directions.

#815B GRAND CENTRAL SAUNA & HOT
TUB CO.

☐ 845 Lincoln     (303) 837-8827
Denver, CO 80203     PR

One of a chain of urban locations, established by Grand Central, a pioneer in the private-room rent-a-tub business.

Private-space pools using chlorine-treated tap water are for rent to the public by the hour. There are 20 private rooms, each including a sauna, with pool-water temperature maintained at 102° to 104°.

A juice bar is available on the premises. No credit cards are accepted.

Phone for rates, reservations and directions.

#815C SHERATON DENVER TECH CENTER
☐ 4900 DTC Parkway    (303) 779-1100
Denver, CO 80237    Hydropool MH

#815D EXECUTIVE TOWER INN
☐ 1405 Curtis St.    (303) 571-0300
Denver, CO 80202    Hydropool MH

#815E THE CLARION HOTEL—DENVER AIRPORT
☐ 3203 Quebec St.    (303) 321-3333
Denver, CO 80207    Hydropool MH

#815F DENVER GRANADA ROYALE HOMETEL
☐ 7625 E. Hampden Ave.    (303) 696-6644
Denver, CO 80231    Hydropool MH

#815G HOLIDAY INN DENVER—NORTHGLENN
☐ 10 E. 120th Ave.    (303) 452-4100
Denver, CO 80234    Hydropool MH

#815H DENVER PARK SUITE HOTEL
☐ 1881 Curtis St.    (303) 297-8888
Denver, CO 80202    Hydropool MH

#815I BEST WESTERN LANDMARK INN
☐ 455 S. Colorado Blvd.    (303) 388-5561
Denver, CO 80222    Hydropool MH

#815J DENVER MARRIOTT SOUTHEAST
☐ 6363 Hampden Ave.    (303) 758-7000
Denver, CO 80222    Hydropool MH

#815K DENVER MARRIOTT—CITY CENTER
☐ 1701 California St.    (303) 297-1300
Denver, CO 80202    Hydropool MH

#815L GRANADA ROYALE HOMETEL
☐ 7525 E. Hampden Ave.    (303) 696-6644
Denver, CO 80231    Hydropool MH

#815M HOWARD JOHNSON'S MOTOR LODGE—
DENVER SOUTH
☐ 6300 E Hampden Ave.    (303) 758-2211
Denver, CO 80222    Hydropool MH

#815N WESTIN HOTEL—TABOR CENTER
☐ 1672 Lawrence    (303) 572-9100
Denver, CO 80202    Health club MH

#815O WRITER'S MANOR HOTEL
☐ 1730 S. Colorado Blvd.    (303) 756-8877
Denver, CO 80222    Health club MH

#816P RODEWAY INN—AIRPORT
☐ 4590 Quebec St.    (303) 320-0260
Denver, CO 80216    Hydropool MH

#815Q SHERATON DENVER AIRPORT HOTEL
☐ 3535 Quebec St.    (303) 303-7711
Denver, CO 80207    Hydropool MH

#815R HOLIDAY INN
☐ 7390 W. Hampden Ave.    (303) 980-9200
Denver. CO 80227    Hydropool MH

#815S DOUBLETREE HOTEL
☐ 13696 E. Cliff Pl.    (303) 337-2800
Aurora, CO 80014    Hydropool MH

#815T HOLIDAY INN—DENVER EAST
☐ 13650 E. Colfax    (303) 364-2671
Aurora, CO 80011    Hydropool MH

#815U SHADY MEADOWS AND RV PARK
☐ on Potomac St.    (303) 364-9483
Aurora, CO 80011    Hydropool CRV

#815V HOLIDAY INN—SOUTHEAST
☐ 9009 E. Arapahoe Rd.    (303) 790-1421
Englewood, CO 80112    Hydropool MH

#815W HERITAGE HOTEL,
☐ 5150 S. Quebec St.    (303) 796-8966
Englewood, CO 80111    Hydropool MH

#815X PRIME RATE MOTEL—DENVER WEST
☐ 10101 S. I-70 Service Rd.    (303) 424-8300
Wheatridge, CO 80033    Hydropool MH

#815Y QUALITY INN ROYAL
☐ 3270 Youngfield St.    (303) 238 7701
Wheatridge, CO 80033    Hydropool MH

#816A HOLIDAY INN—WEST
☐ 14707 W. Colfax    (303) 279-7611
Golden, CO 80401    Hydropool MH

#816B DENVER WEST MARRIOTT HOTEL
☐ 1717 Denver West Blvd.    (303) 279-9100
Golden, CO 80401    Health club MH

## #817　INDIAN SPRINGS RESORT

■ P.O. Box 1300　　　　　(303) 623-2050
　Idaho Springs, CO 80452　PR + MH + CRV

Popular historic resort just off of Interstate 70 in the Arapahoe National Forest. Elevation 7,300 ft. Open all year.

Natural mineral water flows out of three underground springs at 124°. Within the men's cave are three walk-in soaking pools ranging in temperature from 104° to 112°. Within the women's cave are four similar pools. There are 12 private-space soaking pools large enough for couples or families, with temperatures ranging from 104° to 112°. All of the above pools operate on a flow-through basis so no chemical treatment is necessary. A minimum of chlorine treatment is used in the large, landscaped indoor pool, which is maintained at 96° in the winter and 90° in the summer. Bathing suits are required in the swimming pool and prohibited in the caves.

Locker rooms, massage, chiropractor, dining room, hotel rooms, overnight camping and RV hook-ups are available on the premises. It is five blocks to a store and service station. Visa and MasterCard are accepted.

Directions: From I-70 take the Idaho Springs exit to the business district, then follow signs south on Soda Springs Road to resort.

▲ *Indian Springs Resort:* A tropical garden has grown up under the famous translucent roof which covers this large main pool.

---

#818　H & H MOTOR LODGE
☐　P.O. Box 1359　　　　　(303) 567-2838
　　Idaho Springs, CO 80452　Hydropool　MH

---

#819　ALPENGLO MOTOR LODGE
☐　P.O. Box 35A　　　　　(303) 726-5294
　　Winter Park, CO 80482　Hydropool　MH

---

#820A　BEST WESTERN FOXPINE INN
☐　　154 Wheeler　　　　(303) 968-2600
　　　Dillon, CO 80443　Hydropool　MH

---

#820B　HOLIDAY INN AT LAKE DILLON
☐　　P.O. Box 669　　　　(303) 668-5000
　　　Dillon, CO 80435　Hydropool　MH

---

#820C　SNOWSHOE MOTEL
☐　　521 Main St.　　　　(303) 668-3444
　　　Dillon, CO 80443　In-room hydropools　MH

---

#820D　SILVERTHORNE LODGE AT LAKE DILLON
☐　　P.O. Box 368　　　　(303) 468-6200
　　　Silverthorne, CO 80498　Hydropool　MH

---

#821A　THE VILLAGE AT BRECKENRIDGE
☐　　P.O. Box 1979　　　　(303) 453-2000
　　　Breckenridge, CO 80424　Health club　MH

---

#821B　BEAVER RUN RESORT
☐　　P.O. Box 2115　　　　(303) 453-6000
　　　Breckenridge, CO 80424　Hydropool　MH

---

#821C　TIGER RUN RV RESORT
☐　　on Hwy 9　　　　(303) 453-9690
　　　Breckenridge, CO 80424　Hydropool　CRV

---

#822A　HOLIDAY INN
☐　　13 Vail Rd. and I-70　(303) 476-5631
　　　Vail, CO 81657　Hydropool　MH

---

#822B　BEST WESTERN VAILGLO LODGE
☐　　701 Lionshead Circle　(303) 476-5506
　　　Vail, CO 81658　Hydropool　MH

---

#822C　THE WESTIN HOTEL—VAIL
☐　　1300 Westhae Dr.　(303) 476-7111
　　　Vail, CO 81657　Hydropool　MH

---

#822D　MARRIOTT'S MARK RESORT
☐　　715 W. Lionshead Circle　(303) 476-4444
　　　Vail, CO 81657　Hydropool　MH

---

#822E　BEST WESTERN RAINTREE INN
☐　　2211 N. Frontage Rd. W.　(303) 476-3890
　　　Vail, CO 81657　Hydropool　MH

---

#823　BEST WESTERN SILVER KING MOTOR INN
☐　　2020 N. Poplar　　　(303) 486-2610
　　　Leadville, CO 80461　Hydropool　MH

*Glenwood Hot Springs Lodge And Pool:* A swim meet can be held in this pool without requiring any regular patrons to get out of the way.

## #824A GLENWOOD HOT SPRINGS LODGE
### AND POOL                    (see map)
P.O. Box 308              (303) 945-6571
Glenwood Springs, CO 81601    PR + MH

A very large commercial resort near the center of town on the north bank of the Colorado River. Elevation 5,700 ft. Open all year.

Natural mineral water flows out of a spring at 130° and is mixed with cold spring water to supply four pools, all of which are treated with chlorine. The two-block-long swimming pool is maintained at a temperature of 98°; the outdoor soaking pool, with jet therapy chairs, at 104°, the water slide catch-pool at 85°, and the indoor hydrojet pool (in the athletic club) at 104°. There is also a sauna and steam bath in the athletic club. Bathing suits are required everywhere.

Locker rooms, cafe, hotel rooms and miniature golf course are available on the premises. It is three blocks to a store and service station, and five miles to overnight camping and RV hook-ups. MasterCard, Diners Club, Visa, Choice and American Express are accepted.

▶ *Glenwood Springs Vapor Caves:* This location is proud of its therapeutic reputation.

## #824B GLENWOOD SPRINGS
### VAPOR CAVES             (see map)
709 E. 6th                (303) 945-5825
Glenwood Springs, CO 81601

Unique health center, one block from the large Hot Springs Lodge complex. Elevation 5,700 ft. Open all year.

Natural mineral water and vapor emerge from several springs within two caves at 115°. There are no soaking pools, but a cold-water hose is available within each cave. Both caves are co-ed and bathing suits are required.

Locker rooms and massage are available on the premises. It is three blocks to a cafe, store, service station and motel, and five miles to overnight camping and RV hook-ups. MasterCard and Visa are accepted.

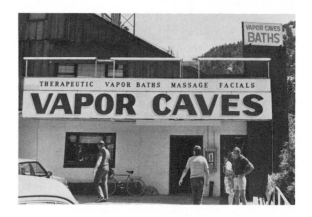

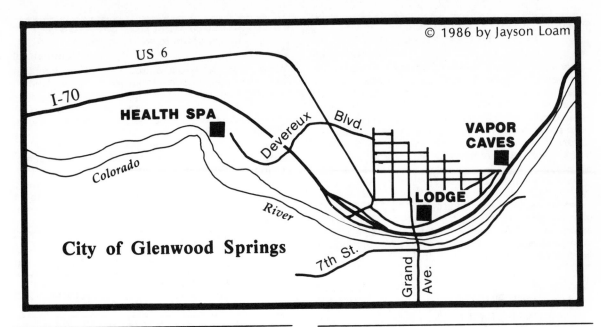

US 6

I-70

**HEALTH SPA**

Devereux Blvd.

**VAPOR CAVES**

Colorado

River

**LODGE**

7th St.

Grand Ave.

**City of Glenwood Springs**

## #824C HEALTH SPA    (see map)
P.O. Box 536    (303) 945-5021
Glenwood Springs, CO 81601    PR

Chiropractic office and bathhouse part of old resort. Elevation 5,700 ft. Open all year.

Natural mineral water flows out of two springs at 110° and 124° and is piped to six individual tubs in private rooms. Customers can control tub temperature up to 112°. Bathing suits are not required in tub rooms.

Chiropractic adjustment and massage are available on the premises. It is ½ mile to a cafe, store, service station and motel, and five miles to overnight camping and RV hook-ups. No credit cards are accepted.

## #824D SOUTH CANYON HOT SPRINGS
**West of the city of Glenwood Springs**
**non-commercial**

A primitive city-owned geothermal spring with a long history of controversy involving nudity, lack of sanitary facilities and the bulldozing of volunteer-built soaking pools. Elevation 5,600 ft. Open all year.

Natural mineral water flows out of a spring at 118°. From time to time, volunteers build masonry soaking pools, then the city tests the water in the pools, finds it to be a health hazard (per state standards) and destroys the pools. The area is not fenced or posted, and there is no recent pattern of harassment. However, the police may choose to respond at any time to a complaint about drugs or nudity.

There are no services on the premises.

Directions: From I-70, west of Glenwood Springs, take the South Canyon exit and go approximately ½ mile up from the mouth of the canyon. You might or might not find a usable pool of geothermal water on the west side of the canyon.

#825A    HOLIDAY INN OF GLENWOOD SPRINGS
1359 US Hwy 6    (303) 945-8551
Glenwood Springs, CO 81601
In-room hydropools  MH

#825B    BEST WESTERN CARAVAN MOTEL
1826 Grand Ave.    (303) 945-8535
Glenwood Springs, CO 81601
Hydropool  MH

#825C    BEST WESTERN ANTLERS MOTEL
305 Laurel St.    (303) 945-8535
Glenwood Springs, CO 81601
Hydropool  MH

#825D    GLENWOOD MOTOR INN
P.O. Box 1386    (303) 945-5438
Glenwood Springs, CO 81601
Hydropool  MH

#825E    THE INN AT GLENWOOD
124 W. Sixth    (303) 945-2500
Glenwood Springs, CO 81601
Hydropool  MH

PLEASE! Don't Walk on The Water

## #826  PENNY HOT SPRINGS
### North of the town of Redstone
**non-commercial**

Primitive riverbank hot spring seasonally flooded by high water. Elevation 8,000 ft. Open all year.

Natural mineral water flows out of a spring at 133° and drops directly into the Crystal River. In between annual high-water washouts volunteers build rock-and-sand pools in which hot mineral water and cold river water can be mixed to a soaking temperature. The location is close to the highway so bathing suits are advisable.

There are no services on the premises. All services are within 25 miles.

Directions: On the east side of CO 133, 0.2 mile south of mile marker 57, there is a small parking area on the east side of the highway. A telephone cable strung across the river is visible from that area, and the springs are almost directly under the cable.

| | | | |
|---|---|---|---|
| #827 ☐ | KOA ASPEN—BASALT<br>on CO 82<br>Basalt, CO 81621 | (303) 927-3532<br>Hydropool CRV | |
| #828A ☐ | INNSBRUCK INN<br>233 W. Main St.<br>Aspen, CO 81611 | (303) 925-2980<br>Hydropool MH | |
| #828B ☐ | ULLR LODGE<br>520 W. Main St.<br>Aspen, CO 81611 | (303) 925-7696<br>Hydropool MH | |
| #828C ☐ | THE ASPEN INN<br>701 Mill St.<br>Aspen, CO 81611 | (303) 925-6300<br>Hydropool MH | |
| #828D ☐ | HIGHLAND INN<br>1650 Maroon Creek Rd.<br>Aspen, CO 81612 | (303) 925-5050<br>Hydropool MH | |
| #828E ☐ | THE GANT<br>610 S. West End St.<br>Aspen, CO 81612 | (303) 925-5000<br>Hydropool MH | |
| #828F ☐ | THE ASPEN<br>311 W. Main St.<br>Aspen, CO 81611 | (303) 925-7650<br>Hydropool MH | |
| #828G ☐ | LIMELITE LODGE<br>228 E. Cooper<br>Aspen, CO 81611 | (303) 925-3025<br>Hydropool MH | |
| #828H ☐ | MOLLY GIBSON LODGE<br>120 W. Hopkins<br>Aspen, CO 81611 | (303) 925-2580<br>Hydropool MH | |

## #829  CONUNDRUM HOT SPRINGS
### South of the town of Aspen
**non-commercial**

Two primitive pools surrounded by spectacular Rocky Mountain scenery in the White River National Forest. Elevation 11,200 ft. Open all year.

Natural mineral water flows out of a spring at 100°, into two volunteer-built rock-and-sand pools. The local custom is clothing optional.

There are no services on the premises. It is eight miles of trail and five miles of rough road to a campground and 20 miles to all other services.

This is a rewarding but hazardous location. Be sure to obtain directions, instructions and information about current trail conditions at a White River National Forest ranger station before attempting the trip.

| | | | |
|---|---|---|---|
| #830A ☐ | ABC MOTEL<br>212 E. Tomichi Ave.<br>Gunnison, CO 81230 | (303) 641-2400<br>Hydropool MH | |
| #830B ☐ | COLORADO WEST MOTEL<br>400 E. Tomichi Ave.<br>Gunnison, CO 81230 | (303) 641-1288<br>Hydropool MH | |
| #830C ☐ | BEST WESTERN TOMICHI VILLAGE INN<br>P.O. Box 763<br>Gunnison, CO 81230 | (303) 641-1131<br>Hydropool MH | |

## #831  YOUMANS STORE & CABINS (CEBOLLA HOT SPRINGS)
**County Road 27**  (303) 641-0952
**Powdernorn, CO 81243**  **MH**

Something special. An old-fashioned soak in a plank-lined spring covered by an authentic log cabin on a rugged mountain slope in central Colorado. Elevation 8,100 ft. Open May to October.

Natural mineral water flows out of two springs at 106° directly up through the bottom planks of two wood-lined pits which have been built within each spring. The odorless geothermal water flows through continuously, maintaining a pool temperature of 105° and eliminating the need for any chemical water treatment. There are no hydrojets but you will feel an occasional gas bubble rising to the surface as you soak in natural silence. The soaking pools and cabin floor are kept very clean, and one of the cabins even has a wood stove. Bathing suits are not required within the cabins.

IMPORTANT NOTICE: These hot springs are reserved primarily for the use of registered guests in the nearby rental cabins. Phone ahead for reservations before attempting to drive to this remote location.

A store, service station, rental cabins and fishing are available on the premises. It is 10 miles to a cafe and overnight camping and 20 miles to RV hook-ups. No credit cards are accepted.

Directions: From US 50, 10 miles west of Gunnison, drive south on CO 149 approximately 15 miles and watch for Powderhorn turn off on left.

*Youmans Store & Cabins:* Each of the authentic log cabins contains a plank-lined soaking pit, but all patrons must share the authentic privy in the middle.

*Rendezvous In The Rockies:* Urban-type fiberglass tubs have been given a rustic deck on the bank of a rushing mountain stream.

## #832   WAUNITA HOT SPRINGS RANCH
**8007 County Road 887   (303) 641-1266**
**Gunnison, CO 81230                    MH**

Older guest ranch, surrounded by Gunnison National Forest. Elevation 9,000 ft. Open all year.

Natural mineral water flows out of a spring at 175° and is piped to a swimming pool and to geothermal heating units in the buildings. The swimming pool is treated with chlorine and maintained at a temperature of 95°. Pool use is reserved for registered guests, with a minimum stay of six days, by prior reservation only. Bathing suits are required.

Guest-ranch services, including rooms, meals, saddle horses and fishing, are available on the premises. It is 15 miles to a store, service station and overnight camping, and 28 miles to RV hook-ups. No credit cards are accepted.

Directions: From the town of Gunnison, go 19 miles east on US 50, then follow signs eight miles north to the ranch.

## #833   RENDEZVOUS IN THE ROCKIES
**P.O. Box 909              (303) 395-6715**
**Buena Vista, CO 81211              PR + MH**

A self-styled "small resort for all seasons/reasons," situated at the mouth of Cottonwood Canyon, surrounded by San Isabel National Forest. Elevation 8,500 ft. Open all year.

Natural mineral water flows out of several springs and wells at temperatures ranging from 72° to 130°. There are three fiberglass hydrojet tubs on enclosed decks overlooking a tumbling mountain stream. Continuous flow-through eliminates the need for any chemical treatment, and temperatures in each pool are controllable.

Bathing suits are required in the lower pool, and are optional in the other two, fully enclosed pools. All pools are available to the public as well as to registered guests.

The mineral water is so pure and odorless that it is used in the resort water supply, so every tub bath within the motel rooms and cabins is also natural mineral water. Additional outdoor and in-room hydropools are planned. Phone for status of construction.

Locker rooms, poolside bar service, massage by appointment, dinner house meals, rooms and cabins are available on the premises. It is six miles to all other services. MasterCard and Visa are accepted.

The resort brochure describes this unique facility as being, "Especially designed for personal and small-group retreats, business meetings, conferences and seminars."

Directions: From US 24, in Buena Vista, go west five miles on CO 306, the road to Cottonwood Pass. Watch for resort signs on the right side of the road.

### #834 MOUNT PRINCETON HOT SPRINGS

County Road 162      (303) 395-2361
Nathrop, CO 81236      PR + MH

Large modern resort surrounded by San Isabel National Forest. Elevation 8,500 ft. Open all year.

Natural mineral water flows out of a spring at 132°. Odorless and tasteless, this water is used in all pipes, including those which water the lawn. The outdoor swimming pool is maintained at 85°, the outdoor soaking pool at 95°. Both are treated with chlorine. There are six individual tubs in private rooms which are drained and refilled after each use, with temperatures controllable up to 110°. All pools and tubs are available to the public as well as to registered guests. Bathing suits are required everywhere except in private tub rooms.

Locker rooms, restaurant, hotel rooms, picnic area, saddle horses, fishing and hiking are available on the premises. It is five miles to all other services. MasterCard and Visa are accepted.

Directions: From US 285 in the town of Nathrop, go west five miles on CO 162 to resort.

### #835 SALIDA HOT SPRINGS

410 Rainbow Blvd.      (303) 539-6738
Salida, CO 81201      PR

Modernized indoor municipal plunge, hot baths, park and playground. Elevation 7,000 ft. Open all year.

Natural mineral water flows out of Poncha Springs at 114° and is piped five miles to Salida. The large indoor swimming pool is maintained at a temperature of 92° to 96°, and is treated with chlorine. There are six private family-size indoor soaking pools which are drained and refilled after each use, and in which the water temperature is controllable by the customer. Bathing suits are required everywhere except in private soaking pools.

Locker rooms are available on the premises. It is less than five blocks to all other services. No credit cards are accepted.

Directions: From the junction of US 50 and US 285, go six miles east on US 50. Look for signs on the north side of the street.

*Salida Hot Springs:* The city of Salida wanted a "hot spring" pool so strongly that it bought a private hot spring and built a five-mile pipeline to this site.

### #836 VALLEY VIEW HOT SPRINGS

P.O. Box 175      (no phone)
Villa Grove, CO 81155      PR + MH + CRV

Unique combination of primitive hot springs and primitive camping facilities, with clothing optional, on the west slope of the Sangre De Cristo mountains. Elevation 8,700 ft. Open all year.

Natural mineral water flows out of several springs at temperatures ranging from 85° to 105°. All pools are supplied on a flow-through basis, so no chemical treatment is needed. The outdoor cement swimming pool is maintained at 89°. The outdoor soaking pool is built right over a spring so the water flowing up through the gravel bottom maintains a temperature of 96° in the pool. The small gravel-bottom upper pool is also built right over a spring, and the pool temperature varies from 80° to 105°, depending on the volume of snow melt running through the gully in which the spring is located. There is also a small soaking pool at 83° inside the wood-fired sauna building. Clothing is optional everywhere on the extensive grounds.

Rustic cabins and tent spaces are available on the premises. It is 12 miles to all other services. No credit cards are accepted.

Note: This is primarily a membership facility, with the premises reserved for members and their guests on weekends. A limited number of guest passes are available during the week by prior arrangement. Write first for permission to enter.

Directions: From the junction of US 285 and CO 17 near Mineral Hot Springs take the gravel road due east seven miles to the location.

### #837 QUALITY INN/INTERNATIONAL SPA

E. Hwy 50 at Dozier      (303) 275-8676
Canon City, CO 81212      Hydropool MH

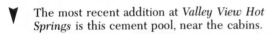 *Valley View Hot Springs:* Geothermal water flowing up through the gravel bottom keeps this pool at 96° summer and winter.

▼ This upper pool at *Valley View Hot Springs* can be reached only via a steep path, but it does have far-reaching view of the valley.

▼ The most recent addition at *Valley View Hot Springs* is this cement pool, near the cabins.

▲ *Mount Princeton Hot Springs:* The newer pools are on a grassy, parklike knoll above the main lodge and individual hot-tub rooms.

167

### #838 DESERT REEF BEACH CLUB

P.O. Box 305      (303) 372-6488
Penrose, CO 81240      PR + CRV

A small recreation resort which has grown up around a geothermal well in the foothills west of Pueblo. Elevation 5,200 ft. Open all year.

Natural mineral water flows out of an artesian well at 110°, directly into a large cement soaking pool on a continuous basis, so no chemical treatment is necessary. During the summer the geothermal water is sprayed into the air to cool it, resulting in a pool temperature of approximately 90°. During winter the geothermal water is directed into small tubs set on the bottom of the emptied main pool. These small tubs can be temperature-controlled by taking or diverting the 110° flow from the well outlet. Bathing suits are required on some days and optional on other days. Phone for information on the current schedule.

Locker rooms, club house, massage, snack bar, indoor/outdoor liquor bar and overnight camping are available on the premises. It is one mile to all other services.

Note: The facilities are reserved for the use of members on the weekends, but a limited number of guest passes are available during the week by prior arrangement.

Phone for information on guest passes, rates, reservations and directions.

### #839 CRIPPLE CREEK GOLD CAMPGROUND

on Hwy 67      (303) 689-2342
Cripple Creek, CO 80813      Hydropool CRV

*Desert Reef Beach Club:* This hot well site has developed its own traditions, including umbrella tables in the pool, a volleyball net, clothing optional days and an outdoor bar.

### #840 SPRING SPA

P.O. Box 1083      (303) 685-5955
Manitou Springs, CO 80829      PR

Historic old spa building being remodeled and restored by new owner, on the main street in downtown Manitou Springs. Elevation 6,200 ft. Open all year.

Natural mineral water flows out of a spring at 68° and is heated as needed. There are three individual one-person tubs, which are drained and filled after each use, so no chemical treatment is necessary, and water temperature in each tub is controllable by the customer. There are four indoor hydrojet pools, in private rooms, holding from two to ten persons. These tubs are normally filled with gas-heated tap water treated with bromine, and are maintained at a temperature of 104°. By prior reservation only, any one of these private-room tubs, for an extra charge, will be drained and filled with natural mineral water, without any chemical treatment. Bathing suits are required in all tubs at all times.

A flotation tank, lockers and massage by appointment are available on the premises. It is less than three blocks to all other services. MasterCard, Visa and American Express are accepted.

The street address is 934 Manitou Ave. in Manitou Springs. Phone for rates, reservations and directions.

| #841A | EAGLE MOTEL |  |
|---|---|---|
| ☐ | 423 Manitou Ave. | (303) 685-5467 |
|  | Manitou Springs, CO 80829 | Hydropool MH |

| #841B | TOWN-N-COUNTRY MOTEL |  |
|---|---|---|
| ☐ | 123 Crystal Park Rd. | (303) 685-5427 |
|  | Manitou Springs, CO 80829 | Hydropool MH |

| #842A | CHEYENNE MOUNTAIN INN |  |
|---|---|---|
| ☐ | 2860 S. Circle Dr. | (303) 576-4600 |
|  | Colorado Springs, CO 80906 | Hydropool MH |

| #842B | CLARION HOTEL |  |
|---|---|---|
| ☐ | 2886 S. Circle Dr. | (303) 576-5900 |
|  | Colorado Springs, CO 80906 | Hydropool MH |

| #842C | HILTON INN |  |
|---|---|---|
| ☐ | 505 Popes Bluff Trail | (303) 598-7656 |
|  | Colorado Springs, CO 80907 | Hydropool MH |

| #842D | EMBASSY SUITES HOTEL |  |
|---|---|---|
| ☐ | 7290 Commerce Center Dr. | (303) 599-9100 |
|  | Colorado Springs, CO 80919 | Hydropool MH |

| #842E | GARDEN OF THE GODS CAMPGROUND |  |
|---|---|---|
| ☐ | on Colorado Ave. | (303) 475-9450 |
|  | Colorado Springs, CO 80904 |  |
|  |  | Hydropool CRV |

| #843 | HOLIDAY INN |  |
|---|---|---|
| ☐ | Rte. 1 Box 426F | (303) 846-4491 |
|  | Trinidad, CO 81082 | Hydropool MH |

| #844 | HOLIDAY INN |  |
|---|---|---|
| ☐ | 333 Santa Fe Ave. | (303) 589-5833 |
|  | Alamosa, CO 81101 | Hydropool MH |

▼ *Spring Spa:* This should be considered to be an urban tap water rent-a-tub location unless you require genuine mineral water, in which case it's available at extra cost.

▲ *Jones Splashland:* The air is seldom hot at 7,500 ft. so a summertime heated pool is nice.

### #845 JONES SPLASHLAND
■ Box J      (303) 589-5151
Alamosa, CO 81101      PR

Large rural-community plunge in the center of a large, high valley. Elevation 7,500 ft. Open May through September.

Natural mineral water flows out of a spring at 106° and is piped to a large outdoor swimming pool which maintains a temperature of 87° to 88°. The water is treated with chlorine. Bathing suits are required.

Locker rooms and snack bar are available on the premises. It is two miles to a cafe, store and service station, and five miles to all other services. No credit cards are accepted.

Directions: Located on CO 17, two miles north of the town of Alamosa.

| #846 | BALLOON RANCH ADVENTURE |  |
|---|---|---|
| ☐ | Star Rte. Box 41 | (303) 754-2553 |
|  | Del Norte, CO 81132 | Hydropool MH |

| #847A | WOLF CREEK SKI LODGE |  |
|---|---|---|
| ☐ | P.O. Box 283 | (303) 873-5547 |
|  | South Fork, CO 81154 | Hydropool MH |

| #847B | UTE BLUFF LODGE RV PARK |  |
|---|---|---|
| ☐ | on US 160 | (303) 873-5595 |
|  | South Fork, CO 81154 | Hydropool CRV |

## #848  4UR GUEST RANCH

■  **P.O. Box 340**          **(303) 658-2202**
**Creede, CO 81130**          **MH**

Modern deluxe guest ranch surrounded by Rio Grande National Forest. Elevation 8,400 ft. Open June 1 to November 15.

Natural mineral water flows out of a spring at 140° and is piped into two pools, where it is treated with bromine. The outdoor swimming pool is maintained at a temperature of 78° and the indoor hydrojet pool is maintained at a temperature of 105°. Bathing suits are required. Pools are for the use of registered guests only and the minimum stay is one week, by prior reservation only.

Rooms, meals, tennis, saddle horses, fishing and hiking are available on the premises. It is four miles to all other services. No credit cards are accepted.

Directions: From the town of South Fork on US 160, go 22 miles north on CO 149 to the village of Wagon Wheel Gap. Just 0.4 mile beyond the Wagon Wheel Gap Cafe, watch for sign and turn left across bridge onto gravel road to the resort.

▲  *4UR Guest Ranch:* The hydrojet pool is located in the building on the right, with the picture windows overlooking the lawn.

## #849  RAINBOW (WOLF CREEK PASS) HOT SPRINGS

■

**non-commercial**
**Northwest of the town of Pagosa Springs**

A primitive riverside hot spring, at the end of a rugged, sometimes dangerous, but very rewarding hike in the Weminuche Wilderness northwest of CO 160. Elevation 9,000 ft. Open all year.

Natural mineral water flows out of a spring at 104° and flows directly into volunteer-built rock-and-mud pools at the edge of the San Juan River. A high rate of geothermal flow maintains a temperature of more than 100° in these pools. The apparent local custom is clothing optional.

There are no services available on the premises. It is six miles to overnight camping and 25 miles to all other services.

The five-mile trail to this location includes fords of Beaver Creek and of the West Fork of the San Juan River. During so-called "low water" these fords are still dangerous, and during "high water' they are impossible. For your own safety, inquire at a San Juan National Forest ranger station before starting this trip, and use the sign-in/sign-out board at the trailhead.

Source map: *San Juan National Forest.*

▲ *Pagosa Springs Pool:* There is no visible difference between the mineral well water in this pool and the spring water used at the Inn.

▲ *Pagosa Spring Inn:* These fiberglass pools have the advantage of a windbreak and a view.

## #850A  PAGOSA SPRINGS POOL

■  P.O. Box 37                    (303) 264-5912
   Pagosa Springs, CO 81147              PR

Older swimming pool and bathhouse formerly reserved for motel guests, now available to the public. Located near downtown Pagosa Springs. Elevation 7,100 ft. Open all year.

Natural mineral water is pumped from a well at 130° and piped to the swimming pool and bathhouse. The outdoor swimming pool is maintained at 90°. The two indoor soaking pools, in separate men's and women's sections, are maintained at 108°. All pools have continuous flow-through so no chemical treatment is necessary. Each of the two bathhouse sections also has its own steam bath. Bathing suits are required in the outdoor pools.

Locker rooms are available on the premises. It is less than three blocks to all other services. Visa, MasterCard and American Express are accepted.

Directions: In Pagosa Springs, on US 160, ½ block west of the high school, turn south across the bridge and watch for pool on your left.

## #850B  PAGOSA SPRINGS INN

■  P.O. Box 1858                  (303) 264-2287
   Pagosa Springs, CO 81147         PR + MH

Historic motel adjoining Great Pagosa Spring, on a bluff overlooking the San Juan River. Elevation 7,100 ft. Open all year.

Natural mineral water flows out of the spring at 156° and is cooled with tap water as it is piped to four outdoor fiberglass soaking pools. Temperatures in the four pools vary from 100° in the coolest to 110° in the hottest. They operate on a flow-through basis so no chemical treatment is needed. The pools are available to the public as well as to registered guests. Bathing suits are required.

Locker rooms, cafe and motel rooms are available on the premises. It is five blocks to a store and service station and five miles to overnight camping and RV hookups. MasterCard, Visa and American Express are accepted for motel rooms.

Directions: In Pagosa Springs, on US 160, ½ block west of the high school, turn south across the bridge and watch for motel on your right.

| | | | |
|---|---|---|---|
| #851A ☐ | WESTERN STAR MOTEL<br>3310 N. Main St.<br>Durango, CO 81301 | (303) 247-4895<br>Hydropool MH | |

#851A ☐ **WESTERN STAR MOTEL**
3310 N. Main St. (303) 247-4895
Durango, CO 81301 Hydropool MH

#851B ☐ **THUNDERBIRD LODGE**
2701 N. Main St. (303) 259-2540
Durango, CO 81301 Hydropool MH

#851C ☐ **RODEWAY INN OF DURANGO**
400 E. Second Ave. (303) 385-4980
Durango, CO 81301 Hydropool MH

#851D ☐ **QUALITY INN SUMMIT**
1700 CR 203 (303) 259-1430
Durango, CO 81301 Hydropool MH

#851E ☐ **LANDMARK MOTEL**
3030 Main Ave. (303) 259-1333
Durango, CO 81301 Hydropool MH

#851F ☐ **GENERAL PALMER HOUSE**
567 Main Ave. (303) 247-4747
Durango, CO 81301 In-room hydropools MH

#851G ☐ **DURANGO TRAVELODGE**
150 5th St. (303) 247-0955
Durango, CO 81301 Hydropool MH

#851H ☐ **COMFORT INN**
2930 Main Ave. (303) 259-5373
Durango, CO 81301 Hydropool MH

#851I ☐ **BEST WESTERN MOUNTAIN SHADOWS**
3255 Main Ave. (303) 247-5285
Durango, CO 81301 Hydropool MH

#851J ☐ **TALL TIMBER RESORT**
SSR Box 90 (303) 259-4813
Durango, CO 81301 Hydropool MH

#851K ☐ **BEST WESTERN LODGE AT PURGATORY**
P.O. Box 2732 (303) 247-9669
Durango, CO 81301 Hydropool MH

#851L ☐ **BEST WESTERN DURANGO INN**
P.O. Box 3099 (303) 247-3251
Durango, CO 81301 Hydropool MH

#852A ☐ **ARROW MOTOR INN**
440 S. Broadway (303) 565-3755
Cortez, CO 81321 Hydropool MH

#852B ☐ **LAZY G MOTEL AND CAMPGROUND**
on CO 145 (303) 565-8577
Cortez, CO 81321 Hydropool MH + CRV

#852C ☐ **KOA CORTEZ/MESA VERDE**
on US 160 (303) 565-9301
Cortez, CO 81321 Hydropool CRV

## #853 DUNTON HOT SPRINGS
■ **Dunton Route** **(no phone)**
**Dolores, CO 81323** **PR + MH**

Historic old resort surrounded by San Juan National Forest. Elevation 8,800 ft. Open May to mid-November.

Natural mineral water flows out of a spring at 107° and is piped to a large indoor soaking pool in its own separate building. It is drained and refilled after each use so no chemical treatment is necessary, and the refilled pool holds a temperature in the range of 104° to 106°. Bathing suits are not required in the soaking-pool building.

Rooms and a restaurant are available on the premises. It is two miles to a campground, and 24 miles to all other services. No credit cards are accepted.

Directions: From the town of Dolores go 13 miles northeast on CO 14, then bear north on FS 535 (gravel) for 22 miles along the West Dolores River to the resort.

▲ *Dunton Hot Springs:* The spring flows at a rate which permits the draining and filling of an indoor pool between patrons.

▲ *Ouray Municipal Pool:* Abundant spring flow avoids chemical treatment in these large pools.

◄ *Wizard Water Works:* If your condominium at Telluride does not have its own hot tub, this is your alternative, with privacy, too.

| #854B | THE VICTORIAN INN | |
|---|---|---|
| ☐ | P.O. Box 217 | (303) 728-3684 |
| | Telluride, CO 81435 | Hydropool MH |

| #854C | RESORT RENTALS | |
|---|---|---|
| ☐ | P.O. Box 1278 | (303) 728-4405 |
| | Telluride, CO 81435 | Hydropool MH |

## #855A OURAY MUNICIPAL POOL

■  **City Hall**　　　　　　　**(303) 325-4638**
　　**Ouray, CO 81427**　　　　　　**PR**

Large, city-owned swimming pool and visitor information complex. Elevation 7,800 ft. Open all year.

Natural mineral water flows out of a spring at 150° and is cooled with city tap water as needed to supply two large outdoor pools. The shallow soaking pool is maintained at 95° to 100° in the summer and 102° to 104° in the winter. The deep swimming and diving pool is maintained at 85° to 95° in the summer and 75° to 80° in the winter. Both pools have continuous flow-through so no chemical treatment is needed. Bathing suits are required.

Locker rooms are available on the premises. All other services are within six blocks. No credit cards are accepted.

Location: The entire complex is easily visible on the west side of US 550.

## #854A WIZARD WATER WORKS

☐  107 N. Fir　　　　　　　(303) 728-3656
　　Telluride, CO 81435　　　　　　PR

A combination rent-a-tub establishment, retail spa sales and TV cassette rental store, just off the main street.

Private-space hot pools, using chlorine-treated tap water, are for rent to the public by the hour. Two indoor redwood tubs and one indoor fiberglass tub are maintained at a temperature of 102° to 104° in the summer and at 104° in the winter. There is also an indoor steam bath maintained at a temperature of 115°.

Visa and MasterCard are accepted.

Phone for rates, reservations and directions.

*Wiesbaden Motel & Health Resort:* This group is dedicating a new deck and fiberglass pool.

An exercise room is part of the extensive health facilities at *Weisbaden Motel.*

## #855B WIESBADEN MOTEL & HEALTH RESORT

P.O. Box 349      (303) 325-4347
Ouray, CO 81427      PR + MH

Health-oriented modern resort in a spectacular canyon area of Uncompahgre National Forest. Elevation 7,700 ft. Open all year.

Natural mineral water flows from two springs at 111° and 117°, supplying two pools on a flow-through basis, without any chemical treatment of the water. The outdoor swimming pool is maintained at 80° to 90°, the indoor soaking pool at 106°. The sauna room includes a soaking pool with temperatures up to 117°. Bathing suits are required everywhere.

Geothermal heat is used in all buildings. Rooms, picnic area, massage, reflexology, facials and exercise equipment are available on the premises. It is two blocks to a cafe, store and service station and eight blocks to overnight camping and RV hook-ups. Visa and MasterCard are accepted.

Location: In the town of Ouray, two blocks east of US 550. Follow signs.

*Box Canyon Motel and Hot Springs:* Hot tubbing in the winter can be quite enjoyable when your nice warm motel room is just steps away.

## #856 LOPA HOT SPRINGS

21945 Hwy 550      (303) 626-5505
Ridgway, CO 81432      PR

Hot bath and chiropractic business operated in the owner's home. Elevation 7,200 ft. Open all year.

Natural mineral water is pumped from a well at 80°, then given additional gas heat as needed. There is one private room, which contains two individual jet-equipped soaking tubs, which can be temperature-controlled up to 106°. Tubs are drained and refilled after each use so no chemical treatment is necessary. Bathing suits are optional in the tubs.

Massage and chiropractic adjustment are available on the premises. It is two miles to a cafe, store and service station and four miles to all other services. No credit cards are accepted.

Location: On US 550, ½ mile south of the junction of US 550 and CO 62.

| #857 | BUTTE MOUNTAIN TRAILER RANCH | |
|---|---|---|
| ☐ | on US 50 | (303) 249-7382 |
| | Cimarron, CO 81220 | Hydropool CRV |
| #858A | QUALITY INN RED BARN | |
| ☐ | 1417 E. Main St. | (303) 249-4507 |
| | Montrose, CO 81401 | Hydropool MH |
| #858B | SAN JUAN INN | |
| ☐ | 1480 US 550 S. | (303) 249-6644 |
| | Montrose, CO 81401 | Hydropool MH |
| #859 | KOA—DELTA/GRAND MESA | |
| ☐ | on CO 92 | (303) 874-3918 |
| | Delta, CO 81416 | Hydropool CRV |
| #860A | HOLIDAY INN | |
| ☐ | P.O. Box 1725 | (303) 243-6790 |
| | Grand Junction, CO 81502 | Hydropool MH |
| #860B | QUALITY INN AIRPORT | |
| ☐ | 733 Horizon Dr. | (303) 245-7200 |
| | Grand Junction, CO 81501 | Hydropool MH |
| #860C | BEST WESTERN HORIZON INN | |
| ☐ | 754 Horizon Dr. | (303) 245-1410 |
| | Grand Junction, CO 81501 | Hydropool MH |
| #860D | GRAND JUNCTION HILTON | |
| ☐ | 743 Horizon Dr. | (303) 241-8888 |
| | Grand Junction, CO 81501 | Hydropool MH |
| #860E | RODEWAY INN-GRAND JUNCTION | |
| ☐ | 2790 Crossroads Blvd. | (303) 241-841I |
| | Grand Junction, CO 81501 | Hydropool MH |

## #855C BOX CANYON MOTEL AND HOT SPRINGS

45 3rd Ave.      (303) 325-4981
Ouray, CO 81427      MH

Modern, off-highway motel, adjacent to Box Canyon falls, in a picturesque mountain town. Elevation 7,700 ft. Open all year.

Natural mineral water flows out of a spring at 140° and is piped to four redwood tubs, where it is treated with bromine. There are four outdoor hydrojet tubs maintained at a temperature of 105°, and reserved for the use of registered guests only. Bathing suits are required. MasterCard, Visa, American Express, Diners Club, Carte Blanche and Choice are accepted.

Location: Two blocks west of US 550 on 3rd Ave.

## #855D BEST WESTERN TWIN PEAKS MOTEL

125 3rd Ave.      (303) 325-4427
Ouray, CO 81427      MH

Modern major hotel in a picturesque mountain town. Elevation 7,700 ft. Open all year.

Natural mineral water flows out of a spring at 156° and is piped to two pools treated with bromine. The outdoor swimming pool is maintained at 84° to 86°, the indoor soaking pool at 104°. Pools are reserved for the use of registered guests. Bathing suits are required. Visa, MasterCard, American Express, Carte Blanche, Diners Club and Amoco are accepted.

Location: One block west of US 550 on 3rd Ave.

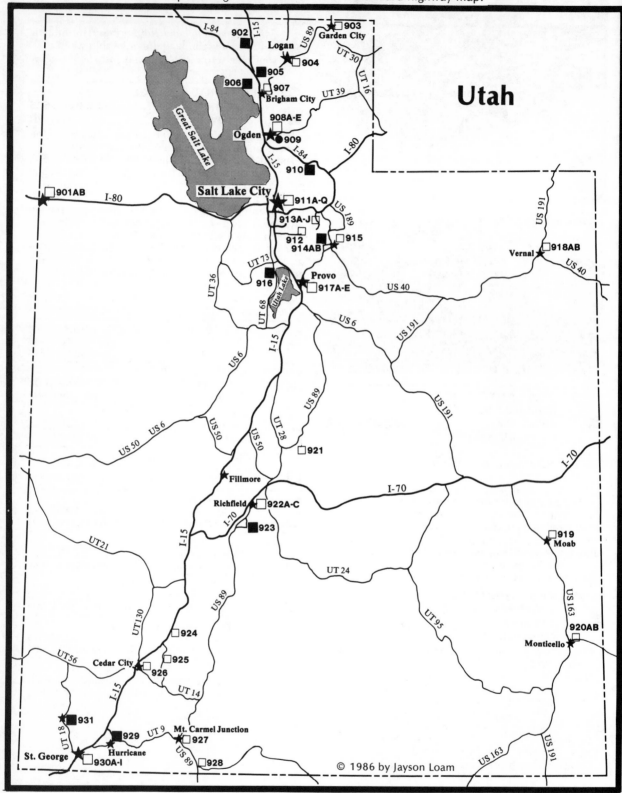

# Utah

Great Salt Lake

I-84  902  I-15  US 89  903 Garden City

Logan  904  UT 30  UT 16

905  UT 39

906  907  Brigham City

908A-E

Ogden  909

I-84  I-80

910

Salt Lake City

901AB  I-80  911A-Q  US 189

913A-J

912  915  Vernal 918AB

914AB  US 40

UT 73

UT 36  916  Provo  917A-E  US 40

UT 68  Utah Lake  US 6  US 191

US 6  US 89

US 50  US 6  UT 28  I-70

US 50  921

US 50  Fillmore

UT 21  Richfield  922A-C  I-70

923  919 Moab

I-15  I-70  UT 24

US 89  UT 95  US 163

924  920AB

UT 130  Monticello

UT 56  Cedar City  925

926  UT 14

931  UT 9  Mt. Carmel Junction

UT 18  929  927

St. George  Hurricane  US 89  928

930A-I  US 163  US 191

© 1986 by Jayson Loam

176

## MAP AND DIRECTORY SYMBOLS

● **Unimproved natural mineral water pool**

■ **Improved natural mineral water pool**

☐ Gas-heated tap or well water pool

——————— Paved highway

- ⌒ - ⌒ - Unpaved road

··········· Hiking route

PR = Tubs or pools for rent by hour, day or treatment

MH = Rooms, cabins or dormitory spaces for rent by day, week or month

CRV = Camping or vehicle parking spaces, some with hookups,
for rent by day, week, month or year

#901A BEST WESTERN WENDOVER MOTEL
☐ P.O. Box 640     (801)665-2211
Wendover, UT 84083     Hydropool MH

# 901B STATE LINE INN
☐ P.O. Box 620     (801) 665-2226
Wendover, UT 84083     Hydropool MH

#### #902 BELMONT SPRINGS
■ Box 36     **(801) 458-3200**
Fielding, UT 84311     **PR + CRV**

Modern commercial plunge, with RV park and golf course, in a treeless northern Utah valley. Elevation 4,300 ft. Open April through September.

Natural mineral water flows out of an artesian well at 131°, and is piped to four outdoor pools, all of which are treated with chlorine. The large swimming pool is maintained at 90°, a soaking pool is maintained at 106° to 108°, and two hydrojet pools are maintained at 106° to 108°. Bathing suits are required.

Locker rooms, picnic area, golf course, overnight parking and RV hook-ups are available on the premises. A cafe, store, service station and motel are available within ten miles. No credit cards are accepted.

Directions: From the town of Plymouth, on I-15, go one mile south and watch for resort sign.

▲ *Belmont Springs:* Free form pools with modern skimmers identify this location as a recent development with completely new construction.

#903     SWEETWATER PARK RESORT
☐     (801) 946-3306
Garden City, UT 84028     Hydropool MH

#904     BEST WESTERN WESTON LAMPLIGHTER MOTEL
☐ 250 N. Main     (801) 752-5700
Logan, UT 84321     Hydropools MH

▲ *Crystal Hot Springs:* Tree-covered slopes on both sides of the pool area give this location the air of being user-friendly.

► *Stinky Springs:* No one knows why this block house was built, or how it survives, but it continues to provide free soaks, 24 hours/day.

▼ There are dozens of shaded tenting spaces at *Crystal Hot Springs* along the grassy ridge just north of the main pool area.

## #905    CRYSTAL HOT SPRINGS

■ 8215 North Hwy 69        (801) 279-8104
Honeyville, UT 84314        PR + CRV

Superbly remodeled historical resort, featuring the world's largest side-by-side hot and cold springs. The property includes spacious tree-shaded lawns for picnics and camping. Elevation 4,700 ft. Open all year.

Natural mineral water flows out of a spring at 135° and is piped to three outdoor hydrojet pools which are maintained at 102°, 104° and 106° on a flow-through basis, requiring no chemical treatment. A large outdoor soaking pool of natural mineral water is maintained at 100°, with a minimum of chlorine treatment. Another large soaking pool uses chlorine-treated spring water maintained at a temperature of 95°. Similar water is used in the catch-pool at the bottom of two large water slides. Bathing suits are required.

Locker rooms, snack bar, overnight camping and RV hook-ups are available on the premises. It is four blocks to a store and service station and 15 miles to a motel. No credit cards are accepted.

Directions: From I-15, take Honeyville exit. Go one mile east on UT 240 to UT 69, then 2½ miles north to resort on west side of highway.

## #906   STINKY SPRINGS
**West of the town of Brigham City**
**non-commercial**

A small, partly vandalized cement-block bathhouse alongside a highway in the flat country north of the Great Salt Lake. Elevation 4,000 ft. Open all year.

Natural mineral water flows out of a spring at 118°, through a culvert under the highway, and into three cement soaking pits in the abandoned building. Temperature within each pool is controlled by diverting the hot-water flow as desired. In recent years volunteers have kept the surrounding party trash to a minimum but the water does have a sulfur-dioxide smell. The apparent local custom is clothing optional within the building.

There are no services available on the premises.

Directions: From I-15, take the Golden Spike exit, then go nine miles west, through Corinne, on UT 83. The building is on the south side of the road shortly before you reach Little Mountain, a rocky hill on the north side of the road.

| | | | |
|---|---|---|---|
| #907 ☐ | RED BARON MOTEL 1167 S. Main St. Brigham City, UT 84302 | (801) 723-8511 | Hydropool MH |
| #908A ☐ | BEST WESTERN COUNTRY INN 1335 W. 12th St. Ogden, UT 84401 | (801) 394-9474 | Hydropool MH |
| #908B ☐ | OGDEN HILTON 247 24th St. Ogden, UT 84401 | (801) 627-1190 | Hydropool MH |
| #908C ☐ | RADISSON SUITE HOTEL 2510 Washington Blvd. Ogden, UT 84401 | (801) 627-1900 | Hydropools MH |
| #908D ☐ | PUTNAM'S CREST MOTEL 234 24th St. Ogden, UT 84401 | (801) 627-1332 | Hydropools MH |
| #908E ☐ | BEST WESTERN RED BARON 1825 Washington Blvd. Ogden, UT 84401 | (801) 621-8350 | Hydropools MH |

*Como Springs Resort:* A popular summer resort despite 82° water and therefore no hot pools.

## #909   OGDEN HOT SPRINGS
**East of the city of Ogden   non-commercial**

Small primitive hot spring in a river gorge subject to annual flooding. Elevation 4,800 ft. Open all year.

Natural mineral water flows out of a spring at 130°, and through a pipe to a volunteer-built rock and mud pool at water's edge. Temperature is controlled by diverting flow when desired. The apparent local custom is clothing optional.

There are no services available on the premises.

Directions: From I-15, in Ogden, go east 4 miles on UT 39 to the mouth of Ogden Canyon. The pool is 100 ft. upstream from the water pipe suspended far above. Parking is upriver just past where river crosses under road for first time.

## #910   COMO SPRINGS RESORT
**Box 386**                    **(801) 829-3489**
**Morgan, UT 84050**          **PR + MH + RV**

Older rural plunge and recreation park in the foothills northeast of Salt Lake City. Elevation 5,000 ft. Open Memorial Day to Labor Day.

Natural mineral water flows out of a spring at 82° and is piped to three outdoor pools, which are treated with chlorine and maintain a temperature of approximately 80°. There is a large swimming pool, a small wading pool, and a catch pool for a small waterslide. Bathing suits are required.

Locker rooms, picnic area, cafe, motel rooms, overnight camping, RV hook-ups, skating and trout fishing are available on the premises. It is two miles to a store and service station. No credit cards are accepted.

Directions: Take Morgan exit from I-84. Immediately after going through railroad underpass turn left (south) on Commercial Street, which runs directly into the resort entrance.

179

## #911A SOAK YOUR BODY

☐ 3955 S. State St.          (801) 264-TUBS
Salt Lake City, UT 84107          PR

Basic rent-a-tub establishment on a main street in southern Salt Lake City. Open all year.

Private-space hot pools, using bromine-treated tap water, are for rent to the public by the hour. Six indoor fiberglass hydrojet pools are maintained at temperatures ranging from 102° to 104°. Visa and MasterCard are accepted.

Phone for rates, reservations and directions.

### #911B WORLD MOTOR HOTEL
☐ 1900 S. State St.          (801) 487-7801
Salt Lake City, UT 84115          Hydropool  MH

### #911C SHILO INN
☐ 206 S.W. Temple          (801) 521-9500
Salt Lake City, UT 84101          Hydropool  MH

### #911D SALT PALACE TRAVELODGE
☐ 215 W. N. Temple          (801) 532-1000
Salt Lake City, UT 84103          Hydropool  MH

### #911E SALT LAKE SHERATON HOTEL AND TOWERS
☐ 255 S.W. Temple          (801) 328-2000
Salt Lake City, UT 84101          Hydropool  MH

### #911F SALT LAKE HILTON HOTEL
☐ 150 W. 5th S.          (801) 532-3344
Salt Lake City, UT 84101          Hydropool  MH

### #911G SALT LAKE AIRPORT HILTON
☐ 5151 Wiley Post Way          (801) 539-1515
Salt Lake City, UT 84116          Hydropool  MH

### #911H QUALITY INN-SOUTH
☐ 4465 Century Dr.          (801) 268-2533
Salt Lake City, UT 84107          Hydropool  MH

### #911I THE MARRIOTT HOTEL
☐ 75 S. W. Temple          (801) 531-0800
Salt Lake City, UT 84101          Hydropool  MH

### #911J LITTLE AMERICA HOTEL
☐ 500 S. Main          (801) 363-6781
Salt Lake City, UT 84101          Hydropool  MH

### #911K HOLIDAY INN-DOWNTOWN
☐ 230 W. 6th S.          (801) 532-7000
Salt Lake City, UT 84101          Hydropool  MH

### #911L FRIENDSHIP INN SKYLINE MOTEL
☐ 2475 E. 17th S.          (801) 582-5350
Salt Lake City, UT 84108          Hydropool  MH

### #911M COMFORT INN
☐ 8955 S. 255 W.          (801) 255-4915
Salt Lake City, UT 84070          Hydropool  MH

### #911N BROCK RESIDENCE INN
☐ 765 E. 400 S.          (801) 532-5511
Salt Lake City, UT 84102          Hydropool  MH

### #911O AIRPORT INN
☐ 2333 W. N. Temple          (801) 539-0438
Salt Lake City, UT 84116          Hydropool  MH

### #911P BEST WESTERN SANDMAN INN
☐ 380 W. 7200 S. St.          (801) 561-2256
Midvale, UT 84047          Hydropool  MH

### #911Q RODEWAY INN—SOUTH
☐ 280 W. 7200 S. St.          (801) 556-4141
Midvale, UT 84047   In-room hydropools MH

### #912 RUSTLER'S LODGE
          (801) 742-2200
☐ Alta, UT 84092          Hydropool  MH

### #913A PROSPECTOR SQUARE HOTEL
☐ 2000 Sidewinder Dr.          (801) 649-7100
Park City, UT 84060          Hydropool  MH

### #913B COPPER BOTTOM INN
☐ 1637 Shortline Rd.          (801) 649-5111
Park City, UT 84060          Hydropool  MH

### #913C BLUE CHURCH LODGE AND TOWNHOUSE
☐ P.O. Box 1720          (801) 649-8009
Park City, UT 84060          Hydropool  MH

### #913D STEIN ERIKSEN LODGE
☐ P.O. Box 3177          (801) 649-3700
Park City, UT 84060          Hydropool  MH

### #913E THE YARROW/HOLIDAY INN
☐ 1800 Park Ave.          (801) 649-7000
Park City, UT 84060          Hydropool  MH

### #913F SUN CREEK INN
☐ 1885 Prospector Ave.          (801) 649-2687
Park City, UT 84060          Hydropool  MH

### #913G SNOWCREST
☐ 1510 Empire Ave.          (801) 649-5333
Park City, UT 84060          Hydropool  MH

### #913H SILVER KING
☐ 1485 Empire Ave.          (801) 649-5500
Park City, UT 84060          Hydropool  MH

### #913I PARK CITY VILLAGE
☐ 1385 Lowell Ave.          (801) 649-1700
Park City, UT 84060          Hydropool  MH

### #913J PARK CITY ACCOMMODATIONS
☐ 1510 Empire Ave.          (801) 649-5333
Park City, UT 84060   In-room hydropools MH

▲ *The Homestead:* The small curved pool in the foreground is the only mineral pool in this beautiful new pool-and-sun-deck complex.

▼ The proximity of Midway to several major ski slopes makes this indoor pool at *The Homestead* a popular wintertime attraction.

## #914A THE HOMESTEAD

■ **700 N. Homestead Road  (801) 654-1102**
**Midway, UT 84049          PR + MH + CRV**

Remodeled historic resort, specializing in family reunions and group meetings. Extensive landscaping and minimal use of natural mineral water. Elevation 5,600 ft. Open all year.

Natural mineral water flows from a tufa-cone spring at 98° and is piped to one small outdoor soaking pool, which averages 90° and is not treated with chemicals. All other pools use chlorine-treated tap water. The large outdoor swimming pool is maintained at 82°, the indoor swimming pool at 90°. The outdoor hydrojet redwood tub is maintained at 104°, the indoor hydrojet pools at 98°. There is also a dry sauna available. Pools use is available to the public as well as to registered guests. Bathing suits are required.

Locker rooms, dining room, hotel rooms and overnight camping are available on the premises. It is two miles to a store, service station, RV hook-ups and a golf course. MasterCard, Visa and American Express are accepted for rooms and for dining but not for public swimming.

Directions: From Heber City, on US 189, go west on UT 113 to the town of Midway and follow signs to resort.

### #914B MOUNTAIN SPAA RESORT

■ **800 North 200 East** (801) 654-0721
**Midway, UT 84049** PR + MH + CRV

Historic older resort, formerly known as Luke's Hot Pots. Telephone ahead to determine status of planned remodeling program. Elevation 5,700 ft. Open April to October (mineral baths open all year).

Natural mineral water flows from cone-shaped tufa craters at 110° and is piped to three pools. The outdoor swimming pool is maintained at 90° to 95°, and is treated with chlorine. The indoor swimming pool is built inside a large crater, maintains a temperature of 95° to 100°, and has a continuous flow-through, requiring no chemical treatment of the water. The indoor soaking pool is large enough for eight persons, and is drained after each use, so no chemical treatment of the water is necessary. Pool temperature ranges up to 109°. Bathing suits are required everywhere except in the indoor soaking pool.

One of the planned remodeling projects is an Indian-style steam bath within one of the tufa craters large enough to hold 20 persons.

Locker rooms, cafe, bed and breakfast, rooms, overnight camping and RV hook-ups are available on the premises. No credit cards are accepted.

Directions: From Heber City, on US 189, go west on UT 113 to the town of Midway. Turn north on River Road, go .7 mile and follow signs to resort.

### #915 BUDGET HOST INN GREEN ACRES LODGE

□ **989 S. Main** (801) 654-2202
**Heber City, UT 84032** Hydropool MH

▲ *Mountain Spaa Resort:* Year-round swimming classes are one of the main attractions at this unchlorinated indoor pool.

▲ *Saratoga Resort:* One of the few open-top super slides available in the northwest states. Most of them used closed tubes.

### #916 SARATOGA RESORT

■ **Saratoga Rd. at Utah Lake** (801) 768-8206
**Lehi, UT 84043** PR + CRV

Lakeside recreation resort with picnic grounds, rides and boat-launching facilities. Elevation 4,200 ft. Open May to September.

Natural mineral water is pumped out of a well at 120° and is piped to four outdoor pools, all of which are treated with chlorine. One large hydrojet pool is maintained at 100°. The swimming pool, diving pool and water-slide catch pool are maintained at 75° to 80°. Bathing suits are required.

Locker rooms, snack bar, overnight camping and RV hook-ups are available on the premises. There are also several amusement park rides. No credit cards are accepted.

Directions: From the town of Lehi, on I-15, go west on UT 73 and follow signs to resort.

| #917A | BEST WESTERN COTTONTREE INN | |
|---|---|---|
| ☐ | 2230 N at University Pkwy. | (801) 373-7044 |
| | Provo, UT 84604 | Hydropool MH |

| #917B | ROYAL INN | |
|---|---|---|
| ☐ | 55 E. 1230 N. | (801) 373-0800 |
| | Provo, UT 84604 | Hydropool MH |

| #917C | PROVO HOLIDAY INN | |
|---|---|---|
| ☐ | 1460 S. University Ave. | (801) 374-9750 |
| | Provo, UT 84601 | In-room hydropools MH |

| #917D | SAFARI MOTEL | |
|---|---|---|
| ☐ | 250 S. University Ave. | (801) 373-9672 |
| | Provo, UT 84601 | Hydropool MH |

| #917E | PROVO EXCELSIOR HOTEL | |
|---|---|---|
| ☐ | 101 W. 100 N. | (801) 377-4700 |
| | Provo, UT 84601 | Hydropool MH |

| #918A | BEST WESTERN DINOSAUR INN | |
|---|---|---|
| ☐ | 251 E. Main St. | (801) 789-2660 |
| | Vernal, UT 84078 | Hydropool MH |

| #918B | SHERATON INN | |
|---|---|---|
| ☐ | 1084 W. Hwy 40 | (801) 789-9550 |
| | Vernal, UT 84078 | Hydropool MH |

| #919 | RAMADA INN | |
|---|---|---|
| ☐ | 182 S. Main St. | (801) 259-7141 |
| | Moab, UT 84532 | Hydropool MH |

| #920A | CANYONLANDS LODGE | |
|---|---|---|
| ☐ | 389 N. Main St. | (801) 587-2266 |
| | Monticello, UT 84535 | Hydropool MH |

| #920B | KOA—MONTICELLO CANYONLANDS | |
|---|---|---|
| ☐ | on Park Rd. | (801) 587-2884 |
| | Monticello, UT 84535 | Hydropool CRV |

| #921 | PALISADE LODGE | |
|---|---|---|
| ☐ | P.O. Box R | (801) 835-5413 |
| | Sterling, UT 84665 | Hydropool MH |

| #922A | RICHFIELD TRAVELODGE | |
|---|---|---|
| ☐ | 647 S. Main St. | (801) 896-9271 |
| | Richfield, UT 84701 | Hydropool MH |

| #922B | ROMANICO INN | |
|---|---|---|
| ☐ | 1170 S. Main St. | (801) 896-8471 |
| | Richfield, UT 84701 | Hydropool MH |

*Monroe Hot Springs:* This hot spring also supplies geothermal water for use in a space-heating project at the high school.

| #922C | QUALITY INN | |
|---|---|---|
| ☐ | 540 S. Main St. | (801) 896-5465 |
| | Richfield, UT 84701 | Hydropool MH |

### #923 MONROE HOT SPRINGS
**575 East First North**     **(801) 527-4014**
■ **Monroe, UT 84754**     **PR + CRV**

RV park with restaurant, swimming pool and hillside soaking pool overlooking an agricultural valley. Elevation 5,500 ft. Open all year, except swimming pool open only from Memorial Day to Labor Day.

Natural mineral water flows from a spring at 135° and is piped into a heat exchanger, then into a soaking pool, where the temperature ranges from 100° to 105°. The outdoor swimming pool and hydrojet pool use chlorinated tap water, heated in the geothermal heat exchanger to approximately 90°. Bathing suits are required.

Locker rooms, dinner-house meals, store, picnic area, overnight camping and RV hook-ups are available on the premises. It is a short walk to the large and colorful Red Hill Spring, and to the adjoining tropical fish pond. A service station and motel are within four blocks. MasterCard and Visa are accepted.

Directions: From the town of Richfield, on I-70, go nine miles south on UT 118 to the town of Monroe. Follow signs to resort.

| #924 | BEST WESTERN VILLAGE MOTEL | |
|---|---|---|
| ☐ | 580 N. Main St. | (801) 477-3391 |
| | Parowan, UT 84761 | Hydropool MH |

*Pah Tempe Hot Springs Resort:* An abundance of user-friendly geothermal water gushes out of both sides and the bottom of this canyon carved out by the Virgin River.

| #925 | BRIAN HEAD HOTEL | |
|---|---|---|
| ☐ | Rte. 143 | (801) 677-3000 |
| | Brian Head, UT 84719 | Hydropool MH |

| #926 | BEST WESTERN EL REY INN | |
|---|---|---|
| ☐ | 80 S. Main St. | (801) 586-6518 |
| | Cedar City, UT 84720 | Hydropool MH |

| #927 | BEST WESTERN THUNDERBIRD INN | |
|---|---|---|
| ☐ | US 89 at UT 9 | (801) 648-2262 |
| | Mount Carmel Junction, UT 84755 | |
| | | Hydropool MH |

| #928 | BEST WESTERN RED HILLS MOTEL | |
|---|---|---|
| ☐ | P.O. Box 758 | (801) 644-2675 |
| | Kanab, UT 84741 | Hydropool MH |

### #929 PAH TEMPE HOT SPRINGS RESORT
■ 35-4 (801) 635-2879
Hurricane, UT 84737 PR + MH + CRV

A unique resort, being remodeled by new owners, featuring a spectacular flow of geothermal water out of the sides and bottom of the Virgin River canyon. Elevation 3,000 ft. Open all year.

Natural mineral water flows out of rock grottos, and up out of the riverbed, at temperatures of 105° to 110°. There is one shaded outdoor swimming pool which averages 100°. The seven riverbank soaking pools range from 102° to 106°, and the two private indoor hydrojet pools average 105°. The flow-through rate in all pools is sufficient to eliminate the need for chemical treatment of the water. Bathing suits are required.

Locker rooms, massage, bed & breakfast, cabins, overnight camping and RV hook-ups are available on the premises. It is two miles to a cafe, store and service station. MasterCard and Visa are accepted.

Directions: From the town of Hurricane, go two miles north on UT 9 and follow signs to resort.

| #930A | REDLANDS RECREATIONAL VEHICLE PARK | |
|---|---|---|
| ☐ | I-15 Frontage Road | (801) 673-9700 |
| | St. George, UT 84770 | Hydropool CRV |

| #930B | BEST WESTERN THUNDERBIRD LODGE | |
|---|---|---|
| ☐ | 1000 E. 150 N St. George Blvd. | |
| | | (801) 673-6123 |
| | St. George, UT 84770 | Hydropool MH |

| #930C | FOUR SEASONS RESORT AND MOTOR INN | |
|---|---|---|
| ☐ | 747 E. St. George Blvd. | (801) 673-4804 |
| | St. George, UT 84770 | Hydropool MH |

| #930D | THE HERITAGE INN | |
|---|---|---|
| ☐ | 1165 S. Bluff | (801) 628-4481 |
| | St. George, UT 84770 | Hydropool MH |

| #930E | HILTON—ST. GEORGE | |
|---|---|---|
| ☐ | 1450 Hilton Inn Dr. | (801) 628-0463 |
| | St. George, UT 84770 | Hydropool MH |

| #930F | REGENCY INN | |
|---|---|---|
| ☐ | 770 E. St. George Blvd. | (801) 673-6119 |
| | St. George, UT 84770 | Hydropool MH |

| #930G | WESTON'S LAMPLIGHTER MOTEL | |
|---|---|---|
| ☐ | 460 E. St. George Blvd. | (801) 673-4861 |
| | St. George, UT 84770 | Hydropool MH |

| #930H | ST. GEORGE TRAVELODGE—WEST | |
|---|---|---|
| ☐ | 60 W. St. George Blvd. | (801) 673-4666 |
| | St. George, UT 84770 | Hydropool MH |

| #930I | BEST WESTERN CORAL HILLS MOTEL | |
|---|---|---|
| ☐ | 125 E. St. George Blvd. | (801) 673-4844 |
| | St. George, UT 84770 | Hydropool MH |

▼ Soaking pools have been built in grottos and along the cliffs at *Pah Tempe* for day-rate use as well as by registered guests.

▲ *Veyo Resort:* Nothing fancy—just a warm pool with clean dressing rooms, a snack bar and tree-shaded picnic tables next to a stream.

### #931    VEYO RESORT

■ Veyo Star Route 107      (801) 574-2744
Central, UT 84722                          PR

Older community plunge and picnic park with a small running stream. Elevation 4,600 ft. Open Memorial Day to Labor Day.

Natural mineral water flows out of an artesian well at a temperature of 98°. There is one outdoor swimming pool, which is chlorinated and maintains a temperature of 85°. Bathing suits are required.

Locker rooms, snack bar, volleyball court and picnic area are available on the premises. It is one mile to a store and service station, eight miles to overnight camping and RV hook-ups, and 12 miles to a motel. No credit cards are accepted.

Directions: From the city of St. George, on I-15, go 19 miles north on UT 18 to the town of Veyo and follow signs to the resort.

The alphabetical master index contains several dozen locations labeled NUBP (Not Usable by the Public), with no further information. On the basis of our research we have determined that a NUBP location is not operational, is not legally accessible by the public, or is no longer in existence. Space does not permit including all NUBP locations in this index, but we chose to include some examples to convey the fact that we did not simply overlook them. The photographs in this section were chosen to illustrate the NUBP status of several such locations.

During the early stages of our research we tried to determine the history of all commercial sites, especially those which had been open to the public at one time. However, we learned that some places had been defunct for so many years that no one clearly remembered what had happened. If we asked four different people, we got four different answers, none of them verifiable. Eventually, we concluded that the only significant fact, for the purpose of this book, was that a specific site was no longer usable, regardless of the reason. We decided to let the historians speculate about what happened at those places where we *can't* go, and concentrated on what is presently happening at the places where we *can* go.

# ALPHABETICAL MASTER INDEX
## of Mineral Water Locations

This index is designed to help you locate a hot spring or resort listing when you start with the location name. Turn to the page given for that name and look for the listing information under the location number. Then, if you want to see where that is, turn to the key map for that state or province and look for that location number on that map.

### Key Maps

▲ *Gold Fork Hot Springs:* This scene is now only a memory since new ownership removed these tubs and pools, making the location temporarily NUBP. Their plans to reopen under the name *Gold Fork Retreat* are on page 128

*Corwin Hot Springs:* This Montana location is on all springs lists and still appears on many maps, but it is now merely a relic on a fenced and posted private cattle ranch.

*Wasatch Warm Springs:* The Salt Lake City Parks and Recreation Department operated this plunge for many years, but it has been closed to the public for more than two decades.

| Name | Page Number | Area Key Map | Location Number |
|------|-------------|--------------|-----------------|
| PAGOSA SPRINGS POOL | 171 | CO | #850A |
| PAH TEMPE HOT SPRINGS RESORT | 184 | UT | #929 |
| PANTHER CREEK HOT SPRINGS | 87 | ID | #511 |
| PARADISE INN | 107 | ID | #552 |
| PENNY HOT SPRINGS | 164 | CO | #826 |
| PINE BURL HOT SPRING | 125 | ID | #583B |
| PINE FLATS HOT SPRING | 122 | ID | #576 |
| PINKERTON HOT SPRINGS | | CO | NUBP |
| PISTOL CREEK HOT SPRINGS | 91 | ID | #522 |
| PLAZA HOTEL AND APARTMENTS | 145 | WY | #707D |
| PREIS HOT SPRING | 98 | ID | #538 |
| QUINN'S HOT SPRINGS | 132 | MT | #601 |
| RADIUM HOT SPRINGS | 32 | BC | #216 |
| RADIUM HOT SPRINGS | 60 | OR | #405 |
| RAINBOW (WOLF CREEK PASS) HOT SPRINGS | 170 | CO | #849 |
| RED RIVER HOT SPRINGS | 86 | ID | #508 |
| RENDEZVOUS IN THE ROCKIES | 165 | CO | #833 |
| RENOVA HOT SPRINGS | | MT | NUBP |
| RIGGINS HOT SPRINGS | | ID | NUBP |
| RIVERDALE RESORT | 102 | ID | #547 |
| RIVERSIDE INN | 105 | ID | #549B |
| ROBINSON BAR HOT SPRING | | ID | NUBP |
| ROCKY CANYON (ROBERTS) HOT SPRING | 124 | ID | #580 |
| ROOSEVELT HOT SPRINGS | | UT | NUBP |
| ROYSTONE HOT SPRINGS | | ID | NUBP |
| RUSSIAN JOHN HOT SPRINGS | 96 | ID | #532 |
| SACAJEWEA HOT SPRINGS | 119 | ID | #572 |
| SALIDA HOT SPRINGS | 166 | CO | #835 |
| THE SARATOGA INN | 146 | WY | #716A |
| SARATOGA RESORT | 182 | UT | #916 |
| SAWTOOTH LODGE | 118 | ID | #571 |
| SCENIC HOT SPRINGS | | WA | NUBP |
| SHEEP CREEK BRIDGE HOT SPRINGS | 116 | ID | #568 |
| SHOWER BATH HOT SPRINGS | 91 | ID | #525 |
| SILVER SPRINGS PLUNGE | 124 | ID | #581 |
| SKILLERN HOT SPRINGS | 98 | ID | #539 |
| SKOOKUMCHUCK HOT SPRINGS | 44 | BC | #254 |
| SLATE CREEK HOT SPRING | 93 | ID | #527 |
| SLEEPING CHILD HOT SPRINGS | 141 | MT | #628 |
| SLIGAR'S THOUSAND SPRINGS RESORT | 108 | ID | #555 |
| SLOQUET CREEK HOTSPRINGS | 45 | BC | #255 |
| SMITH CABIN HOT SPRINGS | 114 | ID | #567 |
| SNIVELY HOT SPRINGS | 61 | OR | #409 |
| SODA (HOOPER) HOT SPRINGS | 101 | ID | #544 |
| SOL DUC HOT SPRINGS RESORT | 50 | WA | #331 |
| SOUTH CANYON HOT SPRINGS | 163 | CO | #824D |
| SPA MOTEL | 136 | MT | #614 |
| SPRING SPA | 168 | CO | #840 |
| SQUAW HOT SPRINGS | | ID | NUBP |
| STANLEY HOT SPRINGS | 84 | ID | #505 |
| STAR PLUNGE | 145 | WY | #707C |
| STARKEY HOT SPRINGS | | ID | NUBP |
| STATE BATH HOUSE | 144 | WY | #707B |
| STEAMBOAT SPRINGS HEALTH AND RECREATION | 156 | CO | #803 |
| STEELE HOT SPRINGS | | WY | NUBP |
| STINKY SPRINGS | 179 | UT | #906 |
| STRAWBERRY PARK HOT SPRINGS | 155 | CO | #802 |
| SUGAH HOT SPRING | 127 | ID | #585 |
| SULLIVAN HOT SPRINGS | Omitted by owner's request | | |
| SUMMER LAKE HOT SPRINGS | 64 | OR | #415 |
| SUNBEAM HOT SPRINGS | 93 | ID | #528 |
| SUNFLOWER FLATS HOT SPRINGS | 89 | ID | #514 |
| SYMES HOTEL AND MEDICINAL SPRING | 133 | MT | #602 |
| TEEPEE POOLS | 144 | WY | #707A |
| TERRACE LAKES RECREATIONAL RANCH | 123 | ID | #579 |
| TERWILLIGER (COUGAR RESERVOIR) HOT SPRINGS | 72 | OR | #428 |
| THERMO HOT SPRINGS | | UT | NUBP |
| TRAIL CREEK (BREIT) HOT SPRINGS | 126 | ID | #584A |
| TRIMBLE HOT SPRINGS | | CO | NUBP |
| TWIN SPRINGS RESORT | 116 | ID | #569 |
| UMPQUA WARM SPRING | 66 | OR | #422 |
| UPPER HOT SPRING | 28 | AB | #210A |
| UTAH HOT SPRINGS | | UT | NUBP |
| VALE HOT SPRINGS | | OR | NUBP |
| VALLEY VIEW HOT SPRINGS | 166 | CO | #836 |
| VEYO RESORT | 185 | UT | #931 |
| VULCAN HOT SPRINGS | 127 | ID | #584C |
| WARFIELD HOT SPRING | 97 | ID | #536 |
| WARM SPRINGS RESORT | 118 | ID | #570 |
| WASATCH HOT SPRINGS | | UT | NUBP |
| WASHAKIE MINERAL HOT SPRING | | WY | NUBP |
| WAUNITA HOT SPRINGS RANCH | 165 | CO | #832 |
| WEATHERBY HOT SPRINGS | | ID | NUBP |
| WEIR CREEK HOT SPRINGS | 84 | ID | #506 |
| WEISBADEN MOTEL & HEALTH RESORT | 174 | CO | #855B |
| WELLSVILLE WARM SPRING | | CO | NUBP |
| WEST PASS HOT SPRING | 92 | ID | #526B |
| WHITE ARROW HOT SPRINGS | | ID | NUBP |
| WHITE LICKS HOT SPRINGS | 128 | ID | #587 |
| WHITEHORSE RANCH HOT SPRING | 62 | OR | #411 |
| WHITEY COX HOT SPRINGS | 91 | ID | #517 |
| WILSON HEALTH SPRINGS | | UT | NUBP |
| WOLF CREEK PASS (RAINBOW) HOT SPRINGS | 170 | CO | #849 |
| WORSWICK HOT SPRINGS | 98 | ID | #537 |
| YOUMANS STORE & CABINS (CEBOLLA HOT SPRINGS) | 164 | CO | #831 |
| ZIM'S HOT SPRINGS | 131 | ID | #591 |